REFERENCE

REVOLT IN ATHENS

REVOLT IN ATHENS

THE GREEK COMMUNIST "SECOND ROUND," 1944-1945

BY JOHN O. IATRIDES

With a Foreword by William Hardy McNeill

PRINCETON UNIVERSITY PRESS

PRINCETON, NEW JERSEY

Publication of this book has been aided
by a grant from the Ford Foundation

LCC: 76-39052
ISBN: 0-691-05203-4

This book has been composed in Linotype Caledonia

Printed in the United States of America by
Princeton University Press

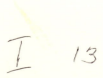

To Nancy

CONTENTS

ABBREVIATIONS

EAM (Ethnikon Apeleftherotikon Metopon): National Liberation Front

EDES (Ethnikos Demokratikos Ellinikos Syndesmos): National Republican Greek League

EKKA (Ethniki Kai Koinoniki Apeleftherosis): National and Social Liberation

ELAS (Ethnikos Laikos Apeleftherotikos Stratos): National Popular Liberation Army

KKE (Kommunistikon Komma Ellados): Communist Party of Greece

PEEA (Politiki Epitropi Ethnikis Apeleftherosis): Political Committee of National Liberation

X (Khee): Extreme royalist armed group

FOREWORD

By WILLIAM H. MCNEILL
ROBERT A. MILLIKEN DISTINGUISHED SERVICE PROFESSOR OF
HISTORY, UNIVERSITY OF CHICAGO

ODD THOUGH it may sound, I have experienced the events
with which Professor Iatrides deals in this book no less
than three times: once as an eyewitness in 1944-45; once as
a writer and historian in 1946-47; and now for a third time
as a reader in 1970. Each experience carried its own
poignancy.

As an eyewitness I saw and heard a small part of what
took place in Athens during the revolt of December 1944.
Some events of greatest import, like the demonstration in
Constitution Square on December 3, which touched off
large-scale fighting in Athens, manifested themselves as a
series of more or less disconnected encounters, separated
from one another by periods of quiet when nothing happened within the range of my personal observation.

In such moments of crisis, normal patterns of communication break down; the eyewitness, if he pauses to reflect,
must realize how little he really knows about what is going
on. But everyone, even high military commanders, is in
nearly the same position. For even if the command and
communications net functions smoothly, it functions only
within the pattern of everyday channels, linking headquarters with headquarters up and down the line. The desperate
confusion "out there," where thousands of angry, frightened
people are doing things and having things done to them,

where individuals and small armed groups can use their weapons in fear or in anger or inspired by both, and where isolated representatives of authority—policemen, guards, clerks—either stick to routine or flee from their accustomed posts without notifying headquarters: "out there," where unpredictable behavior is at its peak, remains by definition inaccessible to any form of regular information-gathering system. Even if agents are everywhere (a situation unlikely ever to prevail) they cannot report until later, when their information, even if accurate (another situation unlikely ever to prevail), can only be used to reconstruct what happened after the event.

Hence the eyewitness experience, though it left numerous vivid scenes etched into my memory, added up to chaos. Confusion, excitement, and uncertainty as experienced by individual observers and participants were resolved for many simply by accepting one or another official line of propaganda. One could believe that the Greek Communists had plotted a *coup d'état* as soon as they saw how few Allied troops had come to Greece; or one could accept the EAM interpretation which held that the British together with Greek Monarcho-Fascists were attempting to foist an undemocratic regime on Greece by plotting to disarm the resistance fighters of ELAS. But no one *at the time* had access to information that sufficed by any sort of logical standards to prove either the one contention or the other. Belief, often passionately held, had to take the place of truth, which is notoriously the first victim of war.

My second experience of these events was therefore inspired by an effort to put together a more adequate picture of what had happened. By gathering written records (somewhat haphazardly) and by interviewing individuals who had taken prominent parts in the events, I was able to reconstruct the pattern and sequence of happenings. I undertook this enterprise in 1946 and wrote my first book,

Greek Dilemma: War and Aftermath (Lippincott, 1947), on the basis of these inquiries.

One thing became quite clear to me in writing my book. Circumstantial evidence proved that neither the Greek Communists nor the British authorities had planned on fighting in Athens. Elementary consideration of how unprepared each side was for the hostilities that broke out seemed adequate proof of this proposition. It followed, of course, that both of the official propaganda lines were false. Instead, both sides had misjudged the situation and been surprised (perhaps even dismayed) at the result. Working toward this conclusion by fitting together what data I had at hand, comparing it to my remembrance of the experiences I had personally encountered during those hectic days and locating them within the larger pattern of events as a whole, was in its way as engrossing an experience as the initial eyewitnessing itself.

Yet important dimensions of the whole affair in Athens remained unknown to me in 1946-47. In particular, I knew nothing of the deal between Churchill and Stalin, concluded in Moscow early in October 1944, whereby Greece was assigned to the British sphere of influence. The springs of Russian passivity and of British aggressiveness both became clearer when the terms of this agreement first came to my attention. Other bits and pieces of evidence came to public knowledge during the years that followed, but I soon gave up the effort to keep track, and never found time to test and revise my understanding of what had taken place in Athens in 1944-45 against the new data that had come to hand.

It was, therefore, with a keen sense of anticipation that I began reading Professor Iatrides' pages. For he has painstakingly gathered and woven together new and old evidences of what happened. The scattered entries captured in a Communist record of dispatches sent to regional headquarters in the days before December 3, 1944 proves by documentary evidence how hesitant and unsure the party leaders were as the crisis approached. Insight into the British side is also possible now, what with the publication of Churchill's key messages, and of memoirs by Macmillan, Eden, and Leeper.

Overall, the effect of the new data is to confirm the conclusion I reached long ago: to wit, that neither side expected or was prepared for the battle that actually occurred. To discover documentation in support of conclusions reached largely by guess work is always pleasurable. Reading this book gave me this kind of pleasure, in its way almost as intense as the quite different kinds of satisfaction derived from my two previous experiences of these events.

Other readers will not have such a special relation to Professor Iatrides' work. They can, however, here find a careful and judicious study of an episode, small in itself, but typical of the way in which mutual misunderstanding and miscalculation leads to situations that no one wanted or foresaw. Politics, and human life in general, is like that. Here is a slice of it, carefully described and deftly analyzed. Anyone who cares to inquire about what happened in Athens in the fall of 1944 can here find out—not everything, of course, but the political-diplomatic moves and countermoves, and the professed motives and calculations of most of the principal actors, insofar as available evidence allows us to know.

Some important mysteries remain. The role, if any, of Tito and the Yugoslav Partisans can only be surmised. The decisions of the Greek Communist Party after December 3, 1944 are unclear. Likewise, the relations among the disparate groups that made up the EAM coalition cannot be reconstructed from the evidence available to Professor Iatrides. On the other hand, he did have access to the personal and official records kept by Lincoln MacVeagh, United States Ambassador to Greece. This book therefore plays its own part in adding to the data available to historians for reconstructing the events of that troubled period.

To be sure, no surprising new data emerges from Mr. MacVeagh's papers. It is nonetheless interesting, in view of what we know was to happen later, to observe how the United States Ambassador on the scene was already beginning to urge Washington to take a more active role in Greek affairs. Such advice—under quite different circumstances—led in little more than two years' time to America's first effort to "contain" Communism by sending aid to Greece on a scale that would have seemed inconceivable in 1944. In 1947 the United States thus took over the role Great Britain played in 1944-45. By revealing the first impulses that led eventually to this reversal of roles, Professor Iatrides' book contributes significantly to the sum of what is known and knowable about the revolt in Athens and its larger historical significance.

William H. McNeill

September 28, 1970

ACKNOWLEDGMENTS

THIS SMALL volume is the early by-product of an extended research project dealing with United States policies toward postwar Greece, culminating in the Truman Doctrine. In this bigger undertaking I have been assisted by a number of individuals in and out of government service in the United States, Britain, and Greece. I am especially indebted to Mr. Arthur G. Kogan of the Historical Office, Department of State; Mr. James O'Neill, Director of the Franklin D. Roosevelt Library at Hyde Park; Mr. Alexander P. Clark, Curator of Manuscripts at the Princeton University Library; Mr. R. A. Winnacker of the Office of the Assistant Secretary of Defense; Mr. Philip C. Brooks, Director of the Truman Library; Mrs. Domna Visvisi-Dontas, Archivist of the Greek Ministry of Foreign Affairs; and Mr. E. G. Boxshall of the British Foreign and Commonwealth Office.

I am most grateful to retired Ambassador Lincoln MacVeagh and his family for permission to quote from his letters to President Roosevelt, and for allowing me to examine and cite his personal diary. I hope to be able to produce much of this valuable historical material in a separate volume soon.

Mr. Sanford G. Thatcher, Social Science Editor of Princeton University Press, was very helpful from the first draft to the completion of this book. I am greatly indebted to Mrs. Virginia L. Lloyd whose efforts in turning out the several versions of the manuscript were clearly beyond the call of duty. My wife offered many helpful editorial suggestions and much encouragement. Of course, responsibility for the contents of these pages is mine alone.

J.O.I.

Cheshire, Connecticut
December 1971

REVOLT IN ATHENS

GREEK POLITICAL REALITIES

THE "Government of National Unity" which reached liberated Athens on October 18, 1944 represented an elaborate compromise and a balance of forces whose intricacy defies simple analysis. It had brought together men without a demonstrable power base or a coherent program and with a popular appeal yet to be determined. It had been the product of the complete collapse and demoralization of the country's political parties since the mid-1930's, of sharp clashes inside and outside occupied Greece, of the menacing spectre of a powerful Left and of persistent British pressure for some semblance of unity while the war was still in progress. Even under the best of circumstances such a government could be expected to serve only as a temporary accommodation until the country's political life could be revived and its component parts had regained their confidence and individuality.

The legacy of past failures and bitter partisan divisions did not augur well for Prime Minister Papandreou's frail coalition. The war had found Greece's political forces in a state of enforced paralysis, and foreign occupation had done nothing to heal old sores. Instead, new explosive issues aggravated traditional rivalries, mixing fundamental discord with fear, mutual suspicion, and petty vituperation. The psychological damage which the first Great War had caused had never been repaired. The tug-of-war between Prime Minister Eleftherios Venizelos and King Constantine before Greece finally joined the Entente in 1917 had crystallized into a schism which profoundly affected the country's internal development and foreign relations. The forced departure of the pro-German King and Venizelos' impressive diplomatic accomplishments at the Paris Peace Conference had seriously weakened the royalist cause but had left unanswered the "constitutional question" of the throne's prerogatives regarding the expression of the national will. Although Constantine returned triumphant following the plebiscite of December 5, 1920, his image remained tarnished, particularly since the Allied powers would no longer accord him formal recognition, and withdrew their support from the Greek military campaign into Turkey. That disastrous Anatolian adventure and the consequent frantic search for scapegoats culminating in the hasty execution of six prominent figures had deepened the Venizelist-royalist cleavage and had unleashed powerful emotions destined to reverberate for decades.[1] The dream of *Megali Idea*, of a Greater Greece vaguely reminiscent of Byzantine glories, had now turned into a horrible national nightmare. While Venizelos, whose Liberal Party had suffered a crushing defeat in November 1920, watched sullenly from abroad, Constantine left the country once again (in September 1922), this time never to return. His eldest son and successor, George II, fared no better: following the military coup of Colonel Nikolaos Plastiras, a rising republican tide forced the new monarch to accept exile. In May 1924 the country became officially a republic, remaining one until 1935. By the mid-1930's several more coups made a shambles of party alignments, confirmed the military as a powerful although deeply divided political force, added many more prominent names to the lists of the purged, and discredited the parliamentary system in the eyes of the public.

The exchange of populations with Turkey, Greece's heavy price for defeat in 1922, had not been without its beneficial

[1] Alexander A. Pallis, *Greece's Anatolian Venture and After* (London, 1937).

aspects.[2] In the northern provinces of Macedonia and Thrace, where most of the refugees were settled, the Greek element was permanently solidified, and valuable skills and professions enriched the nation's economy. The abandonment of *Megali Idea* had a sobering effect upon future governments which were now compelled to pursue more modest foreign objectives and devote more of their energies to domestic problems. But the immediate result of that tremendous upheaval had been untold human suffering and the straining to the breaking point of the meager resources of an already exhausted state. The country's unhealthy reliance upon foreign factors was made even more apparent, while at home a new dimension was added to political division: the more republican and progressive northern provinces began to challenge the more royalist and traditionally dominant south-central "Old Greece." Throughout the 1920's and early 1930's a parade of weak and often corrupt governments, coups, and countercoups by factions within the military, wholesale personnel changes in the public services dictated by narrow patronage, and continued foreign pressures succeeded in keeping the country in a state of almost constant turmoil, raising the most serious doubts about the viability of the democratic process and the ability of the ruling elites to effectively deal with the country's social and economic ills.

Superficially, and despite the predominant royalist–republican feud, there were enough parties to span the entire political spectrum. At the extreme left a small but vociferous and disciplined Communist Party, founded in 1918 as the Socialist Labor Party, directed its appeal to the poorly paid industrial laborer and the tobacco workers of the north, but attracted mostly impoverished elements of the professions and "intellectuals," many of whom were

[2] Dimitri Pentzopoulos, *The Balkan Exchange of Minorities and Its Impact Upon Greece* (Paris, 1962).

11

refugees from Asia Minor. The more reformist and largely ineffective Left was represented by such tiny and ephemeral organizations as the Agrarian Socialist Party, the Union of Popular Democracy, and the Socialist Party. The center was personified by Venizelos' large and at times powerful Liberal Party whose followers came from all walks of life. Welded together by his dynamism and fierce nationalism, the Liberals lost their cohesion after his demise and gravitated around lesser and widely divided figures. Many of the older families, on the other hand, representing aristocratic tradition and wealth, as well as the country's more conservative elements, tended to identify their fortunes with those of the monarchy and supported the Populist Party at the far right. For the most part, however, political parties were defined by the personal and emotional following of this or that prominent figure, never in power long enough to do much more than remove from public office the protégés of the previous regime. They contributed to a climate of opportunism, excesses, and flagrant disregard for constitutional rules. The public at large appeared destined to play the role of the passive and often victimized observer. Meager or poorly utilized resources and an ineffectively managed economy heavily burdened by foreign debts contributed to chronic unemployment and one of Europe's lowest living standards. Traditionally a country of independent farmers employing backward methods, and small-scale entrepreneurs with little capital, Greece had to import foodstuffs as well as industrial goods.

The depression of the early 1930's further aggravated the country's severe economic plight, while the rising star of fascism gave new impetus to undemocratic tendencies. When the Venizelist-republican camp boycotted the elections of June 1935, protesting the obstructionist tactics of their opponents and the sentencing to death *in absentia* of Venizelos and Plastiras for their involvement in the abortive coup of March 1935, the royalist-Populist forces gained control of Parliament and presided over the return of King George. The efforts of the young and politically inexperienced monarch to bring about unity and order proved totally ineffective. New elections were held in January 1936, giving the royalists a total of 143 seats, against 141 for the republicans. With its fifteen seats the Communist Party appeared to hold the balance and to have every intention of exploiting it. When it was discovered that both royalists and republicans were prepared to negotiate a deal with the extreme Left the military leadership advised King George that a coalition government which included Communists would be opposed by whatever means necessary. To prevent yet another military coup the King appointed the leader of the small Monarchist Party, General John Metaxas, Minister of War. While the move succeeded in keeping the armed forces under control it also aroused powerful fears in both the royalist and republican camps because the German-trained Metaxas had been an avowed supporter of dictatorship. When the nonpolitical Prime Minister Constantine Demertzis suddenly died on April 13, he was immediately succeeded by General Metaxas. In making the appointment without consulting the nation's leaders, as tradition if not constitutional provisions required, the King had been motivated by a healthy dislike for the political intrigue in which the two major political factions appeared to indulge almost habitually and by the fear that given the opportunity the Communists would completely destroy the very stability and order which he was genuinely anxious to restore. When Parliament gave Metaxas a vote of confidence, the King's tactic appeared to have been vindicated. Widespread labor strikes accompanied by violence, especially in the Thessaloniki region, convinced the monarch that he had little choice but to resort to strong measures if chaos were to be averted. Though not an admirer of Metaxas' pseudo-fascist philosophy, King George gave ready endorsement to his Prime Minister's dictatorial regime, which was officially proclaimed on August 4, 1936. This was to be the dawn of a "new civilization" designed to purify the Greeks and elevate them to the status of a modern society. Parliament was dissolved, the constitution was declared suspended, and the usual paraphernalia of a police state soon began to impose a carefully controlled reign of terror directed primarily against the Communists, trade-unionists, intellectuals, and others known for their strong republican leanings. Thousands of citizens faced dismissal from their positions, brutal interrogation, and imprisonment. If the King had acted in the belief that he was protecting the country's social order, he nevertheless emerged as the symbol of an oppressive dictatorship and the one who presided over the death of democracy in Greece. The stigma of his association with the Metaxas period, whether deserved or not, was to prove indelible.

The full record of the Metaxas regime has yet to be established with any degree of objectivity. Its practical achievements were by no means negligible. A highly centralized and relatively efficient bureaucratic machine instituted public works in the cities and the countryside, designed to improve agriculture and the economy generally. Stability and order removed some of the anxieties of everyday life. Under Metaxas' personal direction there was a serious attempt to combat corruption in public service and to improve the lot of the common man. Above all, the armed forces received much-needed attention and the country's state of military preparedness was greatly improved, despite the adverse effects of the systematic purging of all republican elements from the officers' ranks. On the other hand, the harsh methods of the regime and the crudely corporate ideology modeled after Mussolini's made it thoroughly unpopular with the vast majority of its politically conscious citizens, while the fascist-inspired Youth Movement (EON) failed to create the cadres of a more sympathetic following. In the long run the Metaxas rule represented little more than the temporary freezing of virtually every explosive issue, and instead of removing the causes of factionalism and unrest it gave them new vigor. The prolonged enforced political abstinence left the country potentially even more vulnerable to irresponsible and self-seeking forces and incapable of tackling its fundamental problems in an orderly, parliamentary manner. The shelving of constitutional guarantees, the oppressive tactics, and the highly personalized style of the regime virtually assured that a "day of reckoning" would come and that, when it did, old scores would most likely be settled by violence. Metaxas cheated his many enemies by dying a natural death in January 1941, leaving behind King George, the hapless legatee of the regime of August 4. Moreover, the republican Left blamed the Metaxas dictatorship not only on the King who had given it his endorsement but on the principal bourgeois parties which had done little to prevent its establishment. Indeed, for the Communists and their sympathizers, the Metaxas regime symbolized the bankruptcy of the country's entire political system.

Despite the general oppression, the nation's vitality was not sapped. For a brief but brilliant moment and in the face of supreme external danger Greeks appeared united once again and capable of truly heroic feats. Although widely regarded as an admirer of Hitler's Germany, and while working to reshape the country's internal order along pseudo-fascist lines, Metaxas had pursued a prudent policy of non-involvement in Europe's brewing power contests. Following the Great Depression, strong economic dependence on Germany and the spectacle of Italian expansionism in the eastern Mediterranean compelled him to remain highly sensitive to the dangers which the Axis powers represented for Greece. At the same time he realistically foresaw the failure of the Balkan Entente to protect the status quo in that region and the hollowness of Britain's unsolicited guarantee (on April 13, 1939) of Greece's territorial integrity. In the belief that a neutralist stance would best serve his country's interests, he studiously avoided any commitments which might provide potential enemies with an excuse for aggression. Yet when, after a series of crude provocations, Italy presented him with an ultimatum demanding complete capitulation (on October 28, 1940), he rejected it without hesitation, accepting instead war with the bellicose ally of the mighty Germans.

The war with Italy, which soon saw Mussolini's proud divisions retreating deep into Albanian territory, sparked a paroxysm of patriotic feeling.[3] Political rivalries and disaffection were apparently submerged in the common effort against the impudent foe. Overnight the much-feared Metaxas became the symbol of national honor and valiant resistance. Yet the real hero of the day was not the "Great Leader" but the simple soldier who chose to fight for his homeland despite, rather than because of, its political leaders. A nation of sullen farmers, arm-waving intellectuals, and frustrated politicians, perennial critics of everyone and everything, suddenly turned into an army of high-spirited, determined fighters. For decades to come all Greeks would proudly remember that at the darkest moment of World War II they had delivered the first victory of the Allied cause and had humiliated Hitler's imperious partner.

Predictably, the feeling of unity and exhilaration was not destined to last. On April 6, 1941, while the overextended Greek forces still faced the Italians in Albania, the Germans attacked through Yugoslavia. The new and overpowering pressure caused a complete breakdown of an already severely taxed supply system. The sudden death of Metaxas (on January 29, 1941) had created a power vacuum which seriously affected morale at the nation's highest councils. The arrival of British troops in March merely served to postpone the inevitable, particularly as the troops were

[3] Theodore Papaconstantinou, *I Mahi Tis Ellados, 1940-1941* (Athens, 1966), pp. 13-55.

totally inadequate for anything but delay action. On April 20, and in clear violation of orders, the commander of the Greek forces in Epirus surrendered to the enemy, signaling the collapse of organized resistance everywhere. Two days earlier, amid rumors of possible treason and clear evidence of defeatism among his associates, Prime Minister Alexander Koryzis had committed suicide. Accompanied by his new Prime Minister, Emmanuel Tsouderos, and a handful of mostly Metaxist figures, King George fled to Crete and after a short stay in South Africa made his way to London where his government-in-exile soon began its drab existence. The darkness of foreign occupation had descended upon Greece.

The long-range importance of the traumatic impact of the combined German, Italian, and Bulgarian occupation cannot be overstated. Its demoralizing effects were to serve as a principal cause of future troubles. An enslaved and starving population could do little more than brood over its mostly painful memories of recent years and search for the deeper causes of its misery. Old feuds seemed to disclose new meanings and the gnawing feeling that the most dangerous enemy was a rival, home-grown political force brought bitterness and suspicion to the surface once again. To the multifaceted division of the past a new dimension was now added: puppet regimes composed of fellow Greeks who appeared to be all too willing to do the conqueror's dirty work.

Unquestionably many who agreed to serve in the occupation governments believed that they were helping their compatriots by creating a much-needed buffer between a brutal foreign enemy and the helpless public. Others collaborated to enrich themselves or because they actually believed that Nazi Germany represented the wave of Europe's political future. Some could not resist the psychological attractions of high office even if this meant serving a foreign master. Still more thought that Slav-dominated Communism had to be combated by any means available because it threatened to destroy national institutions more permanently and completely than the German occupation ever could. However noble or petty their motives, their association with the hated foreign conqueror aroused powerful emotions particularly among those of the Left who found themselves the principal target of the occupation's most brutal measures. The fact that many wartime collaborators had previously served the Metaxas regime was viewed by the entire socialist camp as conclusive evidence that Metaxists and collaborators were one and the same, and that both were "enemies of the people." The crisis over the matter of collaboration became even more acute early in 1943 when the Germans, facing a severe shortage of troops, authorized the puppet regime of John Rallis in Athens to form armed "Security Battalions" to police much of the country. Their declared mission was to rescue the country from the Slav-Communists who would surrender Macedonia to the hated Bulgarians. Yet these same forces were the willing tools of the German authorities who had given Bulgaria control of large Greek territories and were considering the establishment of an "independent" Macedonian state. In fact, their principal task was the destruction of the National Popular Liberation Army (ELAS) which after 1942 appeared to be gaining predominance in the resistance movement and spreading its influence over much of the countryside. Other resistance groups were also hunted down, although not with quite the same enthusiasm. Inevitably the Security Battalions attracted criminal elements and ruffians. But they also succeeded in recruiting some of the survivors of nationalist resistance groups which ELAS had decimated in an attempt to dominate the field. Thus while ELAS terrorized its opponents, the Security Battalions exterminated leftists. Greek was pitted against Greek in a vendetta of unprecedented dimensions and brutality.

At the outset the will to harass and resist the foreign conqueror had been the direct outgrowth of the same patriotism which had made possible the Albanian epic. Greeks in all walks of life felt the urge to demonstrate that despite formal surrender the nation's spirit had not been broken. Heroic acts of sabotage provided release from the frustrations of occupation and proof that the mighty enemy was not invulnerable. Their perpetrators believed that they were performing a patriotic duty and a valuable service to the allied cause. As the cities were in the firm control of the occupation authorities, the natural habitat of the larger resistance organizations soon became the mountains and the open countryside where the enemy's presence was often reduced to token forces. At the same time small units of saboteurs and espionage agents continued to operate in the principal urban centers.

In retrospect it can be argued that the achievements of the resistance movement in Greece were obtained at an incredibly high price, or that the entire effort had little military value.[4] With the exception of very few major operations, of which the most significant were the destruction of the Gorgopotamos and Asopos viaducts (in November 1942 and June 1943 respectively), guerrilla activity had essentially a nuisance value. It very probably compelled the enemy to keep in Greece larger forces than otherwise would have been necessary, particularly as long as an invasion of the Balkans appeared to be a likely allied move. For this, nearly 70,000 mostly innocent persons were executed and more than 1,700 villages completely destroyed. Guerrilla activity was undoubtedly one important factor behind the harshness of the occupation, during which, according to some estimates, 550,000 Greeks perished. Furthermore, as the present study will show, the split within the

[4] Many authorities argue that, on the contrary, the Greek resistance was valuable for the allied cause. See D. M. Condit, *Case Study in Guerrilla War: Greece During World War II* (Washington, D.C., 1961), pp. 212-20.

partisan movement, and the violence which it brought about, aggravated the country's problems more than any other single cause. Yet resistance to a foreign enemy is not based on a calculation of losses against gains or of long-range effects, but on a powerful emotional need that must be satisfied. Since guerrilla warfare is not a gentlemen's sport, all sides were guilty of brutality and excesses.

However, if the urge to fight the enemy was widespread, few were willing to answer the patriotic call to arms. For most, the need to provide for family and protect social standing and material possessions, the fear of capture, torture, and almost certain execution served as a powerful deterrent and kept them in the relative security of their homes. Many vented their feelings of defiance secluded in their livingrooms and waited for clearer signs of what the future might bring before committing themselves. Very few were willing to sacrifice everything, or had little to lose by joining the fighting underground. Thus with some notable exceptions, the middle and upper strata of Greek society, those who had achieved certain prominence in the Greek world of the 1920's and 1930's, and virtually everyone who had served the Metaxas regime but had not become a collaborator, remained cautiously inactive, waiting for the days of danger to pass. The exceptions were mostly military men of supreme patriotic dedication and later on a few intellectuals and professional men. Consequently, from its inception the resistance movement was under the dominant influence of political forces which ranged from the mildly republican to the Communist. Thus the rise of resistance to the enemy was also indicative of the emergence of the forces of the Left. For a long time the very rare royalist sympathies among the underground were not made public for fear of association with the Metaxas dictatorship. But whereas the republicans and leftists provided the numbers, the Communists excelled in organizational skills, conspiratorial tactics, and dedication. While the republican leaders often recoiled in the face of the foreign enemy's most horrible reprisals for acts of sabotage, the Communists usually demonstrated a supreme disregard for the misery thus inflicted upon the defenseless population: violence and human suffering were for many of them an accepted way of life. While the republicans and leftists dreamt of liberation that would restore the country to its pre-Metaxas political institutions, the Communists worked for the coming of a "people's justice" and a "People's Democracy," for an ill-defined "social revolution" which would transform them from disfranchised and hunted conspirators to members of the ruling elite.

This is not to say that the Communist leadership had a definite and precise plan of social action. Their ideas about the future, while crudely Marxist and pro-Soviet, were vague and undeveloped. Aside from the defeat of the foreign conqueror, their immediate objective was the strengthening of their position across the country and, conversely, the undermining of their opponents, so as to be able to play as important a role as possible in deciding the country's political future. The most optimistic among them expected that at the moment of liberation their forces would be in effective control. But for the vast majority of their comrades such a happy turn of events was too much to hope for. They viewed the future with apprehension, mindful of the strong popular distaste for totalitarian forms of organization and of the traditionally powerful influence of the western powers, especially Britain, over Greek affairs. Accordingly, the Communist Party (KKE) sought to base its appeal for popular support not on a clear ideological position but on a coalition of forces stressing time-honored patriotic aims, social justice and republican slogans. In particular, wartime Communist propaganda sought to stress a number of broad themes: relentless resistance to the foreign enemy until national liberation had been achieved; genuine, populist democracy after the war; active cooperation with the peoples of the Balkan region during the war and in the future; and lasting friendship and cooperation with the western democracies as well as with the Soviet Union. Significantly, KKE enthusiastically endorsed the nation's battle against the Italian invaders and when, in January 1941, it was directed by the Comintern to disassociate itself from what Moscow called Greek "fascist aggression" (!) the order was ignored. Thus the stated wartime objectives of the Greek Communists did not differ from those of the more respectable socialists and republican groups. In cooperation with republican-socialist groups a National Liberation Front (EAM) was established, eventually attracting perhaps as many as 700,000 active members whose political leanings were strongly antimonarchist and often socialist, but rarely Communist. In addition to the KKE, the National Liberation Front included the Socialist Party of Greece (SKE), the Union of Popular Democracy (ELD), the Agrarian Party of Greece (AKE), and the United Socialist Party of Greece (ESKE). The Front's ruling body was a 25-member Central Committee which consisted of one representative from each of the above political parties and from various functional and regional organizations of EAM such as the National Popular Liberation Army (ELAS), the National Mutual Assistance (EA), the United All-Greece Youth Organization (EPON), and the Workers' National Liberation Front (EEAM). These auxiliary organizations were carefully controlled by the Communists, thus assuring the KKE a very safe majority support in EAM's all-important Central Committee. On the other hand, the establishment of EAM as a popular front offered positive proof of KKE's inability to organize a genuinely Communist resistance movement. Moreover, with all their organizational talents and strong-arm tactics, the Communists could not have succeeded in making EAM widely popular without the fear, shared by large segments of the population, that the King's dictatorial regime would be restored with Britain's backing.

22

In the areas which came under its control EAM built a system of local self-government under the direction of trusted Communists designated as the *ipefthinoi* ("responsible"). It combined a strong leftist bias with considerable commonsense efficiency, operating mostly through "People's Courts" which dispensed a blend of proletarian justice and political terror. At the same time EAM made no attempt to undermine the traditionally powerful institutions of the Church (indeed, many priests and several bishops became prominent EAM members and a few even served with ELAS), the family, and private property. There was, in fact, no serious attempt to preach a Marxist dogma; it concentrated instead on local practical issues. The Front's propagandists talked endlessly about the evils of the past but were rather circumspect about the future, except to say that the agents of oppression and collaboration would pay dearly for their crimes. With the wisdom of hindsight one can readily see that the small Communist Party succeeded from the outset in effectively controlling the EAM leadership. However, to view EAM as merely the clever creation of the Communists is to fail to appreciate the powerful, if essentially leaderless, anti-monarchist sentiment which permeated the country. In their frustration, political inexperience, and fear of the dictatorship's return, these leftist forces allowed the KKE to lead them by default.

EAM's guerrilla organization was the National Popular Liberation Army, or ELAS, pronounced exactly the same as "Ellas," the word for Greece.[5] Later, in the days of the civil war, these initials were to prove a source of embarrassment to British and American officials whose knowledge of Greek genders (Ellas is feminine, ELAS masculine) was too rudimentary to prevent them from drinking an enthusiastic toast to the glory of ELAS before shocked representatives of

[5] There is at present no good study of ELAS. For the account of one of its principal leaders see Stefanos Sarafis, *Greek Resistance Army: the Story of ELAS* (London, 1951).

23

His Majesty! As in the case of the parent organization, ELAS attracted large numbers of non-Communists, while its leadership, organized along political-military lines, remained under Communist control exercised through a hierarchy of political officers (*capetanioi*) whose authority generally exceeded that of the military commander. By far the largest guerrilla force, ELAS was believed to have had about 50,000 armed men at the time of liberation, in addition to a sizeable reserve. Originally equipped and supplied largely by the British, it was eventually able to function without their support, particularly after September 1943 when it seized the equipment of the Italian Pinerolo Division which surrendered in northern Greece following the collapse of the Mussolini regime. It developed a highly elaborate command structure, established an officers' training school, and maintained relatively effective discipline. Its commander-in-chief was Colonel Stefanos Sarafis, whose republican band was destroyed by ELAS in the spring of 1943, but by far its most notorious leader was Aris Velouchiotis (born Athanasios Klaras), a Communist with definite sadistic tendencies. Because of its political orientation, ELAS' weapons were turned against other guerrilla bands nearly as often as they fired upon the occupation forces. Indeed, its critics charged that it was not above open collusion with the enemy.

Next to the ELAS, the largest resistance movement was the National Republican Greek League (EDES), formally under the direction of a committee of prominent Athenians. Its field commander and true leader, Colonel Napoleon Zervas, had been purged from the army in the mid-1930's because of his republican convictions and his involvement in several military conspiracies against the government. The formal political doctrine of EDES called for a democratic constitution, a popular plebiscite to decide the fate of the monarchy after liberation, and punishment for wartime collaborators. As in the case of their leader, EDES officers were mostly men of liberal democratic, mildly anti-monarchist persuasion. Gradually, however, as the leftist orientation of EAM/ELAS became apparent, and as friction between the two rival guerrilla organizations began to mount, conservative and royalist elements joined EDES, bringing about a significant turn in its practical political outlook. In Athens a bitter feud destroyed the effectiveness of the EDES leaders; in fact, some of its original sponsors eventually displayed definitely collaborationist tendencies. In March 1943 Colonel Zervas, at the urging of British agents upon whom he was by then completely dependent for supplies and financial support, addressed a message to King George and the exiled government complaining that, while EDES was being maligned and its contribution to the allied cause went unappreciated, the Communists were seeking to dominate the field. On the nation's constitutional issue Zervas declared that, if a plebiscite invited the King back, EDES would be the first to welcome him. He added, however, that if the British authorities wished to see the King return even without a plebiscite, EDES would offer no resistance whatsoever. "We are determined," he concluded, "in full cooperation with royalists at home and abroad, to resist any attempt, such as the one already undertaken, to arbitrarily and forcefully impose a Communist regime."[6]

Thus, despite the staunch republicanism of many of his lieutenants and Zervas' own vehement denials that he had in fact offered to assist the Right in fighting the Left, EDES as an organization emerged from the war as a supporter of the King's cause. Moreover, although charges that it collaborated with the enemy were very frequently Communist-inspired, the accusation proved damaging, particularly as the evidence incriminating subordinate commands was at

---

[6] Komnenos Pyromaglou, *O Georgios Kartalis Kai I Epohi Tou, 1934-57* (Athens, 1965), p. 543. Pyromaglou, a staunch republican, was Zervas' deputy and represented EDES at the Lebanon Conference in May 1944. On EDES see also his *I Ethniki Antistasis* (Athens, 1947).

least on some occasions more than circumstantial. In one instance, and according to the commander of the German forces in western Greece, a joint German–EDES operation in the spring of 1944 completely destroyed an ELAS band of about 2,000 men near Karpenision.[7] Although his personal patriotic motives could never be impugned, Zervas' political judgment was the cause of much frustration among many of his advisers, and he found himself a controversial figure without popular appeal. All this made EDES, which at the time of liberation numbered about 12,000 men, an easy target of leftist propaganda.

Another resistance organization of strong republican sympathies, the "National and Social Liberation" (EKKA), was formally established in Athens in July 1941 under the leadership of George Kartalis, a political figure of considerable prominence, but did not field a guerrilla force until the spring of 1943. With powerful British backing it began operations in northern Greece under an able officer, Colonel Dimitrios Psarros, who the previous year had formed his personal band of several hundred armed men. A small force surrounded by more powerful and better established ELAS units, Psarros' "5/42 Regiment" valiantly resisted pressures to incorporate it into the ELAS structure. After several skirmishes a temporary accommodation was reached in July 1943, when British liaison officers succeed in bringing about a formal agreement for coexistence and cooperation among the various guerrilla groups in the mountains of northern Greece. However, the truce proved ineffective as ELAS soon resumed its efforts to eliminate from the mountains all rival organizations. The 5/42 was repeatedly attacked and partially disarmed. Finally, in April 1944, following the small-scale civil war of the previous winter (the "First Round"), Colonel Psarros and a number of his officers were overpowered and subsequently killed, probably on orders from Aris. The men of the 5/42 were scattered; some of them

[7] Condit, pp. 163-64.

joining ELAS as the only means of survival. Other minor resistance groups met a similarly cruel fate at the hands of ELAS.

Of the underground organizations with a clearly conservative outlook the most prestigious was a group called "X." It was headed by Colonel George Grivas,[8] a dynamic and dedicated royalist, and membership was at the outset limited to former officers of the Greek army's Second Division which before the occupation had been based in Athens. To Grivas' chagrin the British refused to support "X," fearing that its openly monarchist program would further inflame the fratricidal tendencies of the Greek resistance. Convinced from the beginning that the country's real and lasting enemy was the Communist Party, Grivas succeeded in obtaining weapons from the puppet Greek government in Athens and in gathering around him monarchist and Metaxist elements. A force of perhaps as many as one thousand armed men was eventually assembled, devoting its efforts to attacking EAM and KKE activists in the capital, with at least the tacit approval of the German authorities. Thus, though not a genuine resistance organization, "X" was a significant factor in the Greek political world as the moment of liberation approached.

Other resistance organizations which were devoted to the restoration of the monarchy included the "National Action," the "Union of Reserve Officers," the "National Revolutionary Corps," the "Agrarian Action," the "Spark," and the "Sacred Phalanx." Operating mostly in the principal urban centers and some with a mere handful of members, they were as concerned with the domestic Communist menace as with the foreign occupation. In 1943 Marshal Alexander Papagos organized the "Military Hierarchy," bringing to-

[8] In the 1950's, Grivas, a Cypriot, headed the Greek resistance organization EOKA which fought the British in the cause of *Enosis*, or union of Cyprus with Greece. Subsequently he became a powerful figure in the Republic of Cyprus.

27

gether army officers anxious to counter the domination of the resistance by republicans and Communists. Metropoletan Chrysanthos, former Archbishop of Athens, was widely regarded as the spiritual leader of these royalist groups and as the King's informal representative in occupied Greece. After the war Prime Minister Tsouderos was to complain that these right-wing organizations had been conspiring together with royalist circles in the Middle East to bring about the King's return, by coup if necessary.[9] According to one Greek source, when the Security Battalions were being denounced from Cairo as traitorous, Metropoletan Chrysanthos urged their officers and men to join the "national" resistance to avoid punishment after liberation. The prelate apparently wanted the Security Battalions preserved so that they might be employed as the "last reserves," presumably against the Communists and their sympathizers.[10]

Even the most sketchy survey of wartime resistance would be incomplete without reference to the allied military personnel who operated in occupied Greece. In October 1942 a small group of British officers and enlisted men, under Brigadier Edward C. W. Myers, was parachuted into Greece to carry out the destruction of the important Gorgopotamos viaduct on the railway line linking the north with Athens and the key port of Piraeus.[11] The Germans were using this route to supply Rommel's forces in North Africa and to transport Greek labor to Germany. When that remarkable mission was accomplished with the grudging cooperation of ELAS and EDES units, the British authorities in Cairo decided that the continued presence of allied agents in Greece would facilitate the expansion and coordination of guerrilla operations. Even after the plans for a Balkan invasion had been abandoned, it remained important to

[9] Pyromaglou, *Kartalis*, p. 575.
[10] *Ibid.*, p. 562.
[11] Edward C. W. Myers, *Greek Entanglement* (London, 1955).

harass the Germans and keep them guessing about the allies' next move. For this, stepped up guerrilla activity was essential. Accordingly, Myers became the chief of the British Military Mission and his subordinates were designated British Liaison Officers. In August 1943 Myers, a professional soldier with no flair for political gamesmanship, was replaced by his brilliant political adviser, Colonel Christopher M. Woodhouse, known to thousands of Greeks as "Colonel Chris."[12] In the fall of the same year two American army officers were attached to the British Military Mission, which was thereby designated Allied Military Mission to Greece. In December 1943 Major Gerald K. Wines became the senior American officer under Woodhouse's command. Scores of American and British demolition teams began operating as separate units in the Greek mountains. At the time of the German withdrawal about 400 allied personnel, mostly British, were fighting in Greece alongside the native resistance forces.

Although ostensibly an allied endeavor, responsibility for supplying and directing the Greek underground was almost entirely British, as indeed was the entire theater of operations in the eastern Mediterranean. Myers and Woodhouse received their instructions from British political and military authorities in Cairo, headquarters of the Middle East Command and, after May 1943, seat of the Greek government-in-exile. Though increasingly unhappy about the handling of Greek problems, American officials confined themselves largely to intelligence-gathering and logistical functions, allowing their British colleagues free reign in making all important decisions.

At first the British Liaison Officers devoted their energies to the procurement of weapons, supplies, and gold sov-

[12] Christopher M. Woodhouse's *Apple of Discord: A Survey of Recent Greek Politics in Their International Setting* (London, n.d.) remains one of the most important sources regarding the Greek resistance movement and British policies toward it.

ereigns for the guerrilla forces in their respective areas of responsibility and to the planning and carrying out of acts of sabotage. They soon discovered, however, that the nature of their mission was rapidly changing from military to political. The mounting rivalry between the major resistance groups threatened not only to destroy their effectiveness but also to engulf the country in a civil war from which only the enemy would profit. Courageous and resourceful, these British men worked hard to harness ELAS and EDES to the allied cause. A few among them, including Lieutenant Colonel Rufus Sheppard, developed strong sympathies for EAM/ELAS and stressed in their despatches its popularity among the common people. Most, however, found its Communist core personally distasteful and a serious menace to both British and Greek long-range interests. On the basis of such reports, and anxious about Greece's position in the postwar balance, the British government repeatedly considered declaring ELAS a force hostile to the allied cause. In the end these British agents found themselves struggling to subdue EAM/ELAS' aggressiveness and to bolster the fortunes of EDES, in the vain hope that a rudimentary power balance between them could be preserved until liberation. It was to prove a most frustrating mission.

Furthermore, these agents were called upon to implement the policies of their military and diplomatic superiors whose aims in Greece could not easily be reconciled. On the one hand, anxious to maximize guerrilla activity against the enemy, the Middle East Command in Cairo insisted that the resistance movement be augmented and supplied without regard for the political leanings and ambitions of its component parts. The only criterion for providing weapons and money was that the group have military prowess. In London on the other hand the Foreign Office tended to deprecate the value of guerrilla action in areas of such limited strategic importance and became increasingly alarmed by what it perceived to be the long-range consequences of the building up of guerrilla forces which were known to oppose the King's return and whose political ambitions were viewed as inimical to Britain's interests in the Balkans and eastern Mediterranean. In the opinion of the Foreign Office, which had the backing of the Prime Minister, it was far more important to use Britain's powerful influence to create those conditions inside Greece and abroad which would enable a strong, British-supported democratic government under King George to return home at the moment of liberation to preside over the country's economic and political recovery. Greece would thus remain London-oriented in the uncertain days ahead. Thus, from the outset British agents in occupied Greece were under orders, unless special circumstances dictated otherwise, to lend their support only to those guerrilla groups which were favorable to the monarchy's return.[13]

Until 1943 the momentum of the war effort allowed the military authorities to pursue their objectives in the Greek mountains. Coincidentally, anti-monarchy sentiment was also mounting. After that year, which represented the turning point in the war in favor of the Allies, the diplomats of London did their best to curb the activities of the left-wing resistance forces and prevent them from dominating the scene. The loss of controlling influence over events in Yugoslavia, where Tito's Communist movement appeared destined to prevail, made the British government even more determined to avert a similar fate for Greece. But the genie of left-wing republicanism would not willingly return to its bottle.

The Greek government which reached London in September 1941 represented a curious mixture of political factions. The new Prime Minister, Emmanuel I. Tsouderos, a colorless but generally respected figure of moderately republican views, headed a cabinet of Metaxist luminaries,

[13] Sir Llewellyn Woodward, *British Foreign Policy in the Second World War* (London, 1962), pp. 353-55.

including Minister of Interior Constantine Maniadakis who at the time of the German attack had been keeping Tsouderos as well as other prominent politicians under house arrest. Although relations between King George and Tsouderos were quite correct, the monarch chose to surround himself with personal friends and political sympathizers who prevented him from sensing the winds of change blowing both inside and out of his country. He was particularly perturbed by Tsouderos' insistence, supported by the British government, that as the most offensive reminder of the dictatorship, Maniadakis had to be removed. Moreover, on November 25, 1941, the British government expressed to Tsouderos the hope that, after the country's liberation, the King would return to Greece to proclaim a democratic, representative constitution. On February 4, the King was prevailed upon to sign a decree declaring Metaxas' regime formally ended. While giving in to these pressures, the Greek monarch viewed the dismissal of his loyal supporters as the prelude to a concerted effort to undermine the very foundations of the dynasty.

A man of integrity but of rather narrow vision, steeped in a tradition which stressed the need for discipline, respect for established authority, and paternalism necessitated by the political immaturity and irresponsibility of the masses, King George refused to come to grips with the unpleasant fact that in Greece the monarchy was no longer a popular institution.[14] Throughout the war years, despite mounting evidence to the contrary, he continued to believe that the criticism directed against the throne was the work of a few leftist agitators and naïve liberal types among the British military, and that the vast majority of Greeks was anxious to welcome him back. He refused to change his mind even when he was advised that on March 31, 1942 most promi-

[14] For the King's point of view see Arthur S. Gould Lee, *The Royal House of Greece* (London, 1948), pp. 88-190.

nent political figures of every persuasion in occupied Athens had signed a statement declaring their intention to oppose the King's return until a plebiscite had given the public the opportunity to decide whether or not it wished to retain the institution of the monarchy. Convinced of his own higher motives and of the throne's stabilizing influence, he could not entertain the possibility that the interests of the country and of the crown were not eternally identical. The support which Prime Minister Churchill, Field Marshal Jan Smuts, and even President Roosevelt appeared to offer him at every crucial juncture encouraged him to remain adamant in his position.

The government's center of gravity, already altered by the departure of Metaxists, continued to move from right to left. When the Cabinet was brought to Cairo in May 1943, it was exposed to powerful anti-royalist influences emanating from political and military circles of Greeks who had escaped to the Middle East, and from the prominent local Greek communities. A coterie of known and unknown figures gathered around Tsouderos, eager to fill positions whose real functions were all but nonexistent. As a result of several reorganizations, and to the dismay of King George, the Cabinet came to represent a powerful liberal-republican orientation and to reflect the view that the monarchy's future was the most crucial issue confronting the nation. Among its more prominent members were Panayiotis Kanellopoulos and Sofocles Venizelos, son of the great statesman and arch-rival of the King's father. At the same time the Greek government discovered that its very existence, as well as the maintenance of the Greek armed forces assembled in the Middle East, depended entirely upon the support and good will of the British authorities. Even its contacts with occupied Greece had to be arranged through British channels. For its part the British government made it quite clear at every turn that it did not approve of efforts

33

to raise political questions and to undermine the authority of King George, particularly while the war was still in progress.

But if the activities of the government-in-exile were held in check by British pressures, allowing only occasional ministerial changes, the Greek troops proved themselves a much more difficult client to handle. Recruited from Greeks who had managed to escape the surveillance of the occupation authorities and from the numerous Greek communities in the Middle East, they were eventually organized into two brigades, two independent infantry battalions; a tank regiment, and the special Sacred Battalion whose men had all been officers of the Greek army. There was also a sizeable contingent of naval vessels and several airforce units. Of the total of approximately 30,000 men, more than 2,500 were officers, making for a top-heavy, highly politicized army. It was equipped, trained, and supplied by the British authorities who, nevertheless, displayed a rather curious reluctance to employ it on a regular basis. The First Brigade fought valiantly at the battle of El Alamein, and the Sacred Battalion participated in the capture of Tunis. Otherwise, the Greek armed forces languished in inactivity, engaging instead in political intrigue.

Commanded at first by officers who had served under the Metaxas regime, these units were soon staffed by republican elements which gradually made their way from occupied Greece. Already in October 1941 American diplomatic circles in Cairo were reporting "growing dissension" and "feuding" among Greek emigrés there. To prevent such disaffection from undermining their discipline the Greek army units had been transferred to more remote bases in Palestine to complete their training. Mounting political friction broke into the open in March 1942 and forced Tsouderos to come from London and remove from key positions certain staunchly royalist officers. The following February mutinous activity in both brigades again brought Tsouderos to Cairo, this time accompanied by the King, to preside over a major reshuffling of prominent military and political figures.[15] Allied sources in Cairo generally attributed the disturbances to the growing cleavage between leftist and royalist officers, to the disruptive activities of republican politicians, and to the widespread belief that plans to merge the two brigades into a single division under the royalist General Zagouris were an attempt to prepare the army to reimpose a monarchist dictatorship after liberation. Thus fear and hatred of still-active Metaxist senior officers reportedly were at the heart of the problem. On the other hand a British source identified Vice Premier Panayiotis Kanellopoulos as a principal troublemaker.[16]

Once more the royalists found themselves on the losing side. However, despite a lull in the simmering crisis, it was no longer possible to ignore the powerful pro-republican sentiment in the army and navy, or the increasing influence of EAM, particularly among lower ranks. Indeed, after the spring of 1943, it appeared that large numbers of those escaping from Greece and making their way into the armed forces were EAM sympathizers. Many were leftists; few were Communists. They were soon organizing themselves into groups which, ignoring every principle of military discipline, demanded that the government accede to their political wishes. Specifically they argued for the "democratization" of the Tsouderos government by the inclusion in the Cabinet of more liberal figures and the removal of the remnants of the Metaxist regime and for the application of similar measures to the military commands. Furthermore, they

[15] Emmanuel I. Tsouderos, *Ellinikes Anomalies Sti Mesi Anatoli* (Athens, 1945), pp. 25-32.

[16] The Department of State, *Foreign Relations of the United States, Diplomatic Papers, 1943. IV: The Near East and Africa* (Washington, D.C., 1964), 124. Hereafter cited as *FR* (1943).

demanded a commitment by King George that he would not return to Greece until a plebiscite had been held.[17]

On July 1, 1943, in order to calm political tempers, the Tsouderos Cabinet formally decided to advise the King that immediately following its return to Greece, it would submit its resignation, thus paving the way for general elections to a national assembly which would then be called upon to settle the crucial constitutional question of the dynasty's future. Replying to this move King George declared over Radio Cairo on July 4 (in an open message to Colonel Zervas) that at the end of the war the Greek people would be "invited to decide by popular and free vote the institutions with which Greece must endow herself in sympathy with the forward march of democracy."[18] He made no mention of the timing of his return. However, in a telegraphic message to political leaders in the homeland, Prime Minister Tsouderos made it clear that his government would return to Greece accompanied by the King.[19]

While trying to defuse the constitutional issue, the Prime Minister was astonished and dismayed to learn on August 4, 1943 that without consulting him the British were bringing to Cairo from occupied Greece representatives of the principal resistance forces. The group, which reached Cairo on August 10 escorted by Brigadier Myers, consisted of four spokesmen for the leftist-Communist EAM coalition (E. Tsirimokos, P. Roussos, A. Tsimas, and K. Despotopoulos), one representative of EDES (Zervas' republican deputy, K. Pyromaglou) and the leader of EKKA, G. Kartalis. Another political figure, G. Exindaris, who had traveled from Athens to Cairo via Turkey, had been authorized to represent the pre-war parties of the democratic center. According to Myers, who was instrumental in organizing the mission, its

---

[17] Department of State Records, 868.00/1209, April 5, 1943. Hereafter cited as *DSR*. Date of document given only when not appearing as part of the document's number.

[18] *FR* (1943), 135.   [19] Tsouderos, p. 62.

principal task was to forestall rivalry among the guerrilla groups by having them officially recognized by the Cairo authorities as units of the Greek armed forces and by introducing in the Greek General Staff liaison officers representing the resistance. Correspondingly, in order to avert political friction in the days ahead, the Myers mission wished to see incorporated into the Greek Cabinet representatives of "Mountain Greece" and to have one or two ministers sent to liberated areas to speak for the entire government and prepare for its return to the homeland upon liberation.[20] Thus a firm bond was to be established between the resistance movement at home on the one hand and the exiled government on the other.

Instead of inspiring unity, the Cairo talks of August 1943 served to aggravate existing division and intensify mistrust within Greece's political world. It also brought to the surface for the first time the widening gulf separating the majority of Greek leaders from the British. Efforts to improve coordination between the guerrillas and the military authorities in Cairo were abandoned almost immediately as political issues overshadowed everything else. Brigadier Myers was ordered to return to London where he was promptly relieved of his assignment to Greece. Prime Minister Tsouderos, encouraged by Ambassador Leeper, rejected all suggestions for including in his Cabinet representatives of the resistance organizations. Nor would he agree to send any of his ministers to the liberated areas of the homeland. The only issue upon which all Greeks present—as well as all political parties including the Populists (with the exception of their leader, Constantine Tsaldaris)—readily agreed was the demand for a signed and unequivocal statement from King George that he would return to Greece only if a national plebiscite had invited him back. According to an American diplomatic source, the spokesmen for the resistance organizations had insisted that the political climate in

[20] Myers, pp. 228-66.

Greece dictated that the monarch await the result of a plebiscite on the issue of his return. In the meantime he could continue to function as the chief representative of the country in relation to other governments. A formal declaration on this point was addressed to Tsouderos and on August 19 the Cabinet unanimously concurred that, "to avoid disturbances and possible bloodshed," the King must agree to remain abroad until the future of the dynasty had been decided by a plebiscite.[21]

Rejecting this request of his government, King George formally appealed to the leaders of Britain and the United States for support in his determination to defy the demands of the nation's spokesmen. The result was the first of a long series of instances throughout the war when Greek leaders found themselves consigned to the role of passive observers in the manipulation of their national issues. In a round of talks on August 20-21 senior British and American officials informed the Greek leaders assembled in Cairo that any further declarations on the part of the King beyond his vague promise of July 4 were unnecessary and unwise. The American Ambassador to the Greek government, Alex. C. Kirk, reported that together with his British colleague he had "counselled the King and Tsouderos to make every effort" to convince all concerned "that this was not the moment to raise such an issue as it was not immediate and that such agitation would only serve to detract from the effort of Greece to aid the United Nations in the fight against aggressors and for the liberation of Greece." Kirk also informed his superiors that the British government had made it plain that it would not allow the Greek King to consent to a plebiscite prior to his return to Athens.[22] All this despite the very obvious fact that to the Greeks themselves the

[21] Tsouderos, p. 65.
[22] *FR* (1943), 142. See also Kirk's reports of August 20 and 22, 1943, on the Greek crisis, in *ibid.*, 145-46, and in *DSR*, 868.00/1267, Sept. 2, 1943.

matter of the plebiscite was both "immediate" and the very basis for further concerted efforts to harass the enemy and contribute to the allied cause. When the more outspoken leaders of the republican Left protested this interference in Greek affairs, General Henry M. Wilson, Allied Commander-in-Chief for the Middle East, personally and brusquely reminded the resistance representatives that they were under his direct authority and ordered them to return to Greece at once. Their refusal to board their plane merely delayed for a few days their expulsion. Such highhanded treatment of the spokesmen of an allied resistance movement and the support expressed by the British for the King's cause had the most profound effect upon the entire political world of Greece, but especially the republican Left. In mid-November, while denying widespread rumors that the men of the Greek resistance had been imprisoned or even murdered by the British, American diplomatic sources in Cairo observed that the civil war which had recently broken out in the Greek mountains was in part the outcome of the hostile attitudes which the EAM, EKKA, and EDES representatives had encountered in Cairo.[23]

Churchill's personal reply to the King's appeal for support was received on August 26, several days after the top-level Anglo-American conference at Quebec (August 22, 1943). Military decisions reached at that meeting made it clear that at the moment of liberation no significant allied forces would be present in Greece to restore order and prevent any precipitous political action which the republican Left might be contemplating. Consequently, if the resistance organizations operating in the Greek mountains were not to impose their own political aims, their influence would have to be counterbalanced while the country was still under enemy control. Thus the British leader declared that the King's statement of July 4 represented the line of thought that was designed to serve the interests of Greece

[23] DSR, 868.01/409, Nov. 14, 1943.

best and that, at least for the present, the King should refuse to make further pronouncements regarding his position
at the time of liberation. Whatever his decision, Churchill
concluded, King George could count on the "greatest possible support" from the British government.[24] President
Roosevelt's message to the Greek monarch took the same
position without, however, a similar pledge of support. The
President wrote: "I hope that in the interest of our common
war effort all Greeks will accept the program announced in
Your Majesty's radio address of July 4 as a guarantee that
they will have full opportunity freely to express their political will at the earliest practicable moment and that they will
meanwhile subordinate other considerations to the urgent
necessity of winning the war and liberating their homeland."[25]

Encouraged by such manifestations of sympathy for his
position, King George addressed a letter to his Prime Minister on November 8 restating his views on the constitutional
issue. He asserted that at the moment of liberation, guided
by the political and military situation prevailing in the
country, and taking into consideration the national interest,
he would review once more the question of his return. He
promised to consult with his government before reaching
a decision.[26] This, of course, was no substitute for the signed
statement demanded by virtually every political faction,
that he would definitely not return to Greece pending a
plebiscite. However, this debate over the dynasty's future
was suddenly overtaken by a most dramatic sequence of
events, first on the Greek mountains and, soon afterward,
in the Middle East. Thus in retrospect it can be argued that
the Cairo talks of August 1943 had represented a major and

[24] Tsouderos, pp. 67-68.
[25] *FR* (1943), 151. Significantly, the Department of State was
reluctant to give the President's message any publicity for fear that
it would antagonize the Greek Left and contribute to further controversy (*DSR*, 868.01/387, Sept. 17, 1943).
[26] Tsouderos, pp. 72-74.

genuine opportunity to harness all political factions to a common national cause and avoid the bloodshed that was soon to come. When the talks failed each side chose to interpret the failure in its own narrow way and prepared to act accordingly.

The collapse of the Cairo talks was followed almost immediately by the resumption of ELAS attacks upon rival resistance organizations in Epirus and elsewhere on a scale so large that the entire affair later came to be known as the "First Round" in what appeared to be a Communist struggle to seize power by force.

It is now clear that the First Round was in fact sparked by many factors which had contributed to the collapse of the precarious balance existing among the quarreling resistance groups. From its early days ELAS had shown little tolerance for other guerrilla bands, insisting that they should place themselves under its authority in the interests of unity and greater effectiveness against the enemy. Although it was frequently the instigator of incidents, there were exceptions, particularly in areas where ELAS's strength was not clearly superior. In the Athens-Piraeus region EAM followers and ELAS recruiters often fell victim to the terror tactics of right-wing organizations which feared the likelihood of a Communist-imposed regime at least as much as they hated the German occupation. Moreover, after the summer of 1943 British attitudes toward the various resistance organizations were interpreted by the EAM/ELAS leadership as an open attempt to bolster its rivals and curtail republican-leftist influence across the country. In the fall of 1943, in one of the most bizarre episodes of the occupation, a New Zealander, Captain Donald Stott, sent to Athens on an espionage and sabotage mission, arranged instead to enter into negotiations with the German authorities. Though very little is known about this affair, and although there is every reason to believe that Stott's actions went beyond the scope of his orders, his probable intention was to assist anti-Communist organizations to assume power in the capital at the moment of the German withdrawal. Nothing came of his efforts and he was quickly recalled to Cairo. Nevertheless, as the chief of the Allied Military Mission to Greece has recorded, Stott's secret dealings had already done enough "to convict British policy, in the eyes of malevolent critics, of collusion with the enemy" for the purpose of frustrating EAM's postwar aims.[27] The suspension of deliveries of supplies to ELAS offered further weight to the argument that a widening conspiracy against EAM/ELAS did in fact exist. Clever German propaganda did much to inflame suspicions and hatred. Finally, British-inspired rumors that Greece was about to be liberated had served as the catalyst for the several months' fighting which ensued.

In October 1943 isolated incidents led to full-scale assaults by ELAS upon its rivals. Vastly outnumbered and confused, the forces of EDES and EKKA suffered considerable losses in personnel and equipment. In all, several hundred men were killed and many more wounded. EKKA's military arm, the 5/42, was completely destroyed. To make matters worse, the Germans took advantage of the situation to launch a large-scale operation and to regain control of the more vital lines of communication across northern Greece. By December EDES had been confined to a small area of Epirus. Both sides appeared exhausted and ready to listen to the most urgent pleas from Cairo and elsewhere that they put an end to fratricide. However, while Colonel Woodhouse was trying to arrange a truce, and in an apparent attempt to strengthen its position before the impending negotiations, EDES launched a counteroffensive. Fighting was resumed in earnest, despite new appeals from Prime Minister Tsouderos, King George, and the British. After repeated proddings, Moscow also issued a half-hearted state-

[27] Woodhouse, p. 39.

ment on January 4, declaring: "As the British Government, on the basis of the information available to it, considers that a reconciliation of the rivalry among the partisan groups in Greece is now possible, the Soviet Government considers it expedient, with the aim of strengthening the struggle against the German invaders, to support the creation of a unified front of all partisan groups in Greece."[28] The results of such pressure from every quarter were not immediately apparent. ELAS once again took the initiative and EDES was forced to retreat further. Finally, on February 4, 1944, a cease-fire was arranged, followed by a conference under the auspices of the Allied Military Mission. The result was the Plaka Agreement of February 29, negotiated personally by Zervas for EDES, Aris for ELAS, and Woodhouse for the allies, in the midst of the most confusing and explosive round of talks. Under its terms ELAS and EDES accepted the "final cessation of hostilities" between them, agreed to exchange prisoners and hostages, and to confine themselves to the areas which they occupied at the time of the truce. They assumed the obligation "of fighting the Occupation and its collaborators with all their forces, either independently in their respective areas or in common by prearranged agreement." A common plan of operations was to be worked out, and the Allied Military Mission was requested to provide "the maximum possible supplies for the forces of all organizations in Greece, on the basis of their operations against the Germans and in proportion to the real requirements of the war." At the request of Colonel Woodhouse a "secret clause" was also included, stipulating that all resistance groups would cooperate in the execution of

---

[28] Department of State, *Foreign Relations of the United States. Diplomatic Papers. 1944. V: The Near East, South Asia, and Africa. The Far East* (Washington, D.C., 1965) 85. Hereafter cited as *FR* (1944). See also report from Ambassador Lincoln MacVeagh from Cairo, Jan. 5, 1944, in *ibid.*, 85-86.

operation "Noah's Ark," the allied plan for the liberation of Greece.[29]

Although the Plaka Agreement signaled the end of the First Round, friction and skirmishes continued. As already mentioned in mid-April EKKA's military leader, Psarros, whose forces had already been scattered, was captured and killed. Even though serious fighting did not break out again, the bitterness of division continued, and so did the suspicion that the Communists in EAM/ELAS were biding their time, waiting for the right moment to launch the "Second Round."

In March 1944 there appeared to be further cause for alarm. An EAM-sponsored "Political Committee of National Liberation" (PEEA) was formed in territory controlled by ELAS in what appeared to be a move to monopolize power at the end of the occupation.[30] The official communique of March 16, issued at the ELAS headquarters and addressed to Tsouderos in Cairo, announced the establishment in "Free Greece" of the Political Committee of National Liberation for the purpose of "uniting the national forces for the coordination of the national liberation struggle by the side of the Allies, for the administration of the areas in Greece already free or being freed, and for safeguarding after liberation a smooth and free political life throughout the country." More particularly, PEEA would seek to establish "the firm foundation of a government of general national unity, interpreting the manifest desire of the people and their armed forces." The message concluded with an appeal to Tsouderos "to realize the imperative national needs and make an effective contribution to the formation of a government of general national unity."[31]

[29] For the text of the Plaka Agreement of Feb. 29, 1944, see Appendix A. Pyromaglou's *Kartalis* (pp. 195-267) contains the author's extensive "minutes" of the Plaka Conference.

[30] Editorials in *Rizospastis*, March 24 and 30, 1944.

[31] Sir Reginald Leeper, *When Greek Meets Greek* (London, 1950),

This announcement appeared to echo the demands of the resistance organizations of the previous August for a broadening of the government abroad and the despatch of one or two of its members to the mountains of Greece. Alarmed by this development Prime Minister Tsouderos warned his colleagues in Cairo that the situation in Greece would have to be watched very closely, particularly if the allies failed to denounce PEEA for fear that EAM/ELAS might once again resort to hostile acts.[32] While the Greek government watched helplessly from Cairo, PEEA proceeded to form a "Cabinet" of its own under Colonel Euripides Bakirdzis, a staunch republican, who assumed the title of "President" and "Minister of Foreign Affairs." Later he was succeeded in both titles by Alexander Svolos, the respected Professor of Constitutional Law at the University of Athens. Communists became "Ministers" of Interior, Justice, and Agriculture. Elections were held in ELAS-controlled areas, and in May 1944 a "National Assembly" was convened. EDES and other organizations were invited but, to no one's surprise, refused to take part in the formation and operations of this "Government." Thus the Greeks now appeared "blessed" with three governments: the puppet regime in Athens, the EAM-sponsored Political Committee in the mountains, and the Tsouderos government in Cairo. Moreover, matters were destined to become worse.

The position of the British and American governments regarding the future of the monarchy—a crucial element in

---

pp. 39-40. The author served as British Ambassador to the Greek government during 1943-46.

[32] B. P. Papadakis, *Diplomatiki Istoria tou Ellinikou Polemou, 1940-1945* (Athens, 1957), p. 327. On the other hand, MacVeagh reported from Cairo on March 31 that Tsouderos ". . . is not worried about developments in Greece since he has had a second message from the Committee couched like the first in conciliatory terms and only urging speed in the negotiations for a government of national unity; and he believes that the Committee not only lacks popular support but is aware of the lack" (*FR* [1944], 89).

the unfolding drama—has already been alluded to above and will be examined in some detail in later chapters. When in December 1943 the British government appeared to modify its stand and pressured King George to publicly declare that he would await the verdict of a plebiscite before returning to Greece, President Roosevelt unexpectedly sided with the King and encouraged him to reject such a recommendation, despite the fact that it had been endorsed by the British and Greek governments and had been strongly advocated by American diplomatic circles. Disappointed by this turn of events which could only prolong the crisis, Tsouderos submitted his resignation and recorded in his diary: "The King has not come out the winner from this business. . . ."[33] However, he was prevailed upon to continue in office, and on December 13 he prepared a broad plan designed to shelve the constitutional issue and in cooperation with the British authorities prepare for the country's liberation.

According to the protocol of December 13 the King was to decide the timing of his return in consultation with his government, as indeed he had already promised to do in his letter to Tsouderos of November 18, 1943. Meanwhile "all discussion and misunderstanding concerning the matter of the King's return to Greece must be considered definitely ended. . . ." Hereafter all political questions pertaining to the armed forces and resistance groups were to be handled jointly by the Greek government and the appropriate British authorities. The Archbishop of Athens, Damascinos, was to be entrusted to form a secret advisory committee of notables and to personally act as the government's "representative" in the still-occupied country. Some of his advisers might be brought into the government so as to strengthen the feeling of solidarity between Athens and Cairo and to pave the way for peaceful and free elections.[34] Significantly, Tsouderos' protocol made no provision for the

[33] Tsouderos, p. 78. [34] *Ibid.*, pp. 79-80.

guerrilla forces of "Mountain Greece." Clearly, this statement of purpose, which Prime Minister Churchill heartily endorsed, represented a reaffirmation of the King's position and a set-back for those who continued to regard his intention to return to Greece before a plebiscite as the seed of future troubles. It also constituted a determined effort to keep the political initiative during the approaching critical moments of liberation in the hands of the official government—and its designated representatives in Athens—and to discourage EAM from seeking to establish a *de facto* authority in Greece.

It now became necessary to ascertain the reactions of those in Athens (but not those of "Mountain Greece") to the December 13 proposed plan of action. The contents of the protocol were communicated to Archbishop Damascinos by a secret courier, Colonel Emmanuel Fradellos, who made his way to Athens during the first week of January 1944. Even before his return, however, there were serious complications. In the midst of the First Round EAM formally requested Cairo to send to the mountains a representative to negotiate the formation of a new government of "national unity." The government replied that no political talks were possible as long as the shooting continued. Moreover, in the exchanges which ensued, the Prime Minister expressed himself willing to consider the broadening of the Cairo government by the inclusion of leftist elements but remained adamant in his position that his Cabinet was the only legitimate government of Greece. Within a few weeks, however, there could be no doubt that EAM, through the recently established "Political Committee of National Liberation," intended to compete with Cairo for legitimacy and power.

Nor was trouble emanating from the Greek mountains alone. On March 1 Tsouderos telegraphed the King in London that in his view it was "imperative" to have the First Brigade transferred immediately from Cairo to the Italian theater in order to keep it from coming under the influence of various individuals arriving from Greece who intend to raise "political issues which may affect military discipline." Such disruption would constitute a "national disaster" because the prestige of Greece in allied circles rested upon the national forces now stationed in the Middle East. Tsouderos reported that the movement of the Brigade to Italy had evidently been postponed or even permanently blocked and that certain of its officers, "apparently for political reasons," wished to keep the unit in Cairo on the pretext that it would thus be closer to Greece and would be better able to take part in the country's liberation.[35]

Colonel Fradellos returned to Cairo on March 6, the bearer of many reports, letters, and personal impressions. Tsouderos immediately informed British Ambassador Reginald Leeper that the messages received from the Archbishop and others left no doubt that the King must not return before the people had declared themselves on the constitutional question. However, "this time the King is not [merely] being requested to make a new statement to this effect, but to sign a decree appointing as of now a regent who will undertake to regulate the country's political life as soon as the enemy has evacuated Athens." All political parties and resistance organizations without exception concurred on this point; and they unanimously recommended the Archbishop for the office of regent. The outcome of every other major issue, including the reorganization of the guerrilla forces, was believed to depend upon the satisfactory settlement of the matter of the regency. Accordingly Leeper was advised that the Cairo government would recommend the appointment of Archbishop Damascinos as regent. On a related question, the political groups whose views had been solicited regarded the Cairo Cabinet as the only national government. However, whereas the leftists recommended once more that it be expanded, and that four of its members (presumably the representatives of the

[35] *Ibid.*, p. 85.

Left) be located in Greece, other political factions thought that no more than two representatives of the Left might be included and that, in any event, the entire government should remain in Cairo until the moment of liberation. The matter of the government's composition, Tsouderos concluded, would be solved without much difficulty if the regency were first established and if certain political figures in Greece whose groups were not in the present Cabinet were brought to Cairo. However, if the King refused to appoint a regent, the situation would not develop "normally."[36]

On March 8 Tsouderos presented the same information to the King by letter and on behalf of his government urged him to appoint Damascinos regent. He stressed that such a move would insure a normal and peaceful transition after liberation. Otherwise, difficulties were certain to arise, and in all probability they would begin in Cairo. He expressed the conviction that in Greece public opinion was being guided by "leftist elements of every kind, and by the armed forces in the mountains." Furthermore, "the country's youth, of both sexes, almost in its entirety, but especially in the towns, has joined the leftists and the enemy occupation has accustomed it to expressing its ideas without fear and to support them by every means available. I conclude, therefore, that in view of this situation in Greece, we cannot anticipate that developments will be favorable for us if we oppose [public opinion] in such a vital matter" as the regency question. Conversely, the appointment of a regent would eventually bring about a climate favorable to the monarch, whose self-restraint would have been recognized and appreciated.[37]

Tsouderos' advice fell on deaf ears. In his brief response of March 10, King George informed his Prime Minister that he would study the information arriving from Athens before deciding his course of action. He added: "However, I

[36] *Ibid.*, pp. 85-87.   [37] *Ibid.*, pp. 87-91.

can state to you now that I find unacceptable the suggestion regarding the appointment at this time . . . of Archbishop Damascinos Regent." Furthermore, as the "emissary of the Greek people," he felt called upon "to continue the struggle against the enemy" and to preserve the nation's rights "throughout the period in which it finds itself under a foreign yoke and unable to express itself freely." The King concluded: "I do not wish, nor do I have the right, to lay down this mandate and to negotiate with anyone before the Greek people has decided sovereignly, freely, and unswayed."[38] And on March 18, having been informed of PEEA's overtures for a new government of national unity, King George once again telegraphed from London directing his Prime Minister to refrain from undertaking any commitments which might bind the monarchy, pending a more careful study of the situation.[39]

A written report and detailed recommendations from Archbishop Damascinos reached Cairo on April 6. He reiterated the view that the King must not return before the plebiscite. After conducting extensive consultations, the prelate had also concluded that the suggestion that he become the government's "representative" in occupied Greece was entirely useless. Instead he urged the immediate appointment of a regent to assume all royal prerogatives and to exert a stabilizing influence in the critical days ahead. He was prepared to accept the office at the King's request. Otherwise, he argued, a patchwork government would be called upon to preside over the difficult transition from occupation to elections, with possibly disastrous results. On the matter of the composition of the government, Damascinos advised the Prime Minister to reject the leftist demands as dangerous and expressed himself satisfied with the complexion of the existing Cabinet.[40] The Archbishop's report was forwarded to the King in London, with no apparent results.

[38] *Ibid.*, p. 87.   [39] *Ibid.*, p. 121.   [40] *Ibid.*, pp. 91-97.

Damascinos' views coincided with those expressed by an impressive number of prominent political figures in Athens whose separate letters and other messages were also brought to Cairo by Colonel Fradellos. The aging leader of the Liberal Party, Themistoclis Sofoulis, wrote that unless the King remained abroad pending a plebiscite, suspicions would intensify and the Communists would emerge as the defenders of political freedom and civil rights. The result would be civil war. The President of PEEA, Professor Svolos, wrote that, despite personal differences with EAM/KKE, he was compelled to agree with them that they represented the only forces actually fighting the foreign enemy and therefore qualified to speak for the people. He declared the old political parties defunct and warned about the powerful "new currents" sweeping the country. At the same time he sought to assure the Cairo government that the leftists desired democratic solutions to the country's problems, a guarantee of basic political freedoms and the establishment of genuine national unity. To accomplish this, however, a new government would be needed.[41]

Word that the King would not appoint a regent, and would not promise to stay away from Greece until the plebiscite, reached the Greek armed forces in the Middle East almost immediately. At the same time, the announcement that PEEA had been formed in the Greek mountains was received with great excitement and, by some, as the signal for action. Republican and Communist propaganda, combined with prolonged inactivity and low morale, sparked a new crisis. On March 9 British military authorities drew the attention of the Greek government to increased political activity among the Greek troops and expressed the fear that March 25, Greek Independence Day, might be used to precipitate unrest and demonstrations, with the most serious consequences for Greek national interests.[42]

March 25 passed without incident. Three days later, how-

[41] *Ibid.*, pp. 101-3.   [42] *Ibid.*, pp. 124-25.

51

ever, the Minister of the Army, Byron Karapanayiotis, urged Tsouderos to prevail upon the King to cancel his impending visit to Cairo because his presence there "would magnify the difficulties against which we have been struggling and I fear we shall be unable to suppress demonstrations directed primarily against him." He hinted that if the King ignored this advice, he might have to resign from the Cabinet.[43] Although Karapanayiotis was not an especially able member of the Cabinet, his alarm was well founded. A few days later Tsouderos telegraphed the King in London that in certain army and naval units there had been open and provocative declarations of pro-EAM and pro-PEEA sentiment.[44] As it soon developed, these were the rumblings of the fast-approaching storm. On March 31, a "committee of national unity of the Greek armed forces in the Middle East," consisting of republican officers, demanded to see Tsouderos and presented him with a memorandum whose tortuous language amounted to a declaration that unless the Cairo government recognized PEEA as the legitimate authority in Greece and agreed to merge with it, civil strife could not be averted.[45] The Prime Minister, who agreed to see them only when his Ministers of the Army (Karapanayiotis) and Marine (Venizelos) admitted that they no longer controlled their subordinates, rejected the officers' demands and warned them about the grave consequences of their deed. Following this encounter mutiny broke out in the First Brigade and spread quickly to other units of the Greek armed forces. As in the past, the only notable exception was the Sacred Battalion which remained loyal to the government throughout the upheaval.

The mutiny of April 1944 was the product both of a clumsily prepared plot and of the combustive forces in Greece and in Cairo which had caused earlier disorders. Pro-EAM elements among enlisted men and lower ranks

[43] *Ibid.*, pp. 123-24.   [44] *Ibid.*, p. 127.
[45] *Ibid.*, pp. 131-33.

were largely responsible for conspiratorial activity and the creation of political cells within many units. At the same time republican officers, aware of these developments, did nothing to stop them in the belief that they would be able to harness this powerful anti-government feeling to their own purposes. They were confident that the mutiny would force the King and his Cabinet to accede to their demands. Thus collusion between republicans and leftists in the armed forces was based on a common hostility toward the monarchy and suspicion of its intentions for the country's political future. It was precipitated by the King's refusal to act on the advice of Tsouderos and Damascinos to appoint a regent and promise not to return until invited by the people of Greece. Once mutiny broke out it quickly spread, in part because of the highhanded manner in which the British authorities dealt with the entire affair: men who had not joined the mutineers did so when ordered to surrender their weapons and march off to detention.

Contrary to scattered rumors, and despite British Ambassador Leeper's complaint that "the Russians could stop the trouble in a minute if they would,"[46] there is no evidence that Soviet influence was involved either in the outbreak or the course of the mutiny. Although Moscow's press was critical of the British and the Soviet Ambassasor in Cairo expressed considerable interest in the matter of the mutiny, leading to speculation that perhaps "Russia aspires to supplant Britain as the dominating foreign power in Greek affairs,"[47] his conduct remained entirely correct. On the other hand, in dealing with the crisis, Prime Minister Churchill instructed Leeper "on no account [to] accept any assistance from American or Russian sources, otherwise than as specially enjoined by me."[48] Moreover, when order

[46] *FR* (1944), 101.　　　　　[47] *Ibid.*, 100.
[48] Winston S. Churchill, *The Second World War* (Boston, 1951), v, 546. When MacVeagh inquired whether the Americans could help in any way, Leeper replied: "I think not. We have the military re-

had been restored President Roosevelt, complying with a plea from London, wrote to Churchill expressing support for his handling of the matter, and added: "As one whose family and who personally has contributed by personal help for over a century to Greek independence, frankly I am not happy over the situation as it is at present and hope that everywhere Greeks will retain their sense of proportion and will set aside pettiness. Let every Greek show a personal unselfishness which is so necessary now and think of their glorious past. . . ."[49] While satisfying the British, the President's message caused much grief to many a Greek who felt that, deliberately or otherwise, the real causes of the crisis had once again been conveniently ignored.

Faced with superior British force and determination, the leaders of the mutiny accepted surrender, detention, and eventual court-martial. The last units to capitulate after brief skirmishes were the First Brigade (which had in fact been scheduled to leave for Italy in a few days) and the Navy. Casualties were few, as in many cases cooler heads prevailed. Nevertheless, the result of the mutiny was the disintegration of the Greek forces in the Middle East. After months of interrogation by the British, those who had not participated in the uprising, and whose political leanings were established as being strongly anti-Communist, were grouped into a new unit labeled the "Third Brigade." In the summer of 1944 this new unit took part in the Italian campaign and captured the town of Rimini, thus becoming known as the "Rimini" or "Mountain Brigade." Its arrival in Athens was destined to serve as an important part of the background to the Second Round. Of those not so selected more than 10,000 faced long internment and hardships in the interior of Egypt, Libya, and Eritrea.

---

sponsibility and must go ahead. As to mediation, we can't have that" (MacVeagh Diary, entry dated April 19, 1944).

[49] FR (1944), 99.

On April 3, while the crisis was still in its initial stage, Sofoclis Venizelos, Minister of Marine, who was apparently in cahoots with the mutinous republican officers, advised Tsouderos that bloodshed could still be averted if he, Venizelos, became Prime Minister. Although Tsouderos politely declined the invitation to resign, he telegraphed the King in London that he was prepared to step down in favor of Venizelos who continued to insinuate that he had the backing of the principal figures in the mutiny.[50] King George replied on April 4, asking Tsouderos to remain in office for the time being and requesting that Venizelos go to London to account for his role in the matter. Refusing to comply, Venizelos now announced that he was no longer interested in heading a government. Finally, on April 10, the King arrived in Cairo to preside personally over the settlement of the Cabinet crisis. On April 13, at the recommendation of Tsouderos, King George appointed Venizelos Prime Minister, in the apparent belief that he was the only one capable of restoring order and forming a viable government. This change, however, proved totally ineffective: Venizelos had even less influence over the mutineers than his more able predecessor. His grandiose appeal to the principal Allied powers to assist him in bringing about unity among his compatriots—and the intimation that the Soviet Union had been the major cause of the recent crisis—bore no fruit. The American Ambassador was "sympathetic" but warned against harsh punishment for the mutineers. Privately, MacVeagh interpreted the whole affair as merely the latest phase of the steady swing to the left which had been in progress since the death of Metaxas. He was convinced that the Greek politicians in Cairo, the King, the republican officers, and the British had all contributed to the crisis.[51] The British government suggested to Venizelos that it was raising the matter with Marshal Stalin, but Foreign Secretary

[50] Tsouderos, p. 141.
[51] MacVeagh Diary, entries dated April 3, 4, 10, 15, 18, 1944.

Eden admitted that he was far from convinced that there had been Soviet interference in Greek affairs. Venizelos complained to the Soviet Ambassador in Cairo about the inflammatory manner in which the news agency TASS had been describing the events surrounding the mutiny and appealed for assistance in dealing with his country's problems. The Soviet diplomat retorted that his government was already providing such "assistance": the rapidly advancing Soviet armies were contributing to the liberation of Greece. He added that although Russia had been favorably disposed toward Greece, the matter of the mutiny and its handling might cause a change in this policy.[52] Having failed to generate support for his leadership Venizelos resigned on April 24, the same day that the mutineers of the First Brigade surrendered. Two days later (the 25th, a Tuesday, a black day in Greek tradition, would not do for the oath-taking ceremonies) Greece had a new Prime Minister: George Papandreou.

[52] Papadakis, pp. 345-47.

IN SEARCH OF NATIONAL UNITY

GEORGE PAPANDREOU, whom British Ambassador Leeper welcomed as "the man of the hour" and a "breath of fresh air in the over-charged atmosphere of Greek Cairo,"[1] was hardly a new discovery in Greek political circles. One of the brightest young followers of Eleftherios Venizelos, he had acquired a reputation for progressive ideas and impressive oratorical powers as a Cabinet member during the brief years of the Republic. Ideologically to the left of Venizelos' Liberals, Papandreou had eventually formed his own party, the Social Democrats, which had held 24 seats in the 1935 Parliament. Tall, gaunt, imperious in his ways and a brilliant conversationalist, he was looked upon by many moderates as one of the country's most promising leaders.

His socialist convictions were apparently strengthened by his experiences under the Metaxas regime and the German occupation. He was among the more prominent signatories of the Protocol of March 31, 1942, in which representatives of the political world in occupied Athens had declared that King George must await the results of a popular plebiscite before returning to Greece. Although he cultivated his contacts within the EAM leadership, he refused to join that organization and remained inactive until the spring of 1944, when he was called to Cairo to take part in a reorganized Cabinet. The mutiny found him traveling the difficult road from occupied Athens to the freedom of the Middle East, reaching Egypt in mid-April. He was immediately seized upon by the British authorities as the *deux ex machina* who, brushing aside the shambles of the Tsou-

---

[1] Leeper, p. 47.

deros government, would unite political and military factions at home and abroad. A well known Venizelist of vague socialist leanings, he could presumably draw support from republicans and the moderate Left. As a respected member of bourgeois circles he was expected to prove successful with the more conservative and anti-Communist groups in Athens as well. For the British government and King George, Papandreou represented the responsible, "nationalist" center of the political spectrum and an assurance that power would not pass to the militant Left. For his part Papandreou, upon arriving in Cairo, solemnly confided to allied officials his conviction that EAM was definitely planning to establish a Communist dictatorship in Greece.[2] There is even a rather intriguing, although wholly unsubstantiated and not particularly convincing story, related by Tsouderos in 1955, according to which before leaving Athens for Cairo Papandreou had secretly pledged himself to work for the King's return without benefit of plebiscite.[3]

The overriding need to bring unity and cooperation to diverse and quarreling elements, as well as a certain conviction that the moment called for inspired personal leadership rather than for a clearly defined program of action, soon exposed Papandreou to the harsh charge of opportunism. He was accused of trying to be all things to all men, of thinking that he could charm problems away. There is no doubt that his politics were not easy to discern, though in this he was no different than most of his fellow politicians. The British Prime Minister who in the winter of 1944 likened him to the great Venizelos, called Papandreou "a man of the left, a democrat, a socialist, not a Liberal or anything like that, in fact almost everything that is supposed to be correct nowdays. . . ."[4] Komninos Pyromaglou, a prominent

[2] MacVeagh Diary, entry dated April 19, 1944.
[3] Pyromaglou, *Kartalis*, pp. 573-76.
[4] Great Britain, *Parliamentary Debates* (Commons) 402 (1943-44), 942.

member of EDES who had known Papandreou before the war, found him in July 1944 changed by his new position of prominence, "distant," "pontifical," and prone to regard Greece "as his purely private affair."[5] At times the Communists, in their usual sloganeering fashion, called him a crypto-fascist and an agent of the hated monarchy. But by far the most serious comment on his political philosophy was provided by Lincoln MacVeagh, the American Ambassador to the Greek government, who wrote to a colleague in the Department of State in May 1944:

> Mr. Papandreou described himself to me . . . as having sympathies which would have made it quite possible for him to accept the leadership of EAM, had he not suspected that decidedly leftist organization of intentions to establish a dictatorship. This, in addition to his advocacy of "social" democracy for many years past, would appear to me to justify putting him on the left side in Greek politics. However, it all depends on how you want to divide the latter up. Personally, I would put the old-line Liberals in the center, with the right running from the Popular Party to the Metaxists, and the left from the Social Democrats, Agrarians etc. to the communists. I suppose you could, technically, just as well include in the center such good men and true as Papandreou . . . Only in doing so you would perhaps miss giving notation to something essential in their views. I should rather call them the right wing of the leftist group than the left wing of the center, because they aim not at preserving Greek democracy substantially as we have known it, but at altering it profoundly in a socialistic direction. However, if the left is to be considered composed only of communists, anarchists, nihilists or what else have you which advocates altering the structure of society by direct action, Mr. Papandreou is certainly no leftist. He clearly hopes to see

[5] Pyromaglou, *I Ethniki Antistasis*, p. 121.

"social justice" achieved by the democratic process and constitutional means. So I leave it to you, but in the future I'll call him simply the social democrat he is. . . .[6]

On the other hand, in a rather strange departure from his government's routine position that it lacked information about the Greek government, Nikolai Novikov confidently predicted to MacVeagh that if the British made Papandreou Prime Minister they would be harming their own best interests because he was not likely to prove himself capable of solving the Greek problem.[7]

After May 1944 the essence of the Greek problem could be stated quite simply: would Papandreou's efforts acquire sufficient momentum so that, after liberation and with British support, he could remain in control of a highly volatile situation and guide the nation over the dangerous path of recovery and stability? In the months ahead his personal leadership would be put to the most severe test.

Despite powerful British backing and the King's nod, Papandreou faced no easy task. Other political figures in Cairo, having been ignored in this latest appointment, would have nothing to do with him. For many it was a matter of time before he too had to step down, making room for them at the top. Although all factions in Greece, including EAM and KKE, had already agreed to send delegates to a general conference to deal with the country's burning issues, many were understandably doubtful that anything constructive would result from such a meeting. Thus for a few weeks the new Prime Minister was in fact a one-man government.

In his first declaration to the nation, Papandreou designated himself a "crusader for national unity" whose principal task was the formation of a government in which all political parties and resistance groups would participate.

[6] *DSR*, 868.01/585, letter to the Chief, Division of Near East Affairs, May 23, 1944.
[7] MacVeagh Diary, entry dated April 24, 1944.

He promised that the impending consultations would be made public: "If they succeed, the nation will celebrate. And if they fail, the nation will know who is to blame. The motto will be one country, one government, one army. United, Greece will march forward to greatness. Divided, she will fall into the abyss of disaster." In a moving appeal to national pride he recalled for his compatriots the lines from Solomos' "Ode to Liberty," the Greek national anthem:

> If hatreds divide them,
> They do not deserve to be free.[8]

During May 17-20 a colorful array of representatives of the country's badly splintered political and guerrilla factions gathered at the Grand Hotel du Bois de Boulogne in the village of Douhr esh Schoueir outside Beirut, away from the mutinous atmosphere in Cairo. In addition to Papandreou, who had issued the invitations and who presided, the conference included such dignitaries as S. Venizelos, G. Exindaris, P. Kanellopoulos, J. Sofianopoulos, A. Svolos, S. Sarafis, and K. Pyromaglou. In all, 28 delegates came, representing some 17 parties and organizations.[9] Many of those attending had been literally at each other's throats until summoned to Lebanon. In particular, the dele-

---

[8] Papadakis, p. 348.

[9] The official delegates to the Lebanon Conference were as follows: *Social Democrats*: George Papandreou (Prime Minister), Themistoclis Tsatsos, Lambros Lambrianidis, Charalambos Zgouritsas. *Liberals*: Sofoclis Venizelos, Constantine Rentis, George Exindaris, Gerasimos Vasiliadis. *Populists*: Dimitrios Lontos. *National Populists*: Spyridon Theotokis. *Progressives*: George Sakalis. *Agrarian Democrats*: Alexander Mylonas. *National Unity Party*: Panayiotis Kanellopoulos. *Union of Leftists*: John Sofianopoulos. *Socialists*: Dimitrios Stratis. *Communists*: Petros Roussos. *PEEA*: Alexander Svolos, Angelos Angelopoulos, Nikolaos Askoutsis. *EAM*: Miltiadis Porfyrogenis, Stefanos Sarafis. *EDES*: Komninos Pyromaglou, Stavros Metaxas, Alexander Metaxas. *EKKA*: George Kartalis. *"National Dynamic Organizations"*: Constantine Ventiris, A. K. Stathatos. Philip Dragoumis attended as an independent. (Papadakis, pp. 356-57.)

gates of EKKA and of ELAS had to be restrained in the opening sessions of the conference: the field commander and the staff of the former had just been exterminated by the latter. Understandably, and even by Greek standards, it was a stormy gathering. As the British Ambassador put it, "The delegates in this sequestered spot either had to come to terms or murder one another."[10]

Much of the credit for averting the collapse of the conference—and perhaps the resumption of a miniature civil war right in the corridors of the Grand Hotel—belongs to Papandreou, who lectured and cajoled his compatriots until basic agreement was possible. With the knowledge that he had powerful supporters in the British government, he minced no words in placing the blame for many of the country's current ills squarely on the extreme Left. "The situation in our land," he told the assembly, "resembles hell":

The Germans are killing. The Security Battalions are killing. The guerrillas are killing. They kill and burn. What will remain of our unhappy country? EAM's responsibility arises from the fact that it did not restrict itself to the liberation struggle. It has included in its targets the control of the state by force following the liberation. For this reason it has sought to monopolize the national struggle. . . . It has also sought the intimidation of its opponents. It has identified itself with the state. EAM's enemies have been considered enemies of the country. But this can only occur under fascism, where the party is identified with the state. In democracies, the party does not subjugate the state; and the Army does not belong to a party but to the nation. By its terroristic actions EAM/ELAS created the psychological climate which permitted the Germans to succeed during the third year of slavery of our nation in what they had not managed before: the creation of the

[10] Leeper, p. 49.

Security Battalions, whose sole purpose is civil war. In this fashion, we were led into the vicious circle by virtue of which our people are going through a major trial to-day . . . From this vicious circle we must emerge as fast as possible. And this can be achieved in only one way: the elimination of the class army and the institution of a national one.[11]

Significantly, in private talks with non-Communist resistance leaders Papandreou repeatedly inquired whether EDES could attack and destroy ELAS. He was told that any such move would precipitate another civil war (the "First Round" had been halted only a few weeks earlier) which the people would not tolerate. Instead, EDES representatives proposed that their organization in the mountains be strengthened by the inclusion of men from the Greek forces in the Middle East so as to create an effective balance between EDES and ELAS, keeping the latter in check and incapable of pursuing unilateral solutions. Papandreou remained cool to the idea, leading the EDES spokesmen to conclude that he feared that the further build-up of the resistance groups at home would diminish his own prestige and authority since he had no effective control over them. The following verbal exchange was recorded by the principal EDES representative, Komninos Pyromaglou, just prior to the opening of the Lebanon Conference, and after the Prime Minister had been told the EDES would not attack ELAS:

PAPANDREOU: "In that case I shall dissolve ELAS myself, with the help of the British.
PYROMAGLOU: Before or after liberation, Mr. President?
PAPANDREOU: After liberation.
PYROMAGLOU: But, in that case, Mr. President, it will no

[11] Quoted in Andreas Papandreou, *Democracy at Gunpoint: The Greek Front* (New York, 1970), pp. 51-52.

63

longer be a matter for the Middle East Command, but
an allied affair. And it could cause international
complications.

PAPANDREOU: No, no; have faith in me . . .[12]

The leftists appeared to be subdued and off balance. Even
the KKE representative, Petros Roussos, could only offer a
rather meek defense of EAM/ELAS activities in recent
months. He disclaimed responsibility for the mutinies and
insisted that his Party had never wished to dominate the
national resistance movement.

If in the course of the Lebanon conference Papandreou
emerged as a national leader, he could not have succeeded
in his difficult mission were it not for British determination
to see him prevail. The Greek delegates held their sessions
under the watchful eye of the British Ambassador who
coached Papandreou throughout the deliberations. Although Ambassador Leeper told Papandreou that he "was
not going to intrude on what was to be a purely Greek discussion,"[13] he established himself and his staff between the
hotel where the Greeks had gathered, situated on a hill, and
the city of Beirut below, as if to insure that no one got away
before agreement had been reached! Every delegate, but
especially those of the Left, knew only too well who had
been the real sponsor of the conference and on whose authority Papandreou ultimately spoke. As the EDES delegate,
Pyromaglou later caustically recalled: "We were assembled
to hellenize the decisions of the British regarding Greece.
Everyone, instead of formulating their position according
to a correct assessment of the Greek problems, wanted to
know 'what Leeper wants' before expressing their views.
One might say that the . . . British Embassy each morning
regulated even the expressions of the delegates to the Con-

[12] Pyromaglou, *I Ethniki Antistasis*, p. 122.
[13] Leeper, p. 49.

ference. Mr. Papandreou had to emerge from the Conference as the new Eleftherios Venizelos . . ."[14]

Significantly, the American Ambassador to the Greek government and a veteran at his post, Lincoln MacVeagh, had rejected a Department of State suggestion that he might also travel to Lebanon for the conference. He was of the opinion that Leeper's presence there might well prove counterproductive. "It is possible that his attendance within a few miles of the conference," MacVeagh speculated, ". . . will prove a mistake on his part in view of the prevalent and growing Greek distrust and suspicion of British 'meddling.' " He continued:

> But for us to be there too would seem certain to compromise our established policy which couples aloofness from internal politics with interest in the welfare of the whole nation. . . . Strict observance of our traditional policy has hitherto maintained great American influence in Greece. Recently, however, it has become increasingly difficult to keep this policy clear in Greek eyes owing to our military solidarity with Britain and the consequent too easy assumption that all British policy in this region is also Anglo-American. To hang around the outskirts of this conference along with the British could only further increase this difficulty. . . .[15]

The "Lebanon Charter" of May 20, 1944 provided for the reorganization of the Greek armed forces in the Middle East and the unification of all resistance groups under the authority of Papandreou's Government of National Unity. The "reign of terror" in the Greek countryside was to cease immediately and the "personal security and political liberty of the people" were to be firmly reestablished as soon as the enemy had been driven out. Collaborators were to be pun-

---

[14] Pyromaglou, *I Ethniki Antistasis*, pp. 117-18.
[15] FR (1944), 106-7.

ished severely, and preparations were to be made to provide food, medicine, and other essentials to insure that "the material needs of the Greek people shall be satisfied immediately after liberation." There was also enthusiastic agreement to insist upon the "full satisfaction" of the country's "national claims" and on the creation of a "new, free and Great Greece."

On the explosive issue of the King's return the conferees could simply declare that after liberation, and once order and freedom had been established, the Greek people would be given the opportunity to "sovereignly decide both on the constitution and the social regime and on the government which they want." In a masterfully neutral comment designed to placate the Left Papandreou declared that, "On the question of the Supreme Ruler all the political leaders have expressed views and, while joining the Government of National Unity, they naturally retain the same views. One of the aims of the National Government will be to make these views clear."[16]

Considering the fundamental and personal differences involved, the Lebanon Charter of May 1944 was a remarkable achievement, made possible in large measure by the resort to "agreements" which were clearly open to various interpretations. From the outset and despite its participation in the discussions and the resulting agreement EAM, whose share in the new government was to be 5 yet unspecified seats in a 20-member Cabinet (EAM originally understood that the Cabinet was to have 15 members), viewed the Lebanon formula as a very poor bargain. A typical complaint was that EAM, purportedly the most influential force in Greece, had been allotted the same number of seats as the virtually defunct Liberal Party. From April to August 1944, *Rizospastis*, KKE's newspaper printed clandestinely in occupied Greece, remained critical of Papandreou and his

[16] Leeper, p. 54. For the major principles of the "Lebanon Charter" as stated by Papandreou see Appendix B.

efforts for national unity. As will be seen, this situation raised serious questions about the apparent inconsistency between Communist policies as expounded on the Greek mountains and as carried out by KKE's representatives at the conference. Nonetheless, the Lebanon accord held out the hope that personal antipathies and political differences would be held in abeyance until the moment of liberation when all important issues would be placed before the entire nation.

On May 22 Papandreou returned to Cairo where, having presented to the King the results of the Lebanon conference, he submitted his resignation. As expected, he was immediately requested to form a government based on the recently concluded agreement. The majority of the Cabinet's 20 members took the oath of office on May 24.

Despite the Prime Minister's diplomatic dexterity, his government was still one of "national unity" in name only. EAM would not officially enter it until a "clear solution of the constitutional question" had been found.[17] On June 4 the British government informed the Department of State that "the Greek politicians in Cairo are beginning to intrigue against M. Papandreou and that EAM may repudiate agreements reached by its representatives at the Lebanon Conference." Moreover, this time the Foreign Office requested American assistance in averting "renewed chaos" by supporting the Greek Prime Minister in a public statement.[18] To this urgent appeal the Acting Secretary of State, Edward R. Stettinius Jr., replied that the United States "have not and do not desire to intervene in Greek internal affairs and in view of our lack of detailed current information are particularly reluctant to risk involvement in supporting any individual or faction." Nonetheless, "within these limitations," the American government would use its "friendly influence to promote Greek unity." To this end,

[17] *FR* (1944), 115; Papadakis, pp. 357-61.
[18] *FR* (1944), 116.

the American Ambassador in Cairo would be instructed to "consult his British colleague and to take any appropriate steps to help the Greeks settle their differences among themselves."[19]

Fully aware that the principal obstacle to his success continued to be the unsettled issue of the monarchy, and fearful of a broad alignment with EAM and against himself of all forces hostile to the crown, Papandreou took a bold step. On June 12, 1944, acting essentially on his own, he declared that the King would not return to Greece until after a plebiscite had found in his favor.[20]

This pledge appeared to mollify all but EAM which soon demanded further commitments from the Prime Minister before entering his government. As for King George, he viewed Papandreou's recent statement as necessary under existing circumstances, but confided to the American Ambassador that since the statement had not come from him personally, and as he expected public sentiment to change soon in his favor, he did not regard himself finally and irrevocably committed on the subject of the plebiscite. The King, reported MacVeagh, "seemed chiefly concerned with convincing himself that his personal position remains unchanged and that he still has a chance of entering Greece *before the plebiscite* if he so wishes. Unfortunately for his state of mind, however, public opinion appears to be taking the opposite view. . . ." The Ambassador's report continued:

> In a long talk which I had with the King . . . , he said that the Prime Minister had persuaded him to consent to the Government's recent declaration . . . by showing it to be an advisable immediate move in the campaign for national unity, but that he does not himself regard it as necessarily final or as having been so presented to him. He said that since he has personally made no declaration

[19] *Ibid.*
[20] Leeper, pp. 57-58. See also George Papandreou, *I Apeleftherosis tis Ellados* (Athens, n.d.), pp. 92-95.

in the matter (and will not do so) he remains free to urge his Government to alter its present attitude and, furthermore, that he believes it may well do this later under stress of changing circumstances, with or without his instigation. In this connection, he said that he feels that Royalist sentiment is still very strong in Greece, and may become much stronger if EAM continues its opposition and the danger of a Leftist dictatorship becomes clearer to the population at large. In addition he appears genuinely to believe that among the delegates to the Lebanon Conference, from among whom the present Government has been largely constructed, only the extreme Leftists and a couple of radical Republicans without any real following in the country were against his returning to Greece before the plebiscite. He said that Mr. Papandreou himself told him this.[21]

At the Lebanon Conference there had been no doubt that the EAM delegates had been authorized to speak for the entire EAM coalition, including the Communist Party, and that they had committed themselves by the acceptance of the final accord. Nevertheless, on July 3 Papandreou received a telegram from the EAM leadership accusing him of having violated the spirit as well as the letter of the Lebanon Charter. The following day EAM's spokesmen in the Middle East were instructed from the mountains of Greece to present Papandreou with a set of firm demands labeled "our final terms for participation" in the new government. These conditions were: (a) the blame for the "First Round" had to be placed entirely on Zervas' EDES, which should be ordered to return to its original area in Epirus; (b) there had to be a public denunciation of the German-sponsored Security Battalions in occupied Greece; (c) the King must personally declare that he would not return until after a plebiscite had ruled in his favor (this demand could be met *after* EAM had

[21] FR (1944), 123-24. Emphasis mine.

joined the government); (d) retraction of statements by Papandreou and members of the government regarding EAM's "terrorism," statements which allegedly violated the Lebanon accord; (e) a definite clarification of what had actually been decided at Lebanon concerning ELAS, whose character and organization must be preserved until liberation; meanwhile General Othonaios, a former Chief of Staff and a very able officer of liberal-republican views, would be acceptable as supreme commander of all guerrilla forces under the authority of the new government; (f) no executions of participants in the recent mutiny must be permitted, and a general amnesty must be granted following EAM's entry into the government; (g) out of a Cabinet of 15, 6 ministries and 1 under-ministry had to be EAM's share in the government; and, finally, (h) a definite agreement that a portion of the Cabinet would be sent to "Free Greece" at once, whereupon the EAM-sponsored PEEA and its "national Council" would be dissolved.[22]

In retrospect it is not clear why EAM had failed to insist that these terms be clearly and specifically incorporated in the Lebanon Charter before its representatives accepted it. Perhaps the EAM delegation, unable to foresee the course that the conference would follow and lacking more precise instructions, had been reluctant to emerge from the meeting as the single factor that had rendered national unity impossible on the eve of liberation. Since the Lebanon affair was far from orderly and businesslike, EAM's spokesmen may have chosen to "accept" what in their own anxious minds appeared to emerge as a vague gentlemen's agreement. Perhaps they were momentarily swayed by Papandreou's strong-arm tactics and British "pressures." Also, the possibility of serious disagreement and confusion within the EAM leadership scattered between "Free Greece" and Lebanon, and even poor communication and inadequate preparation for the crucial meeting cannot be discounted. Whatever the

[22] *DSR*, 868.01/8-1244.

case, it is safe to say that had EAM insisted, on the morrow of the First Round, on a formal acceptance of all these terms by all the delegations present, the Lebanon meeting would have been turned into a ugly brawl. This everyone, including EAM, was anxious to avoid.

Whether in fact EAM's demands of July 4 explicitly violated the terms of the Lebanon Charter, which had been deliberately and necessarily vague, depends in the last analysis on whose proclamations at Lebanon one chooses to accept as constituting "agreement," and on the motives one imputes to EAM in making such demands.[23] At the very least, convinced of its powerful negotiating position due to the conditions prevailing in Greece, and alarmed by the criticism it met in Cairo, EAM was attempting a formal elaboration of the Lebanon accord which would decisively strengthen its hand and render its postwar political aims easier to pursue. The resulting situation was vividly portrayed by one well-informed American diplomat who, on learning of the new EAM demands, characterized them as "voices crying in the wilderness, for on one hand the tone of EAM's most recent telegram, regardless of the character of its demands, is of such belligerence as to suggest the EAM

[23] For specific Communist charges that it had been Papandreou who had consistently violated the Lebanon Agreement see National Liberation Front, *E.A.M. White Book: May 1944-March 1945* (New York, August 1945), p. 5. For the views of a critic of the British policy regarding the implementation of the Agreement see Great Britain, *Parliamentary Debates* (Commons) 402 (1943-44), 1511-16. In his response Foreign Secretary Eden appeared to weaken the Greek government's case when he stated: "The EAM in Greece repudiated the decision of their own leaders, who had gone to the [Lebanon] Conference. *I am not arguing whether there was good reason or not for what happened. . . .*" (*ibid.*, 1547). On the question of the denunciation of the Security Battalions, Leeper's explanation was that "Papandreou and every one of his colleagues were entirely opposed to them, as they were to any form of collaboration with the Germans. But they were not prepared to denounce them purely for the benefit of EAM, because their existence was really due to EAM's class army, ELAS. Many people in Greece sympathised with the Security Battalions from fear and hatred of ELAS . . ." (Leeper, p. 60).

71

leaders intended to provoke a break, while on the other hand it would appear that such a break is far from unsatisfactory to a number of Cabinet members, if not to Papandreou himself."[24] As for the Prime Minister, summing up his views on the impasse he declared that he was "grateful to the committee of the mountains because at long last it has abandoned its evasions and pretenses and has finally revealed its real aims. A complete explanation is now possible. We know what they ask of us. And in response to their demands we take an official, responsible stand. We refuse! They ask that we surrender Greece to them. We refuse! Our mission is not to surrender, but to support our people. . . ."[25]

On July 9, aware that their demands would not be met, the representatives of EAM in Cairo (A. Svolos, P. Roussos, D. Stratis) addressed a long and most interesting letter to Papandreou, reviewing the issues which, they alleged, hindered their efforts to cooperate with him. Their principal complaint appeared to be that the Prime Minister and his entourage were in fact intensifying their public attacks on EAM/ELAS, belittling their contribution to the allied cause, and accusing them of terror tactics and dark ambitions. A speech which Papandreou had made on June 28 was found to have been particularly offensive. At the same time the government would not publicly and unequivocally denounce the Security Battalions which were serving the common enemy at home and tormenting defenseless people. The letter's authors protested that Papandreou's "anti-communist propaganda" constituted a "contradiction to the general policy followed by the Allies and is of benefit only to the enemy." Moreover, the handling of the Greek armed

[24] *FR* (1944), 130. For the minutes of the Greek Cabinet meeting of July 6 regarding EAM's new demands and the reasons they were found unacceptable see Papadakis, pp. 370-79; Papandreou, *I Apeleftherosis*, pp. 106-19.

[25] Papadakis, p. 377.

forces following the recent mutiny was ill-advised and bound to lead to more dissension and unrest in the future, particularly if executions were carried out. Coming to the more practical matters at hand the letter complained that the Prime Minister had not been forthright on the question of the Cabinet's size and EAM's share in it. Furthermore, in selecting his ministers he was systematically ignoring well-qualified figures who were in Greece and who were associated with EAM or PEEA and thus in a far better position to deal with the country's domestic affairs. Denying that EAM's demands represented a "retraction" or "repudiation" of the Lebanon Charter, the letter characterized them as "only a logical interpretation and clarification of the agreement which, after such a poisoning of the atmosphere, was necessary and suitable in order to secure cooperation enjoying some prospect of success. . . ." Complaining that negotiations on all these matters had thus far been meaningless, the authors declared: "Our conscience is clear because *we* are not to blame but the Government which has not understood that unity must be genuine and which had done everything possible to create an atmosphere which would be destined to result in failure." Nevertheless, the message concluded, "In no case, for any reason, must this interruption of negotiations lead us to a break. By our actions we will demonstrate our intention not to abandon the idea and the endeavor to secure unity. . . . A break would help only the enemy and harm the nation. We would never assume such a responsibility." Consequently:

For that reason and at this very critical moment we declare to you that we are ready to leave some of our representatives here with a view to permitting them to be of assistance in the task of paving the way for a new understanding. If you refuse, we have nothing else to do but return to Free Greece, where, on the basis of the Lebanon Agreement, we will strive for real unity by carrying on the struggle against the Germans and Bulgarians and by supporting all Allied military activity for the liberation of our Fatherland. . . .[26]

Whatever EAM's motives, the move failed. The government rejected these demands as violations of the Lebanon agreement. Following a last-ditch effort to force Papandreou to resign, which was successfully resisted with strong British backing, EAM announced on August 17 that it was at long last prepared to join unconditionally the Government of National Unity.[27]

EAM's capitulation is a matter of considerable interest and has often been attributed to Soviet instructions which are said to have reached the Greek Communists at about this time. As a matter of fact, on July 26 a 10-member team of the Soviet military mission to Tito's partisans, headed by Colonel Gregori Popov, reached the ELAS headquarters in Thessaly. They were to remain in Greece until after liberation, functioning as an intelligence-gathering unit and organizing the repatriation of Russian war prisoners.[28] According to American reports, Ambassador Leeper was quite disturbed by the arrival of the Soviet group in Greek territory, after the Soviet government had agreed to leave all operations in that country to the British.[29] The Russians held secret talks with Greek Communist leaders for which no first-hand account has thus far been produced.[30] Never-

---

[26] For the text of this letter see Appendix C.

[27] Leeper, pp. 63-64.

[28] Regarding the Popov mission see D. George Kousoulas, *Revolution and Defeat: The Story of the Greek Communist Party* (London, 1965), pp. 192-93; William Hardy McNeill, *The Greek Dilemma: War and Aftermath* (New York, 1947), p. 145; Woodhouse, pp. 198-99; *Rizospastis*, July 30, 1944, which announced at the same time the impending arrival of an American mission. OSS agents were dispatched to the ELAS headquarters to report concerning the Russians.

[29] *DSR*, 868.01/7-2844.

[30] Not surprisingly, the Institute of History of the Soviet Academy of Science has advised me that it is not in a position to provide any information regarding the Popov mission (letter of Oct. 26, 1967).

theless, Colonel Popov is believed by some to have prevailed upon the Communists to join the Papandreou government, presumably so as not to embarrass the secret Anglo-Soviet negotiations already under way for a division of responsibility in the Balkans. Similar advice is said to have come to EAM via the Soviet Embassy in Cairo.[31]

In the absence of more concrete information about the purpose of the Popov mission it is not possible to assess its significance with any degree of certainty. If Popov knew of the yet-to-be-formalized "percentages agreement" which would place Greece clearly in the British sphere, a most improbable assumption, he said nothing about it to his Greek hosts: a senior ELAS officer appeared unaware of the famous agreement until the 1950's.[32] On the other hand, the change in EAM's attitude toward the government—reluctant and grudging as it was—came so soon after the arrival of the Russians that one cannot lightly dismiss a connection between the two events as sheer coincidence. Thus the tempting conclusion that EAM entered the government under pressure from Moscow, demonstrating the strict obedience of the Greek Communists to the wishes of the "Socialist Fatherland."

With the wisdom of hindsight, however, the significance of the Popov mission can be seen in an entirely different light. There is no indication whatsoever that the Russians brought pledges of material or even moral support for KKE's cause. On the contrary, according to British intelligence reports from the area:

> ELAS, who had expected the Soviet Mission to bring manna from heaven, found Colonel Popov unable to supply his own party with vodka, let alone ELAS with gold,

[31] On July 28, 1944, the American Legation to Greece (Cairo) reported that according to local sources, Soviet Ambassador Nikolai V. Novikov had advised Professor Svolos that EAM should join the Greek government in Cairo (*DSR*, 868.01/7-2844).

[32] Kousoulas, p. 197.

arms and ammunition. On the other hand, the Soviet Mission, which had expected to find an army of at least the same kind, if not the same magnitude, as Tito's partisans, found a rabble thinly veiled by an elaborately centralized command. . . . Colonel Popov and his compatriots, therefore, only saw those features of EAM/ELAS which the KKE expected to impress him most, and which in fact impressed him least. Neither on the military nor on the political level does it seem likely that a favourable report on EAM/ELAS went to Moscow. The Soviet Government was at that time more concerned over the successful prosecution of the war against Germany than over Balkan ideologies. Circumstantial evidence suggests that EAM/ELAS suffered an abrupt shock as a result.[33]

Scattered oss reports from the same area substantiate this view. They suggest that despite EAM's efforts to herald the presence of Soviet officers at ELAS's headquarters as proof of Moscow's interest in the Communist cause in Greece, Colonel Popov discouraged such an interpretation by remaining aloof and totally noncommittal. The same sources led the Assistant Military Attaché of the American Embassy in Athens to believe that during the December 1944 crisis Popov's men "made no gesture to assist the Greek Communists by word or deed," and continued to enjoy the hospitality of the British authorities in the capital.[34] Thus, if there was Soviet influence in the summer of 1944, it most likely took the form of communications to the Greek Communists not as to what to do, but rather as to what Moscow would *not* do for them. From this KKE and EAM were to derive their own conclusions and act accordingly.

If in some perverse way Moscow helped the EAM leaders

[33] Woodhouse, pp. 198-99.

[34] McNeill, p. 145. According to oss reports from Athens, many Russian undercover agents were believed to be in the Greek capital but Colonel Popov's group was confining its activities to those of military observers (*DSR*, 868.00/10-2444).

realize that they had to come to terms with the government of Papandreou, at least for the time being, so did London, in a way which must have been considerably more "shocking" to them.

As suggested in the introductory chapter, throughout the war British policy toward Greek affairs was the product of two basically different and at times incompatible considerations: the immediate needs of resistance to the common enemy, and Britain's long-range interests in the eastern Mediterranean, the Balkans, and the Middle East. Initially, and under the pressures of the war, the first consideration had been paramount, and had resulted in efforts to build up resistance groups regardless of their ideological orientation. Whether intended or not, ELAS had been the principal beneficiary of such a policy. By early 1944, however, with Soviet advances deep into eastern Europe, and with British influence over Tito's movement declining rapidly, the second objective began to receive urgent attention. On May 4, and while Papandreou was struggling to form his Government of National Unity, Churchill directed his Foreign Secretary to prepare a brief paper on the "brute issues" which divided Britain and the Soviet Union in Italy and the Balkans, but above all in Greece, as "evidently we are approaching a showdown with the Russians about their Communist intrigues" in those states.[35] In his memorandum, presented to the Cabinet on June 7, Eden argued that "As regards Greece, we should have to set about now building up a regime which after the war would definitely look to Britain for support against Russian influence."[36] He had already (on May 18) approached the Soviet Ambassador on the need to divide responsibility in the Balkans, thus setting into motion the diplomatic activity which would lead to the

[35] Churchill, VI, 72-73.
[36] *The Memoirs of Anthony Eden*, III, *The Reckoning* (Boston, 1965), 533-34. Parenthetically, Eden's statement belies subsequent claims that the October 9, 1944 agreement had merely been intended for the period of military operations.

famous "percentages agreement," concluded between Churchill and Stalin in Moscow on October 9, 1944.[37] When the Soviet government inquired about the attitude of the United States toward such a deal, Churchill pressured the President to give the matter his blessing.

Warned by his advisers about the probable long-range political consequences for all Europe of an Anglo-Soviet wartime pact on the Balkans, Roosevelt had at first refused to endorse the British proposal. In his telegram to Churchill on June 11 he conceded that the ally responsible for military operations in any given area was bound to make crucial decisions dictated by military considerations. He was convinced, however, "that the natural tendency for such decisions to extend to other than military fields would be strengthened by an agreement of the type suggested." Accordingly, in the American view, such an agreement "would

[37] On the Anglo-Soviet agreement of October 9, under which Britain assumed principal responsibility for Greece, see Churchill, vi, 72-83, 226-35; *FR* (1944), 112-33; Stephen G. Xydis, "The Secret Anglo-Soviet Agreement on the Balkans of October 9, 1944," *Journal of Central European Affairs*, xv (October 1955), 248-71; Stephen G. Xydis, "Greece and the Yalta Declaration," *The American Slavic and East European Review*, xx (February 1961), 6-24; John Lukacs, "The Night Stalin and Churchill Divided Europe," *The New York Times Magazine* (October 5, 1969), 36-49. For a Soviet denial that any such agreement was ever concluded see V. Trukhanovsky, *British Foreign Policy During World War II* (Moscow, 1970), pp. 406-8. According to the author, the official Soviet record of the October 9 meeting reads in part: "Churchill announced that he had prepared a rather dirty and clumsy document that showed the distribution of Soviet and British influence in Rumania, Greece, Yugoslavia, and Bulgaria. The table was drawn up by him to show what the British think on this question." The author concludes: "The Soviet Government understood what the British thought on this score and took note of it. Nothing more. It did not even feel it was necessary to express its attitude to this British proposal. Neither the Churchill table nor any agreement on this issue are mentioned in the Soviet record of the talks. Had such agreement been reached it would unquestionably have been indicated in the record. Churchill's assertion that Stalin had agreed to divide Yugoslavia into spheres of influence is thus a piece of fantasy" (*ibid.*, p. 408).

certainly result in the persistence of differences between you and the Soviets and in the division of the Balkan region into spheres of influence. . . ."[38]

Churchill's immediate response (on June 11) barely concealed his exasperation with Roosevelt's arguments. The Prime Minister expressed great concern lest important action become "paralysed if everybody is to consult everybody else about everything before it is taken." One of the allies, he insisted, must have "the power to plan and act." Otherwise, any allied "consultative committee," which the Americans appeared to favor, "would be a mere obstruction, always overridden in any case of emergency by direct interchanges between you and me, or either of us and Stalin." As a case in point he observed that British initiative in Greek affairs had already resulted in an "immensely improved" situation and, "if firmness is maintained," that country could still be "rescued from confusion and disaster." Although in a few days he was to complain of powerful Soviet support for the Greek Left, and to counter the American argument about dangerous Anglo-Soviet "differences," Churchill assured the President that "The Russians are ready to let us take the lead in the Greek business, which means that EAM and all its malice can be controlled by the national forces of Greece. Otherwise, civil war and ruin to the land you care about so much. . . ." The Prime Minister rested his case with a strong plea: "I always reported to you and I always will report to you. You shall see every telegram I send. I think you might trust me in this. . . ."[39]

The President's information regarding the proposed Anglo-Soviet arrangement for the Balkans did not all come from British sources. On May 29, the American Ambassador to Moscow, Averell Harriman, reported that, according to Marshal Stalin, the yet-to-be-concluded agreement would give the Soviet Union a "free hand" as regards Rumania, in

[38] *FR* (1944), 117-18.   [39] *Ibid.*

return for keeping "hands off" Greece. Such a deal, Harriman commented, would compel the troublesome EAM to support a united front among all Greek political factions.[40]

In the end, the need to uphold the spirit of allied cooperation and the lack of direct American interest in the area in question rather than the persuasiveness of the British arguments had made the difference. Despite strong opposition to such an arrangement from the Department of State, and with obvious personal misgivings, Roosevelt gave his qualified assent on June 13, with the understanding that it was to be tried for a period of three months and then reviewed by the three great powers. "We must be careful," he admonished Churchill, "to make it clear that we are not establishing any post-war spheres of influence."[41]

Signs that the accord was going to have the desired effect appeared almost immediately. On June 23 the American Ambassador to Greece in Cairo was writing to the President that, according to British sources, the Russians were now displaying a "new spirit of cooperation" regarding Greek affairs. MacVeagh speculated that the rumored Anglo-Soviet understanding on the Balkans would serve at least as a "patchwork to cover rifts of fundamental suspicion and distrust. . . ."[42] On the other hand, even after he had given the matter his approval, Roosevelt remained unhappy and perturbed over the entire affair. "I think I should tell you frankly," he telegraphed Churchill on June 22, "that we were disturbed that your people took this matter up with us only after it had been put up to the Russians and they had inquired whether we were agreeable. Your Foreign Office apparently sensed this and has now explained that

[40] The Papers of President Franklin D. Roosevelt, Roosevelt Library, Hyde Park, Map Room Papers (hereafter cited as MRP), 051 Balkans: "Spheres of Influence, 5/19-6/30/44."

[41] *FR* (1944), 121.

[42] MacVeagh letter to the President, June 23, 1944, *Roosevelt Papers*, Personal Secretary's File (hereafter cited as PSF), "Greece: L. MacVeagh."

the proposal 'arose out of a chance remark' which was converted by the Soviet Government into a formal proposal. . . ." However, he concluded, "I hope matters of this importance can be prevented from developing in such a manner in the future." When Churchill refused to admit any wrongdoing and pointed out in his turn that Roosevelt had communicated with Stalin regarding Polish affairs without first consulting London, the President let the matter drop: ". . . both of us," he conceded, "have inadvertently taken unilateral action in a direction that we both now agree to have been expedient for the time being. . . ." What really mattered was that "we should always be in agreement in matters bearing on our Allied war effort."[43]

On a closely related issue the British leader had continued to regard the monarchy of Greece as the one stabilizing factor which, in the midst of seemingly perennial turmoil, would always assure Britain's interests a favorable hearing in Athens. In his view republicanism had in the past perpetuated division and might now contribute to strong pro-Soviet feelings. Churchill hoped that King George would return to his country at the head of a considerable force to drive the enemy off Greek soil, thereby reasserting his moral right to the throne. Support for the King, therefore, became the cornerstone of his Greek policy. Moreover, Churchill sought American support for his plans. On several occasions during 1942 and again in March 1943 the British government had advised Washington that it intended to actively assist the King by "selling" him to the Tsouderos government and to the Greek people. He was confidently expected to rule as a democratic constitutional monarch, and such a regime would provide Greece with a government more stable than "a republican regime which in the past failed to produce anything but weak and unreliable governments."[44]

[43] *FR* (1944), 125-27.   [44] *FR* (1943), 126-27.

The American response to the British position typified the strongly divergent views of the two governments regarding the political problems of Greece. Indeed, King George could count on precious few admirers in the American government. The Department of State had communicated to other agencies its attitude toward the Greek monarchy in June 1942, on the occasion of the impending visit to the United States of the Greek King. Asserting that King George had never been popular, an intra-service memorandum observed that he and his government had at first retained the image of the Metaxas dictatorship, until warned by their British advisors about the powerful opposition they had thus generated in Greece and abroad. More recently the King's professions of devotion to democratic principles were being regarded with much scepticism, and many Greeks remained apprehensive that Britain, perhaps with American support, would attempt to impose him upon the country after the war. Indeed, the royal visit might be offered as proof of American sympathy for the dynasty. Accordingly the memorandum recommended that American officials in their contacts with the royal party express approval of Tsouderos' promises to restore a democratic system. They should also make appropriate references to the Atlantic Charter. Press releases and other official publicity should emphasize United States' sympathy for the people of Greece and play down the King's name. Finally, the Department of State advised strongly against inviting the King to address the Congress.[45]

In December 1942, in response to a British statement of October 12 expressing the hope that after the war a "democratic constitutional monarchy" would be established in Greece, another Department of State intra-service memorandum complained that the British continued to appear committed to the restoration of the King by any methods

[45] *DSR*, 868/001G/102, memorandum dated June 3, 1942.

short of actual force. Such a policy would deny the people of Greece the free selection of their political institutions guaranteed by the Atlantic Charter. According to American sources, the King remained highly unpopular with Greeks everywhere despite public assurances that he had renounced the Metaxas dictatorship. The note challenged the British assertion that the monarchy would contribute to a more stable government than a republican regime and chided London for its intentions to "sell" the King to his own people: such salesmanship was held not to be the business of a foreign government. The memorandum concluded that it was not deemed wise for the American government to appear to be supporting the King and the government-in-exile, although it would be even more awkward to recognize a local government which might emerge in Greece, as such a move would require the repudiation of the official Greek government abroad. Following the country's liberation the most advisable course of action would be to retain an allied military presence in Greece which would not choose political sides but would allow the people to express their will freely under allied auspices.[46] A few weeks later another intra-service memorandum reiterated the position that the principle of continuity definitely precluded the possibility of withdrawing recognition of the Greek government. On the other hand, that government might well stay in London or Cairo until after the plebiscite on the country's constitutional regime. Otherwise, if it were returned to Greece by the allied forces, the United States would be exposing itself to severe criticism at home and might be contributing to serious disturbances in Greece. The author of the note wished to know when the problem of Greece would be discussed with the British, if not with the Russians as well. In the absence of an allied policy on this crucial issue, he reflected, the British would be free to carry

[46] *Ibid.*, 868.01/331-1/4, memorandum dated Dec. 28, 1942.

83

out their plans as soon as Greece had been freed. The result would be a quarrel among the allies and trouble for Greece.[47]

On March 16, 1943 a new intra-service memorandum prepared in the Division of Near Eastern Affairs concluded that on the matter of the monarchy the American government "should not—in fact, cannot—go along with the . . . British policy." The supporting arguments touched on the very heart of the political crisis: "The question of the acceptability of King George II by the Greek people is one that can be determined by the latter, and in view of their known opposition to the King they should be given a chance to express themselves freely on the subject. If the King can 'sell' himself to the Greek people, despite having let them down several times before, well and good. The selling job should not, however, be undertaken by a foreign power." Thus far declarations by the King himself and by Prime Minister Tsouderos had given no assurances that the people would be able to decide the country's constitutional regime. Moreover, "A British campaign to 'sell' the Tsouderos government to the Greek people, besides constituting intervention in Greek internal affairs, seems likely to stir up political dissension and divide the Greek people on the old Royalist and anti-Royalist lines, rather than to create unity." Thirdly, "The British conclusion that only a monarchial regime will assure stable government in Greece, seems to us to be warranted neither by the facts of recent Greek history nor by a reasonable analysis of the present temper of the Greek people." Any attempt to return the King "under the wing of an Allied military occupation" would not only constitute a violation of the Atlantic Charter but might precipitate "serious internal disorders, since it appears from reliable indications that both political and military elements in Greece are organized to oppose a restoration of the King." Under the circumstances, Anglo-American agreement

[47] *Ibid.*, 868.01/333-1/4, memorandum dated Jan. 15, 1943.

should be sought for handling the Greek situation and for establishing a uniform policy toward other governments in exile during the war years. More specifically, the British government should be persuaded that the King and his government must "refrain from returning to Greece until there has been an opportunity for the people to express their will freely under the auspices of an impartial Allied occupation." The memorandum of March 16, which served as the basis of the American position in the talks with Foreign Secretary Eden in Washington in late March 1943, concluded with the admonition: "There is reason to believe that the Greeks realize that the British intend to restore the King; that they are looking to the United States to see that they get the promised opportunity to express their own will; and that, if we fail them, they will turn to Soviet Russia."[48] King George's statement of March 21 that "after his return to Greece," he would "base himself on the will of the people and will follow the opinion which the people will express freely on all questions concerning them"[49] did nothing to soothe apprehensions in the Department of State.

Reacting to American criticism of its Greek policy, the British government reasserted on April 24, 1943, its intention to offer "full support to the King and present Government: such support to be manifested in all its contacts in Greece itself and in their propaganda generally," even though the determination of future political conditions was to be left to the people of Greece. Moreover, because of the need for a strong administration after liberation, "it is *not* the policy of His Majesty's Government to encourage the idea that immediately Greece is liberated a plebiscite shall be organized under British aegis to determine whether the monarchy shall be maintained or abolished. . . ."[50]

As might be expected, the disputation continued unabated, with no apparent progress toward a more uniform

---

[48] *FR* (1943), 126-27. [49] *Ibid.*, 131.
[50] *Ibid.*, 131-34. Emphasis mine.

policy. In its reply of July 2, 1943 the Department of State pointed out that the American government had been urging Greeks to unite, or at least to postpone their quarrels until their country had been liberated. It also insisted, however, that "there exists among the Greek people widespread hostility to the monarchy, and this hostility appears to have developed certain organizational bases within Greece." It would be for the King to "satisfy the Greek people that this hostility is unjustified and that his future role would be in accord with their sentiments and will." Therefore, the American government continued to believe that "the principal Allied Governments should carefully avoid any action which would create the impression that they intend to impose the King on the Greek people under the protection of an Allied invading force or that the Greek people can secure the rewards of the common victory only at the price of accepting the return of the monarchy." Otherwise, it would be "a great tragedy should any civil disturbances arise in Greece as a result of internal opposition to the return of the King, in which it might be necessary for Allied troops to intervene." In sum, "while this Government wishes the Greek King and Government well in any efforts they may make to obtain the support of the Greek people and reenforce their authority in regard to the Greek armed forces, it is not prepared to undertake, or actively associate itself with measures designed to promote these purposes. . . ."[51]

[51] *Ibid.*, 133-34. The Department's Adviser on Political Relations reported to the Under Secretary of State Sumner Welles that the British had been showing a distinct tendency to view Greek political affairs as their private preserve and intended to bring the King back (*DSR*, 868.01/350-1/2, memorandum dated May 15, 1943). And in June American officials in Cairo reported that British policy on Greece as expounded to them by Foreign Office spokesmen included the following objectives: full support for the King and his government; approval of declarations by the King and his government to the effect that at the end of the war the people of Greece would be given the opportunity to decide political matters, not including, however, the holding of a plebiscite on the issue of the monarchy; strengthening

Britain's handling of Greek politics remained a source of irritation for American diplomats. In mid-July reports from Constantinople, a major allied listening post for Greek affairs, suggested that all Greeks regardless of their political loyalties resented London's "dictation" and "interference," particularly on the constitutional issue. As a result republican elements were said to be contemplating resorting to unspecified "independent action." Ambassador Leeper was reported having declared that Greece was clearly Britain's military sphere of responsibility and that the King and his government would be brought to Athens as soon as practicable, following the arrival of allied forces. This despite the fact that the majority of Greeks were known by the British government to be strenuously opposed to such a plan. The British government continued to believe that a constitutional monarchy represented the best guarantee of stability, and that the Greeks would simply have to trust British assurances that the King would faithfully abide by the constitution. All the King's official statements had actually been prepared by British officials. Moreover, to the chagrin of American diplomats, Leeper maintained that Britain's policy had received the full endorsement of Washington as well as Moscow.[52]

In an attempt to fortify its arguments and prepare the ground for the impending talks at the highest Anglo-American level at Quebec, the British government presented its case once again, this time in an aide-memoire delivered in

---

the King's authority over the armed forces, and broadening the basis of his government (*ibid.*, 868.00/1238, June 5, 1943).

[52] *Ibid.*, 868.01/365, July 14, 1943. On July 15 a senior American diplomat in Cairo observed that in his contacts with the Greek government he was handicapped by the lack of instructions as to the United States policy regarding Greece. He advocated a policy of total abstinence, particularly in view of the alleged allocation of Greece to the British sphere which, if true as a temporary measure, might subsequently become subject to modification (*ibid.*, 868.00/1301, July 15, 1943).

Washington on August 4. Britain's principal reasons for supporting the King of Greece were summarized as follows:

(a) He is our Ally, and as such is, in our view, entitled to our full support. He stood by us with the utmost loyalty during the campaign in Greece, and since then he has done nothing to suggest that our confidence in him is misplaced.

(b) He remains the constitutional Head of the Greek State, and it is not in our power to alter this even if we wished to do so. The Greek people are the only authority which can deprive him of this position, but it is clearly impossible for them to pronounce on this question until Greece has been liberated and order restored.

(c) Both from the juridical and from the practical point of view, it is important that the continuity of the Greek Government should be maintained. In the last resort this depends on the King, since no government could be in existence without him. If there is to be a change in the form of regime under which Greece is governed, this can properly take place only when the King has returned to Greece and has summoned a government which can hold elections for a constituent assembly or a plebiscite, by means of which the Greek people can make their views known.

To this fine display of legalistic niceties a new twist was added by the assertion that the King, who would be returning in his capacity as Commander-in-Chief of the Greek armed forces, would *not* be accompanied by any member of the Greek government: ". . . a request from an Allied sovereign to be allowed to return to his country at the earliest opportunity," the British note argued, "cannot be lightly rejected." Conversely, ". . . the military considerations which may make it essential to postpone the return of the [Greek] allied government do not necessarily apply in the case of the Sovereign, provided that he does not insist on exercising his powers of government." Whether Greeks at home and abroad were prepared to see the unpopular King return while their government was deliberately kept away did not appear to concern the British authorities. Indeed, the contents of the August 4 note were not communicated to the Greek Prime Minister, who remained completely in the dark on all these deliberations. Moreover, the King's own authority was held to be considerable: ". . . it was clear," the British government explained, "that if we disregarded the King's wishes in this matter [of his early return], we should stand to forfeit his cooperation, on which we must count in the planning of operations for the reconquest of Greece." Finally, and "after mature reflection," the British government had concluded that "the King's return at this stage and his presence in Greece during the operational phase would simplify rather than complicate the problems which will face both ourselves and the Greek nation." Accordingly, "We are convinced that the King of the Hellenes and the present government, with all *its* faults, are in the best position to rally the forces of Greece against the enemy, and that there is no alternative body which could undertake this task. . . ." Therefore, "If the King and his Government are to be able to carry out their declared intentions, they must be able to rely on our support, and we consider that the interests both of ourselves and of Greece justify us in giving them this support in the fullest measure at our command."[53]

If these arguments were designed to pacify American diplomatic circles, they had the opposite effect. However, without the President's support, the Department of State could do little more than bicker at a low diplomatic level.

Alarmed by mounting evidence of republican sentiment in Greek political circles at home and abroad, and aware of continuing Anglo-American differences regarding his future, King George declared on July 4, 1943, that upon lib-

[53] *FR* (1943), 137-41. Emphasis mine.

eration the Constitution of 1911, suspended by Metaxas in 1936, would be reinstated, the government would resign, and a constituent assembly would be elected to decide the regime's future. At the same time he fully expected to return to Greece with the allied forces at the earliest possible moment.[54] On the last point he had Churchill's enthusiastic blessing. On August 19, the Prime Minister commented to the Foreign Secretary:

> If substantial British forces take part in the liberation of Greece, the King should go back with the Anglo-Greek Army. This is much the more probable alternative. If, however, the Greeks are strong enough to drive out the Germans themselves, we shall have a good deal less to say in the matter. It follows that the King should demand equal Royalist representation with the Republicans. . . . In any case he would make a great mistake to agree in any way to remain outside Greece while the fighting for the liberation is going on and while conditions preclude the holding of a peaceful plebiscite.[55]

On the all-important question of the timing of the plebiscite to determine the fate of the monarchy, Churchill received strong advice from the influential Field Marshal Jan Smuts, a close friend of the Greek dynasty. On August 20 the South African leader telegraphed the Prime Minister that a plebiscite immediately following the country's liberation "should be ruled out as likely to lead to civil strife, if not civil war, in the existing bitterness of feeling." Accordingly, "Allied administration under military occupation could be continued until public opinion has settled down and safe conditions of public tranquility have been established." During such a period of allied control, "King

---

[54] Leeper, pp. 29-30; Tsouderos, p. 62. Explaining the King's statement, Tsouderos wrote to political leaders in occupied Greece that a new government to supervise elections would be formed "as soon as the King had returned to Athens . . ." (*ibid*).

[55] Churchill, v, 536-37.

George and the Royal Family might well return to Greece to lend their moral support and authority. . . ." Smuts voiced grave concern about the "chaos" that may follow liberation "unless a strong hand is kept on the local situation."[56]

The issue appeared to have been temporarily settled at the First Quebec Conference on August 22, 1943, with a compromise which in practice signified an endorsement of the British position. According to the official record of the Conference, at Churchill's request the assembly heard a report from Eden on the Greek political situation and a message from Smuts who urged that "as a matter of fair play, . . . the King of Greece not be precluded from entering his own country and resuming his former position, subject, perhaps, to later decision by the people of Greece as to the future form of the Greek regime." There is no evidence that the President (or Secretary of State Hull) raised any objections whatsoever to the manner in which the British had handled the problems of Greece thus far. On the contrary, Roosevelt and Churchill jointly declared their satisfaction with the King's "contention that he was prepared to return to Greece as soon as possible and submit the question of the Royal House to plebiscite" at an unspecified time after the war.[57] This ruling was, of course, a major setback for republican forces in Greece and elsewhere. In approving it the President had clearly chosen to disregard the position of the appropriate desk officers in the Department of State who viewed the Greek monarchy as the most disruptive element, undeserving of any support whatsoever. Thus a Department of State memorandum dated August 25 observed that the Department was unaware of any commitment to return King George to his throne, as Britain appeared intent on doing. Furthermore, if the King returned with the allied forces, the effect would be most disruptive. Accordingly, it would be unwise for the President

[56] *Ibid.*   [57] *FR* (1943), 147-48.

to offer the King any advice on the issue of his return. The Department advocated the establishment of a small representative commission of Greeks to administer local matters following liberation and prepare the country for the holding of a constituent assembly. Meanwhile the King should remain abroad.[58] However, on October 13, 1943 President Roosevelt commented to the Greek Ambassador in Washington that "After all, King George has a right to return to Greece as Commander-in-Chief of his Army."[59]

Significantly, Churchill and Roosevelt continued for the moment to ignore not only reports from their own subordinates regarding the rising anti-monarchist feeling in Greece, but also the opinion of the Greek Prime Minister. As suggested in the preceding chapter, unaware of the Quebec formula and highly skeptical about the wisdom of the King's stand with regard to his early return, Tsouderos had sent a personal envoy to occupied Greece to sound out Archbishop Damascinos as well as a large number of political personalities in Athens about the need to plan for a temporary, all-party government which could fill the dangerous gap which the withdrawal of the enemy forces was bound to create. The agent (Colonel Fradellos) returned with reports that the King was universally unpopular and that Damascinos was widely regarded as the most suitable person for the position of regent until a plebiscite could determine the question of the monarchy's future. Pending that plebiscite the King should remain abroad.[60] To his dismay Tsouderos discovered that neither the King nor the British were impressed by such reports, although Foreign Secretary Eden thought it desirable to establish in Athens an authority under the Archbishop which could represent the government until it could make its way to Athens.[61] However, Damascinos promptly rejected the suggestion that he

[58] *DSR*, 868.01/379, memorandum dated Aug. 25, 1943.
[59] *Ibid.*, 868.01/412, memorandum dated Oct. 13, 1943.
[60] Tsouderos, pp. 81-115.   [61] Eden, III, 474.

serve as the government's "representative" in occupied Athens. The demand for a regency, voiced by virtually every responsible Greek leader, was anathema to both the King and to Prime Minister Churchill.

Having failed to persuade the President to disassociate himself from Britain's policy on Greece, the Department of State adjusted its stand in accordance with the Quebec decision. A memorandum delivered to the British Embassy in Washington on October 8 declared in part:

> . . . this Government has considered that it would not interpose objection to the return of the King *and Government* to Greece as soon as the military situation should permit, in accordance with the assurances and procedure which they have from time to time announced, notably in the King's radio address of July 4, 1943, unless it should become clear during the military operations that such return would be overwhelmingly contrary to the wishes of the people and could only result in civil warfare.[62]

Obviously, the discrepancy between the British and American positions on the issue of the return of the government—as contrasted to the return of the King—remained. Otherwise, the two allies appeared to have buried their differences on the Greek problem. For most Greeks, on the other hand, the matter of the monarchy's future was anything but settled. None of them were, of course, privy to these important communications which touched upon an issue vital to their country's political system. They simply knew that the King had stubbornly resisted the demand voiced by every party and resistance group that he promise to remain abroad until after the plebiscite. In this he had been backed by the British, and now even the American President seemed to take his side. Many Greeks concluded from this that, regardless of their wishes, the King would

---

[62] *FR* (1943), 152-54. Emphasis mine.

be returned to his throne to stay. Otherwise, why have him come back only to face the risk of rejection by a popular vote? With the King in Athens as the highest symbol of state authority and as Commander-in-Chief of the armed forces, what chance would there be for a fair and free referendum on the monarchy? Thus the charge that the British intended to force the King back upon the country, and that this step might easily lead to the revival of the right-wing dictatorship with which he was widely associated, remained essentially unanswered. Until the last days of 1944, nothing that the monarch himself or the British authorities had said effectively refuted it. And although it was the Communists who made this charge the cornerstone of their propaganda, other leftists and republicans were haunted by the fear that it might in fact be true. The result was an uneasy alliance of the more dedicated anti-monarchists, providing the Communists with a powerful base of support which would not have been theirs to exploit had the issue of the monarchy— and, by extension, the entire matter of the country's future political direction—been resolved to the satisfaction of an overwhelmingly large segment of the Greek public.

Following his meeting with President Roosevelt at Quebec, and speaking to an inquisitive House of Commons early in November, Churchill denied that he had undertaken any commitments on the question of the Greek monarchy. Rather, he asserted that until the Greek people had expressed their will under conditions of political freedom and tranquility, it remained the policy of the British government to support fully the King of Greece as the country's constitutional ruler and an ally.[63] Taking advantage of this favorable moment, King George addressed a letter to his Prime Minister on November 8, restating his position. As already mentioned, the King declared that at the time of liberation and in consultation with his government he would consider anew the matter of the timing of his return,

[63] Tsouderos, pp. 71-72.

taking into consideration the prevailing political and military conditions.[64]

After the summit conference at Teheran in November-December 1943, the British government found it necessary to modify its thinking regarding Greece. There was to be no invasion of the Balkans by Anglo-American forces. Moreover, the course of the war—as well as strong American objections—were making it increasingly clear that no serious fighting would occur in Greece as the Germans withdrew, and that British troops would be needed elsewhere. Nor was it any longer possible to blatantly disregard the rising anti-monarchist sentiment in that country. Accordingly, the War Cabinet approved a new policy for Greece, and on December 3 Foreign Secretary Eden, in the presence of Churchill, presented it to King George in Cairo. In essence the King was now being advised to publicly promise that he would not return to Greece until a plebiscite had found in his favor. In the meantime, a regency council would be formed in Greece, under Archbishop Damascinos. As the American Ambassador reported from Cairo, Eden's proposals "should be taken not as indicating any reversal or even alteration of British policy toward the Greek King but rather as representing a change in tactical procedure for the fulfillment of established policy, prompted by changes in the military and political situation." MacVeagh's analysis continued:

> . . . it seems clear that British policy continues to be based on the hope that the King will be restored to his throne as a constitutional monarch by the will of his people. However, when Allied strategical plans were so changed recently as to make it seem unlikely that any large military force would occupy Greece upon evacuation by the enemy, it occurred to the British Embassy here, which was advised of the growth of anarchy within the country,

[64] *Ibid.*, pp. 73-74.

that the king's early return with only the small forces envisaged would be inadvisable. In the circumstances, as I saw them, which appeared to necessitate a certain lapse of time before conditions of tranquility could be obtained, requisite to the determination of the people's will regarding the regime, it felt that the most hopeful procedure would be to secure some suitable person who had resisted the Axis in Greece and who might be expected to command general respect such as the Archbishop of all Greece to be appointed by the King to head a Regency committee to exercise constitutional authority during the immediate post-liberation era, the King remaining abroad. This idea was I am convinced conceived purely with a view to giving the Royal regime the best possible chance of survival. . . .[65]

The proposed royal pledge, composed by the Foreign Office, would have had King George proclaim that, since he desired nothing more than to serve his people during the war and in the difficult period to follow, he would not return to Greece "until so invited by the clearly expressed will" of the Greek nation. Accordingly, as soon as the country had been liberated, he would appoint a Regency Council to assume the duties of Chief of State until the constitutional matter had been settled. Meanwhile he would continue to represent the nation in allied councils, to insure that "Whatever the decision of the Greek people regarding its future regime, . . . the voice of Greece is heard in peace as it was in war and that the sacrifices of its people in the struggle for man's freedom shall not be forgotten."[66] It was, of course, precisely the formula that the representatives of the resistance organizations had sought in Cairo in August 1943 and the Greek Prime Minister had in vain tried to promote in the preceding months.

Predictably, King George was quite reluctant to concede

[65] *FR* (1943), 158-59. [66] Tsouderos, p. 78.

that the future of his throne was all that uncertain. He was willing to promise to delay his return until after the plebiscite. But the establishment of a regency to be controlled by persons who might well be enemies of the throne appeared to him as likely to lead to the end of his reign and very probably of the dynasty. Moreover, he could not understand the reasons for the shift of the British attitude toward his person, particularly since at the December 3 meeting, while the Foreign Secretary was expounding on the merits of the proposed royal declaration, Churchill had pointedly remarked that he, of course, "remained a royalist."

In rejecting Eden's proposal King George found a powerful if somewhat unexpected friend. President Roosevelt, whom he consulted in Cairo on December 6, suddenly entered the scene by complaining that the Foreign Secretary had been trying to "deprive the King of his crown" and expressing strong disapproval of British policy in the entire matter. This despite the fact that the American Ambassador, acting on instructions from the Department of State, had already encouraged the King to accept Eden's advice.[67] Moreover, following a long discussion of Greek affairs, Roosevelt directed MacVeagh to disassociate himself from British efforts to induce the King to do anything against his will and expressed resentment of any support he may have given the British for this purpose. Subsequently MacVeagh wrote to the President reassuring him that even though he considered Eden's proposal a wise one, he had given the King no advice, encouraging him to decide matters for himself.[68]

[67] Eden, III, 498-99. On December 5 MacVeagh had sent a message to the President in Cairo informing him that the King of Greece was very anxious to see him. The King, wrote MacVeagh, "is distressed in his mind as to whether he should make the declaration which has been suggested to him by the British, and a talk with you would not fail to reassure him and help him come to a decision" (*Roosevelt Papers*, PSF, 1941-44, "Greece.")

[68] Ambassador MacVeagh reported to the Department on December 12: "I am reliably informed that during a long session on De-

The resignation of Tsouderos in mid-April 1944, caused by the mutiny in the Middle East, and the prolonged Cabinet crisis which followed, appeared to cast a new dark shadow upon the controversy surrounding the King's intentions. The monarch's statement of November 8, 1943, pledging to consult with his government at the time of liberation regarding his return, had been in the form of a personal letter to the Prime Minister. With Tsouderos out of office even such a vague promise carried precious little weight. The attitude of the British Prime Minister tended to substantiate such scepticism. Churchill appeared to remain unshaken in what his critics in the House of Commons called his "king-mania." On April 9, 1944 he reminded Ambassador Leeper in Cairo that Britain's relations were established strictly with the "lawfully constituted Greek Government headed by the King, who is the ally of Britain and cannot be discarded *to suit a momentary surge of appetite among ambitious émigré nonentities.*" Moreover, Greece cannot "find constitutional expression in particular sets of guerrillas, in many cases indistinguishable from banditti, who are masquerading as the saviours of their country while living on the local villagers. . . ." Churchill warned that he might "denounce these elements and tendencies publicly in order to emphasize the love Great Britain has for Greece. . . ." Hav-

---

cember 8 with Mr. Churchill and Mr. Eden the King of Greece steadfastly refused to make a declaration proposed by them to the effect that he will not return to Greece unless and until called for by the Constituent Assembly to the formation of which he agreed in his declaration of July 4. I saw the President on December 3 and advised him regarding this proposal and after he had seen the King he desired me not to associate myself with any effort to force him to a course of action against his will. This I have been careful not to do both before and since. I understand that the President told the King that there was no necessity for him to make any declaration whatever unless he so desired" (*FR* [1943], 157). See also *Roosevelt Papers*, psf, "Greece: L. MacVeagh," letter from MacVeagh to the President dated Dec. 13, 1943; letter from the President to Mac-Veagh dated Jan. 15, 1944.

ing thus dismissed the persistent views of virtually every prominent Greek political figure inside and outside Greece as nothing more than the "momentary surge of appetite" of "ambitious émigré nonentities," Churchill hailed the Greek monarch as "the servant of his people" who "makes no claim to rule them": but, rather, "submits himself freely to the judgment of the people as soon as normal conditions are restored." At that time the Greek nation could freely choose between a monarchy and a republic: "Why then cannot the Greeks keep their hatreds for the common enemy, who has wrought them such cruel injuries and would obliterate them as a free people, were it not for the resolute exertions of the Great Allies?" And to his bewildered envoy who had complained that serving near the Greek government was like living on top of a volcano, his mercurial superior fired back: "Where else do you expect to live in times like these?"[69] His attachment to the monarch and impatience with the Greek political situation were flaunted once more on May 4 when, alluding to the recent mutinees, he warned the Greek Ambassador in London that he would not tolerate a recurrence of such trouble, and added: "I fought for you like a tiger, and your King faced the recent crisis with the utmost courage and patriotism." Annoyed, Prime Minister Tsouderos telegraphed London requesting clarification of this statement, asking: "Against whom did he fight for us, and for what purpose?" The Greek Ambassador replied: "I have been officially assured that the phrase 'I fought for you like a tiger' referred to the determined stand of the British Prime Minister against the destructive and divisive elements both in Greece and in Egypt. . . ."[70]

As has been seen, the explosive events of the spring of 1944, both on the Greek mountains and among the Greek

[69] Churchill, v, 544. Emphasis mine. The perplexed Leeper was admonished to "show those qualities of imperturbability and command which are associated with the British Diplomatic Service."
[70] Papadakis, p. 362.

armed forces in the Middle East, finally compelled King George to permit the announcement of part of the formula which Eden had failed to force upon him the previous December. On June 12 the new Greek Prime Minister publicly declared that the King would not return pending the results of the plebiscite. Paradoxically, as already pointed out, although Papandreou had spoken only after consultation with the monarch, the latter continued to regard himself uncommitted on the matter of the timing of his return. Above all, however, he had successfully resisted all efforts to create a regency which would exercise the royal prerogatives while the King remained abroad. There the "constitutional question" rested until the country's liberation.

It might thus be said in review that as the German withdrawal from Greece began to appear imminent the British government concentrated its efforts on the following objectives: strict control of the resistance movement so as to dampen radical political ambitions; strong support for a Greek government which, while moderate and broadly representative, would also be mindful of British interests, and out of the hands of the extreme Left; assisting the King to keep his options open until after the war in the hope that he would soon be returning to his throne; keeping the Soviet Union out of Greek affairs, and obtaining American endorsement of British handling of the Greek situation while encouraging Washington to remain disinterested in such "trivia" within the broader context of allied cooperation. On this last point, when President Roosevelt had complained on June 22, 1944 that Anglo-Soviet discussions regarding a possible division of responsibility in the Balkans had been initiated behind the back of the American government, Churchill had sought (on June 23) to emphasize the seriousness of the situation which had necessitated an early understanding with Moscow. "It would be quite easy for me," he wrote, "on the general principle of slithering to the Left, which is so popular in foreign policy, to let things rip when the King of Greece would probably be forced to abdicate and EAM would work a reign of terror in Greece, forcing the villagers and many other classes to form security battalions under German auspices to prevent utter anarchy. The only way I can prevent this is by persuading the Russians to quit boosting EAM and ramming it forward with all their force. . . ." Accordingly, "I proposed to the Russians a temporary working arrangement for the better conduct of the war."[71]

It had been this remarkable statement in which Churchill, contrary to all available information, blamed EAM's misconduct upon the Soviet Union, that had persuaded the President to drop his objections to the manner in which the British authorities had handled the "spheres of influence" exchange. Quietly the American government admitted that, for all its concern in the matter, it recognized Britain's principal responsibility in Greek affairs.

When EAM attempted to cause Papandreou's fall in August 1944, the British government let it be known that such a development would be entirely unacceptable.[72] Moreover, in the House of Commons Foreign Secretary Eden had already (on July 27) rejected EAM's conditions for joining the government as "unreasonable" and as intended to give its leaders "control over all the guerrilla forces in Greece and over the Greek Army abroad and a representation in the Greek Government out of all proportion to their actual strength. . . ." If they persisted in their refusal to cooperate with the government, EAM's leaders would be held responsible "for the failure to achieve unity of Greek policy and aims at this, the supreme moment of the common struggle. . . ."[73] Several days later Eden told the House of Commons that supplies to ELAS would be withheld if "they per-

[71] FR (1944), 126-27.

[72] Ibid., 132; Papandreou, I Apeleftherosis, p. 131.

[73] Great Britain, Parliamentary Debates (Commons), 402 (1943-44), 898-99.

sist in their present uncooperative attitude," a measure which the British authorities had successfully employed against ELAS during the First Round.[74] Indeed, assistance to ELAS was cut off in August at the insistence of the Foreign Office, despite objections from allied military authorities.

On August 2 Churchill added his own considerable weight to Eden's statements, warning the many critics of his Greek policy in the House of Commons, that "On this line we intend to fight, so far as may be needful, in the House." In the ensuing debate, Churchill was chided for his "intense Royalism" which, as one speaker put it, "must be based on the historical investigation he made into his ancestors," as a result of which "he is doing penance at the present time in supporting kings all over the world. In fact, the Prime Minister cannot see a king without wanting to shore him up. . . ."[75]

At long last, as British pressure on EAM mounted, the leaders of Greece's Liberal, Progressive, Agrarian, and Democratic Parties sent a joint message to EAM through British channels, appealing to EAM to join them without further delay in the Government of National Unity under Papandreou, stressing the dangers that would face them all if unity could not be achieved at the moment of liberation. While showing a copy of this message to an American diplomat, one of the co-signers, Sofoclis Venizelos, expressed strong resentment of the British role in Greek affairs, complaining that Greek unity was "no longer a question between the Government and the mountains, but between Mr. Eden and the mountains."[76]

Under the circumstances, the leaders of EAM found it necessary to yield: on September 2 they entered the government of Prime Minister Papandreou without conditions

---

[74] *Ibid.*, 1357. [75] *Ibid.*, 1483, 1553.

[76] *FR* (1944), 132. Text of cable and reply in *E.A.M. White Book*, p. 6. OSS sources asserted that following receipt of this appeal EAM decided to join the government without insisting that Papandreou resign (*DSR*, 868.01/8-1644).

or further demands. The leftist coalition received the following Cabinet posts: Minister of Finance (A. Svolos), Communications (N. Askoutsis), National Economy (E. Tsirimokos), Labor (M. Porfyrogenis), Agriculture (J. Zevgos), and Deputy Minister of Finance (A. Angelopoulos).

This gradual change of heart toward the government, brought about by the pressures outlined above, can be clearly traced in the editorial line of *Rizospastis*, the organ of the Communist Party, from April to September. This publication, appearing at first clandestinely and irregularly during the enemy occupation, provided not only KKE members but followers of the leftist coalition with information and guidance on every aspect of Greek life. In April, the resignation of Prime Minister Tsouderos had been greeted by *Rizospastis*, as "the first bright victory" of the Political Committee of National Liberation (PEEA), which other prominent figures were now invited to join without delay. Under the sponsorship of PEEA elections to a "National Council" would lead to the "completion of the pan-national coalition. . . ."[77] Thus Communist leaders apparently had hoped that the prolonged crisis in the Middle East would so discredit the King and Greek politicians abroad that EAM would be afforded the opportunity to proceed with the elevation of PEEA to the status of the provisional government of Greece, assuring the country's "socialist" future. On April 24, under the headlines "Hail the National Unity of the Greek People—All Greeks with PEEA," it announced that PEEA had been "reconstituted on a much broader basis" for a variety of reasons and "in view of the impending discussions with the Cairo Government." The following issue (on April 30, 1944) was in large part devoted to the "electoral activity" in Athens and Piraeus (under German occupation) where the "PEEA ticket is being enthusiastically received." Again, "what remains is for the national unity to be

[77] *Rizospastis*, April 10, 1944.

completed, and for the Pan-national Government to be formed quickly." The mutiny, viewed by *Rizospastis* as the struggle of "our army and navy" for "national unity," was actually described on the basis of stories reported in *The Times* of London, the *Daily Herald*, the *Manchester Guardian*, and on the British Broadcasting Corporation.

On the eve of the Lebanon Conference *Rizospastis* began a cautious attack on Papandreou's rising star. Focusing attention on his public denunciation of the mutineers and of what he had repeatedly termed guerrilla "terrorist" activity in Greece, it accused the new Prime Minister of choosing to ignore the atrocities committed by the Germans and the Security Battalions, and of surrounding himself with collaborators and remnants of the Metaxas regime. "Mr. Papandreou must bear in mind," the newspaper's editors warned, "that with these actions he does not facilitate the achievement of national unity." Several weeks later, on July 20, 1944, disregarding the apparently successful conclusion of the Lebanon meeting, *Rizospastis* praised ELAS for "intensifying its blows against the combined forces of the Germans-Bulgarians and the Papandreous. . . ." Linking the Prime Minister with the family name of the Royal House, it denounced the military tribunals of "Glücksborg-Papandreou" which were in the process of trying the mutineers, and declared that "the Greek people will hold personally responsible the Cairo clique and especially the Papandreou Government" for continuing to pursue the "treasonous policy" of the Metaxas dictatorship. Telegrams protesting all this were said to have been sent not only to the Big Three leaders and General De Gaulle, but to Tito, Beneš, and even Hoxha!

Foreign Secretary Eden's statement in the House of Commons on July 27, strongly critical of EAM for refusing to join the Papandreou Cabinet, elicited an immediate and worried response from the Communist leadership. While implying that the British government, however well-intentioned, had not judged the political climate in Greece properly and accurately, the KKE spokesman sought to placate and reassure the authorities in London. Contending that it had been the Communists who had initiated the Greek resistance movement, *Rizospastis* declared that "The Greek people are fighting alongside the allies and England for the aims and ideals proclaimed by all the allies and by England: for its national liberation, for the imposition of the sovereign popular will, for the shattering of the forces of violence. . . ." Moreover, the Political Committee of National Liberation, supported by EAM and the Communist Party, "is the sole organ in Greece entitled to a decisive voice regarding Greek affairs because only PEEA, EAM, and the KKE have fought and are still fighting against fascism, and on the side of the Allies. . . . In accordance with the true facts of Greek life, only PEEA expresses the will of the Greek people, because it represents the absolute majority of the nation." In the interest of national unity and to strengthen the allied cause EAM had already made "major concessions" to Papandreou's "clique" whose reaction, nevertheless, "is hindering our people's struggle." However, ". . . we know that the prestige and influence of the allies and especially of England in Greece are not bolstered by the hated Glücksborg, or by the supercilious crypto-fascists Papandreous . . . [whose scheming destroys] the spontaneously cordial ties of friendship and cooperation . . . which bind our small but proud nation to the great nations of the allies and especially of England." *Rizospastis* concluded: "We are certain that the Great Allies and especially England will recognize the liberational, anti-fascist and democratic struggle of our people, personified in the united and unanimous EAM under the banners of PEEA. This struggle will be served, must be served, by the national unity that will be achieved *in Greece*."[78]

[78] *Ibid.*, July 30, 1944. Emphasis mine. The same issue carried an item under the heading "Papandreou Must Go," according to which,

Contrary to the expressed confidence of KKE's propagandists, it soon became clear that Prime Minister Papandreou would not step down, and that the political center would not suddenly shift to Greece where KKE through EAM and PEEA, might hope to find itself in a position of considerable influence. Therefore, unless EAM went to Cairo to enter Papandreou's government, it would run the risk of being bypassed by the decision-making process that would shape the country's future. Virtual domination of the countryside by ELAS and other leftist organizations offered no sufficient counterweight against a broadly based government sanctioned by the allies and actively supported by the omnipresent British authorities. There is, in fact, no indication that the Communists considered seizing control of the entire country as the enemy withdrew, and confronting Papandreou and the British with a *fait accompli*. Once again the editors of *Rizospastis* had to project the new line, this time tucked away among by-now familiar slogans. Attacking Papandreou as the real enemy of genuine national reconciliation for his refusal to resign, they self-righteously declared that "The nation will be astonished by the attitude of such men who have completely forgotten that they are Greeks and it will vindicate the patriotic superiority of KKE and of EAM and PEEA, *which are compelled by these dramatic hours for Greece to consent to participate in a government even if its Premier is Papandreou.* We do not know if Papandreou will create yet another obstacle to national unity at the last moment. Our Party makes even this concession at the time when the Greek people are defending their

---

". . . in official circles of fighting Greece—of PEEA, EAM and KKE—a single, unanimous view prevails, that for the formation of a unified pan-national government it is necessary first of all for Papandreou to get out of the Cairo Government. Because Papandreou . . . is seeking to impose a unity that will dissolve the national struggle, so that he may succeed in imposing anti-democratic solutions in Greece after liberation."

children and their altars and hearths in the most horrible struggle against the rage of the Germans and Rallides who are fighting in Greece in the name of Papandreou and of Glücksborg. . . ." The message to the party faithful was nevertheless unmistakably clear: "The KKE, EAM, and PEEA have agreed to send representatives to the Government that will have Papandreou as its Premier. . . ." Finally, the indispensable exhortation: "The curse of the nation will eternally burden this man, these cliques, if they persist in playing their awful game with the life, the liberty and the independence of Greece."[79]

With the dispatch of representatives to join the Cabinet in Cairo, PEEA issued a communique on August 23, 1944, explaining once more its latest position, while attempting to retain an identity and a purpose separate from that of the government. "We have been faced," the statement asserted, "with new developments and influences outside Greece whose importance has compelled us, in the interest of our people and of the allied effort, not to insist further on a change in the person of the Premier. . . . While entering the Government and achieving national unity we shall continue the struggle for national liberation, for the crushing of fascism and for the smooth and democratic solution of the country's internal problems."[80] The issue of *Rizospastis* which carried this statement also contained a vehement denial of the "baseless reports" that the decision to enter the Papandreou government "had been taken following the intercession of the Soviet Union and of the Soviet Military Mission."

Thus the legitimacy, the representative nature, and the aims of the Government of National Unity were no longer under attack from the extreme Left. "On the eve of the great battle" for liberation, exclaimed *Rizospastis* on September 10, "the Greeks have a unified Government. This

[79] *Ibid.*, Aug. 20, 1944. Emphasis mine.
[80] *Ibid.*, Aug. 24, 1944.

gives us new wings for battle." Appealing for the dissolution of the Security Battalions, the "various traitor gangs, the last cancers of a shameful occupation," it hastened to point out that such organizations had now been openly denounced by the Greek government in Cairo. As for PEEA, whose reason for independent existence had presumably ended with EAM's entry into the government, "it leads the struggle in the liberated areas [and] continues . . . to be the instrument of the Government until the Government arrives in Greece, which is generally believed to be quite soon. . . ."

The Communist leadership remained sensitive to rumors abroad that it might resort to a coup the moment the enemy had withdrawn. Taking advantage of a short visit to London, John Zevgos, KKE's representative in the Cabinet as Minister of Agriculture, went out of his way to attack as malicious speculation all such reports and to blame them on reactionary elements in Greece and elsewhere. The Communist Party, he declared, had only two objectives: "national liberation" and the "securing of popular sovereignty." He continued:

> KKE has been fighting for these goals for the past three years and will continue to fight for a popular (*laokratiki*) settlement of all domestic issues. I affirm in the most categorical manner that our program . . . is the defense of popular liberties in accordance with the Atlantic Charter and the decisions of our Allies at Teheran. We entered the Government in the pursuit of these two objectives and I believe that all patriotic people will today work together with the KKE and in accordance with the directives of the National Government: for national liberation, the preservation of order, for the people's liberties and for the normal and democratic development of the country.[81]

[81] *Ibid.*, Sept. 27, 1944. Curiously, in this issue the traditional slogan "Proletarians of the world unite!" was replaced by the more innocuous

Reproducing Zevgos' statement *Rizospastis* also reported without editorial comment the following news item: "The Greek Government will be established in Greece together with the Allies, but without the King, who will await the decision of the Greek people in the form of a plebiscite." Finally, on the eve of the arrival of the Papandreou Cabinet in liberated Athens, the Political Office of the Communist Party issued the following ringing proclamation: "Communists! Continue, alongside the National Government and our Great Allies, and with ever greater intensity, the struggle for the liberation of the last inch of our country's soil. For the securing of the independence and territorial integrity of Greece. . . . Long live our National Government!"[82] For the moment, the reconciliation between the government and the extreme Left appeared to be complete.

Despite such protestations of fidelity from the coalition's most powerful and potentially most troublesome partner, the government's road to Athens was still far from smooth. Nor did difficulty always come from the Left. It was to become abundantly clear that the Government of National Unity was a patchwork of conflicting interests and personalities which could survive only as long as its members could see no better chance of furthering their factional aims outside it, and as long as the British authorities gave it their full and unequivocal backing. In addition to the Ministers representing the EAM forces, the Cabinet consisted of mostly colorless figures of a broad and vague liberal-republican spectrum, clinging to Papandreou's prestigious coattails and hoping to revive their own political followings at the earliest opportunity. They were worried men, disturbed by the dangerous prospects ahead.

Their fears were shared by those in a position to take action. On August 17 Churchill requested and obtained

---

"Everything for the crushing of fascism!" The motto of international Communism reappeared in mid-October.

[82] *Ibid.*, Oct. 13, 1944.

American support for the creation of a 10,000-man British force, to be sent to Athens as soon as circumstances permitted, to assist the government in maintaining order in the capital and surrounding towns. The severe shortage of troops indicated that the rest of the country and especially the northern provinces would naturally come under the control of the local resistance groups. Avoiding critics of his Greek policy in the Department of State, Churchill dealt directly with the President once more, seeking to reassure him of Britain's honorable intentions. "You and I," he wrote to Roosevelt, "have always agreed that the destinies of Greece are in the hands of the Greek people and that they will have the fullest opportunity of deciding between a Monarchy or Republic as soon as tranquility has been restored but I do not expect you will relish more that I do the prospect either of chaos and street fighting or of a tyrannical Communist Government being set up. This could only serve to delay and hamper all the plans which are being made by UNRRA for distribution of relief to the sorely-tried Greek people. . . ."[83] The President replied on August 26, giving his consent to the formation of such a British force and authorizing the use of American aircraft for its transport to Greece.[84] This force was destined to play a decisive role in the crucial weeks of the approaching Second Round. Several weeks after the President's endorsement, on September 23, 1944, the American and British ambassadors in Moscow called on Marshal Stalin to deliver a joint message from Roosevelt and Churchill regarding military decisions reached at the Second Quebec Conference. When informed of the contemplated landing by British forces in Greece the Soviet leader expressed his full approval, adding that it was high time that such an operation was carried out.[85]

In mid-August Papandreou traveled secretly to Rome

[83] Churchill, vi, 111-12.   [84] FR (1944), 132-34.
[85] Herbert Feis, *Churchill, Roosevelt, Stalin: The War They Waged and the Peace They Sought* (New Jersey, 1957), p. 425.

(accompanied only by the director of the King's political office) where he met Churchill on the 21st. According to the latter's account, the Greek leader, unaware of the recent decision on this very matter, asked for the early despatch of British troops to Greece where "At present only the wrong people had arms, and they were a minority." Churchill would not commit himself on this point, and warned against public discussion of the matter.[86] As yet without Roosevelt's explicit authorization, Churchill studiously avoided all mention of the British expeditionary force for Greece. He also counseled against the raising of territorial claims at this time. Furthermore, on the question of the monarchy Churchill saw no need for King George to make any further statements since he had already promised that "he would follow his Government's advice about going back to his country. . . ." Although Britain "felt friendly and chivalrous" toward King George, Churchill assured Papandreou that there was no intention of "interfering with the solemn right of the Greek people to choose between monarchy and a republic," as long as no "handful of doctrinaires" attempted to settle this key question in their favor. Observing with satisfaction that EAM had agreed to join the national government, Churchill suggested that "we should wait and see how . . . their representatives behaved before sending any more arms to ELAS." He thought that the formation of a national army should be given highest priority by the Papandreou administration.[87]

At the same meeting Churchill strongly urged Papan-

[86] Churchill, VI, 112-14; Papandreou, *I Apeleftherosis*, pp. 134-41. American military sources in Italy advised the Department of State that the British had requested that the utmost secrecy be observed regarding their military plans for Greece (*DSR*, 740.00119 Control Italy/9-2744). This measure was enforced with particular vigor in the case of the Greek government itself which was told nothing about British troops that might accompany it at the time of liberation.

[87] Churchill, VI, 114. Churchill wrote to Eden after this encounter that he had "liked" Papandreou. On this meeting see also Papandreou, *I Apeleftherosis*, pp. 137-39.

dreou to move his Cabinet from Egypt to Italy at the earliest possible moment so as to facilitate plans for its return to Greece and to get it away from Cairo's "atmosphere of intrigue."[88] Without consulting his colleagues Papandreou readily agreed, thus precipitating yet a new crisis: on August 26 three prominent Liberals in the Cabinet, S. Venizelos, A. Mylonas, and C. Rentis, resigned in protest. Undaunted, Papandreou replaced them (on August 29) with lesser luminaries of the conservative Populist Party: D. Helmis, S. Tsakopoulos, and E. Sofoulis. Significantly, throughout this episode, the Left remained silently obedient. Following the oath-taking ceremonies King George departed for London, having announced that during his stay there his younger brother, Crown Prince Paul, would represent him and serve as "Regent." This casual appointment, unsanctioned by any governmental authority, was hardly designed to inspire confidence in the monarch's intentions. On September 7 the entire Cabinet was officially transferred to Salerno, Italy. Ten days later an American diplomat reported that he had discovered the Greek government "marooned in two miserable hotels in the village of Cava. . . ."[89] It was indeed a devious route to the Greek capital.

The resignation of the three Liberals was an event of considerable significance as it revealed Papandreou's near-total isolation from the country's principal political forces. Even with EAM in the government, his alienation from the Left was by now an accomplished fact and in the future he could expect nothing but trouble from that quarter. Having ad-

[88] Churchill, VI, 113. Macmillan, who after August was to be in charge of British policy in Greece, recalls: "Papandreou accepted enthusiastically, the more so as he wants to keep the five EAM Ministers (who have at last agreed to join) away from the poisonous atmosphere which reigns at Cairo . . ." (Harold Macmillan, *The Blast of War, 1939-1945* [New York, 1967], p. 466; also DSR, 740.00119 Control Italy/8-2744).

[89] DSR, 868.01/1744; Leeper, p. 66.

ditionally antagonized the Liberal Party, which might otherwise have been his principal ally in the Center, he stood virtually alone. Moreover, his gestures toward the numerically
much weaker Populists were not likely to produce more
than opportunistic accommodations because conservative-
monarchist circles remained highly suspicious of his socialist principles. Thus, as the day of liberation drew near,
Papandreou's only solid support was to come from the British government. Characteristically, he made no attempt to
remedy this unhealthy situation, confident that Britain's
blessing, his own charisma, and the adulation he was bound
to receive as the country's "liberator" would more than
make up for the lack of organized support from the old
parties.

A report from one of the three Liberals, in which the reasons for their resignation were reviewed, sheds additional
light on the politically precarious position in which the
Prime Minister had placed himself. Writing to the EDES
leader, Zervas, on September 4, 1944, Rentis charged that
the Cabinet was in fact Papandreou's "personal government." In particular, the participation of the Liberals had
been merely symbolic because they had been given no portfolios and no specific functions, while Papandreou had personally taken over three separate ministries. Their original
decision to cooperate with him had been motivated solely
by the need to maintain a solid front against the forces of
EAM, which, however, were bound to be the principal bene-
ficiaries of his devious tactics. The three had been frustrated in their concerted efforts to deal with a number of
key problems and, in opposing them, Papandreou's men
had been claiming that "the British wanted it that way."
Thus they had in vain protested as unconstitutional a decree which had given the Greek Chief of Staff, General C.
Ventiris, the powers of the Minister of the Army: the British allegedly would not permit its annulment. As a result,
republican officers had been deactivated or otherwise re-

moved from their posts under various pretexts. On a more current issue, Papandreou had lied to his Cabinet (including his Vice President Venizelos) so as to keep his colleagues in the dark concerning his talks with Churchill in Rome and made no attempt to confer with them regarding the move to Italy. Finally, Papandreou wished to serve as Regent in Athens and to prolong his term as Prime Minister after liberation, despite the existing agreement that the present government would be dissolved as soon as elections were possible. Rentis wrote that under no circumstances would the Liberals bow to such demands: "We therefore resigned, believing that cooperation with Papandreou as Prime Minister is not possible because [that office] has gone to his head and he thinks that he too, in his turn, will become Dictator. . . ." As for the transfer of the Cabinet to Italy, "We do not know the meaning of this move. Perhaps it will lose the little freedom it enjoys now. . . ."[90]

While in Italy the Greeks worked closely with Harold Macmillan who, as Chief Commissioner of the Allied Control Commission for Italy and British Minister Resident at the Allied Force Headquarters, Mediterranean Theater, had assumed overall responsibility for British policy in the Balkans but more particularly in Greece. At this time, surveying his latest assignment Macmillan could observe with satisfaction that the United States and even the Soviet Union seemed content to accept Britain's special position and interests in Greece.[91] His principal concern for the moment was the viability of the Greek government. Lamenting the rapid decline of his government's influence in the Balkans generally and particularly in Bulgaria, where the Foreign Office "have 'missed the bus' again," he recorded on September 11: "Already the Greeks are restive and the Communist members of the Papandreou Government may

[90] Text of letter from Rentis to Zervas, dated Sept. 4, 1944, in Pyromaglou, *Kartalis*, pp. 373-75.
[91] Macmillan, p. 475.

easily resign. They are arguing that Greece should be look-ing to the rising sun of the Kremlin, not to the setting orb of Downing Street. . . ."[92]

To minimize the danger of renewed division as the day of liberation approached and to strengthen the govern-ment's control over the resistance forces Macmillan con-vened a conference of Greek political and guerrilla leaders at Caserta. After some heated discussions a formal pact was drawn up and signed by Macmillan as British Resident Minister, General Sir Henry Maitland Wilson, Supreme Allied Commander for the Mediterranean, Prime Minister Papandreou, General Stefanos Sarafis for ELAS, and General Napoleon Zervas for EDES. Under the terms of the Caserta Agreement, the resistance organizations formally placed themselves under the authority of the national government. Agreeing to put an end to past rivalries they declared their intention to form a "national union" to facilitate the co-ordination of their efforts against the common enemy. In turn the Greek government authorized a British officer, Lieutenant General Ronald Scobie, to assume command of the Greek resistance forces. At Sarafis' insistence, the words "to restore law and order in Greece," which had appeared in the original version as defining General Scobie's responsi-bility, were removed from the final text: as far as the Left was concerned, such a crucial mission belonged to the Greeks themselves. The two guerrilla leaders declared that their organizations would refrain from taking the law into their own hands in the areas where they operated, and that any such action would be treated as a crime and punished accordingly. Significantly, the agreement made specific mention of the Athens region, where no action was to be taken except as directly ordered by General Scobie. Clearly this provision reflected the allied decision to have the Brit-ish expeditionary force concentrated in the area of the capi-tal. Presumably in other parts of the country the resistance

[92] *Ibid.*, p. 478.

organizations might enjoy some unspecified freedom of action. The Security Battalions were once again denounced as instruments of the German occupation which would therefore be treated as enemy formations unless they surrendered according to Scobie's orders.[93]

It should be pointed out that the Caserta Agreement, under which the British government for all practical purposes took charge of Greek affairs on the eve of liberation, had no parallel elsewhere in wartime arrangements. Moreover, the policies of the United States and the Soviet Union offered silent though powerful endorsement of this unique decision. Under the circumstances it is hardly logical to contend that the Greek Left was preparing to seize power at the moment of liberation. Any such intention would have rendered the Caserta accord not only anathema but a tactical error of the first order. In particular, the naming of General Panayiotis Spiliotopoulos commander of the Attica Province meant in effect that control of that all-important area was being turned over to General Ventiris, Spiliotopoulos' close friend and former superior. And Ventiris, who as Chief of Staff after the mutiny had purged the Greek armed forces of all leftist-republican officers, was rapidly building for himself a reputation for conservative-monarchist leanings.

Despite the apparent success of the Caserta meeting, Prime Minister Papandreou continued to express privately the fear that unless the government and any accompanying British troops were brought to Greece at once, the Communists were sure to exploit the void which the departure of the Germans would create. On September 22 he telegraphed to Churchill:

> I can assure you that the stability of the Greek Government will be maintained fully in the critical times ahead. We are greatly alarmed, however, by the situation devel-

[93] For the text of the Caserta Agreement see Appendix E.

oping in Greece where the areas evacuated by the Germans are occupied by EAM claiming to act in the name of the Greek Government. I do not know the reasons for Britain's absence. But I regard it my duty to express my conviction that, in view of the critical situation, political counter-measures are no longer adequate. Only the immediate presence of impressive British forces in Greece and beyond to the Turkish shores could change the situation. From my communication with the Commander-in-Chief of the allied forces I know that there are difficulties in this matter. However, your success in this war in so many tasks which others had regarded as impossible justifies the hope of martyrized Greece that your prompt, and determined intervention will rectify the situation.[94]

If the government and sufficient British forces were not present, he told Macmillan several days later, "the Communists would step in and build themselves too strong a position to allow of their subsequent ejection." However, when Macmillan proposed to transport the government to Patras prior to the liberation of Athens, Papandreou and his colleagues "suddenly lost [their] nerve." According to Macmillan's personal account, "They now did not want to go to Patras, or, indeed, to anywhere in the Peloponnese. They could not afford a failure; there were not enough British troops; there were no Greek troops; the relief supplies would be disappointingly small; and so forth and so on. . . ." Exasperated, Macmillan persuaded Ambassador Leeper not to report the matter to London: "We should appear foolish and vacillating in the eyes of the P.M. if one day we tele-

[94] Papadakis, pp. 410-11. When the Bulgarian forces in Greek Macedonia appeared in no hurry to be evacuated, the Greek Prime Minister protested bitterly and warned the British government: "The Greek nation is most alarmed by the situation unfolding in the Balkans. Only the issuance of an order that our territories be immediately occupied by Greeks will bring consolation; otherwise, national desperation will lead to an overthrow of the situation and of our domestic political life" (*ibid.*, p. 416).

117

graph *urgently* for permission to send an expedition and introduce the Government into Patras; and the next day say that we have thought better of it and that we and the Greek Government are now taking counsel of our fears. . . ."[95]

In his new capacity as principal British adviser to the Greek government Macmillan also conferred on September 30 with Crown Prince Paul who expressed his desire to return to Greece at the earliest moment, even if his brother the King could not do so for the time being. In the presence of Ambassador Leeper and General Wilson, Macmillan urged Prince Paul to realize that his return would only destroy the government of Prime Minister Papandreou and would give the Communists the chance to seize control of the country. After the meeting Macmillan recorded in his diary that he had "felt sorry for the Prince," who was "obviously sincere and anxious to do his best for his brother and the dynasty. But I fear he suffers under the usual illusions of royalty. He believes that he has only to show himself in Greece for a 'landslide' to take place. . . ." Significantly, Macmillan discovered that "It was clear that the King does not regard himself as bound by his declaration that he would not go back to Greece without the consent of his Government. . . ." He concluded: "Of one thing I am certain, that even Winston's popularity will not enable him to force a King upon Greece by British arms."[96]

Since the Lebanon Conference in May, which Ambassador MacVeagh would not attend, American officials had been keeping a close and worried eye on the Greek political scene and on British preparations to return the Papandreou government home. Earlier in 1944, in a long letter to the President, MacVeagh in Cairo had urged that allied military operations in southeastern Europe, the "Balkan front" strongly advocated by Churchill, "should be considered more seriously than seems to be the case at present, if relief is to get started." Indeed, he felt that the initiative for such

[95] Macmillan, p. 480.   [96] *Ibid.*, pp. 480-81.

operations should be assumed by Washington and not London. However, as long as American military authorities would not approve an invasion of the Balkans, the United States must first ascertain that the British were prepared to devote sufficient strength and resources, "before we associate ourselves with this in any way." He cautioned the President that "Our old habit of attaching observers to foreign enterprises may be useful under certain conditions, but we should be careful to avoid its leading us into the appearance of responsibility in vital matters over which we have no effective control." He humorously referred to London's "habit and skill" in "putting 'English' on the ball," and added: "The English in Balkan affairs right now is this, that through our association with British schemes we can be handed equal portion of the blame if these go wrong." MacVeagh reported that whereas American agents in the Balkans had been restricting themselves to military matters, the British were "immersed deeply in political maneuvers." However, the people in both Yugoslavia and Greece thought in terms of Anglo-American policies, thus implicating the United States in British "schemes." Furthermore, "British moves are very different from what we conceive as agreed-upon program for the postwar world," and are aimed at "the preservation of Empire connections," as well as "finding where Britain can secure the firmest vantage ground to preserve its stakes in the Balkans, obviating total control of Southeast Europe by any other great power." Nevertheless, such a policy, especially if pursued with inadequate means, could only result in bringing the entire area under Soviet influence. "To keep Britain and Russia from eventually conflicting in this region," MacVeagh continued, "the Balkan states may be reconstituted as genuinely free and friendly to both sides. Only the United States can undertake this task. Are we to fight a war and sacrifice for victory the aims we seek to win? . . . *So let it be known that the United States is running the job.*" Otherwise, the people of the Balkans realize that "the preponderance of power in Europe will certainly drag them to Russia's side if we sell them down the river to the British. . . ."[97]

MacVeagh's wish for an American initiative in the Balkans was to be frustrated. Neither the President nor his principal advisers were inclined to entangle the United States in the problems of postwar Europe generally, but especially of the Balkans, where American interests were virtually nonexistent. On February 21, 1944 the President addressed a note to the acting Secretary of State expressing the conviction that "It would be a great mistake for us to participate in a military campaign against the Balkans at this time." He approved the despatch of "half a dozen observers" to the British forces which were to enter the area but directed that the United States "should do nothing further till later." Ignoring the principal theme in MacVeagh's recommendations, he observed with approval that the Ambassador had strongly advised against *joint* Anglo-American operations in the Balkans.[98]

In mid-May, in another of his personal letters to the President, MacVeagh reported from Cairo that Soviet influence in the Balkans was advancing rapidly because of the presence of Soviet troops, affecting the "thoughts and fears of men." These fears "will doubtless be intensified when Russia is no longer simply one of the great powers but the only great power remaining on the European continent." Consequently, in all of eastern Europe and the Middle East Anglo-Soviet rivalry was destined to replace the competition between Britain and the Axis powers. "Can this be prevented from becoming more than a game? If it leads to war, I suppose we shall again be involved. . . ." As for Greece, re-

[97] *Roosevelt Papers*, PSF, "Greece: L. MacVeagh." Letter to the President dated Feb. 17, 1944. Emphasis mine.

[98] *Ibid.*, MRP, Naval Aide's File "Balkan Countries." Memorandum from the President to the Acting Secretary of State dated Feb. 21, 1944.

sentment caused by British "interference" and the obvious lack of unity among Greeks might well result in a "turning of the eyes towards Moscow." Indeed, MacVeagh believed he had detected in the Greek mutinies the inspiration of "an ideology especially associated with Russia." Obviously alarmed by such a trend his British colleague had remarked that "Greece is now at the cross-roads, the question being whether she is to move into the Russian orbit and lose her independence, or remain a European country under British influence."[99]

Recognizing that his earlier suggestion for an American lead at least in relief operations, designed to "cushion off the impact of British and Russian pressures," had been consistently ignored by his superiors, MacVeagh drew the President's attention to Britain's failure to keep the Soviet Union advised of economic and relief planning for the Balkans. This practice, he warned, may very easily appear to the Russians "as masking an attempt at establishing a postwar zone of influence" and may be equally as dangerous as Soviet propaganda which so alarmed the British. To remedy the situation he recommended that "the Russians . . . be brought more closely into all our long-term planning" for these areas. He observed once again that American efforts "to maintain an independent balancing policy are being heavily handicapped by our good cousins . . . ," who deliberately create the impression that they were implementing joint Anglo-American plans for the entire region.[100] On the other hand, several weeks later MacVeagh informed the President that following exchanges between London and Moscow there now appeared to be considerable easing of Anglo-Soviet tension over the Balkans. Indeed, he had been reliably informed that the two may soon come to an agreement "to recognize each other's 'initiative' in Greece

[99] *Ibid.*, PSF, "Greece: L. MacVeagh.'" Letter to the President dated May 15, 1944.

[100] *Ibid.* Letter to the President dated June 23, 1944.

and Rumania respectively, without of course abandoning their own legitimate interests in these countries." Such an arrangement, the American diplomat speculated, "may be only patchwork to cover up the rifts of fundamental suspicion and distrust, but it is all to the good so far as it goes, and the easing of tension here for the moment is marked. . . ."[101]

In a special report on Yugoslavia and Greece, to which he was officially accredited, MacVeagh noted in early August that the recent attempt by the British government to establish in the Balkans a "division of zones of interest" for the duration of the war appeared to be doomed to failure "largely on account of the [State] Department's doubts as to the advisability of such action in connection with decisions taken at Teheran." Nevertheless, the move indicated that the British government at least appreciated "the dangers inherent in the present situation if suspicions are allowed to grow." In any event, the Balkan region remained susceptible to conflicting Anglo-Soviet pressures. Although Communist ideology had no great appeal there, "the success of Communist-led resistance movements in disorganized and demoralized territories supplies a dangerous opportunity for the imposition of Communist Party dictatorship." MacVeagh summed up allied policies toward Yugoslavia and Greece as follows: the United States wished not to interfere in their internal affairs, while assisting those resistance groups which actively fought the common enemy; on the other hand, Britain and the Soviet Union sought to facilitate the establishment of governments favorable to their own narrow interests in the area. Furthermore, "The British are very active in their direction and manipulation of the Governments-in-Exile. . . ." The Soviet Ambassador in Cairo had complained to him that "the real Prime Minister of Greece is the British Ambassador. . . ." As for

[101] *Ibid.*

the Russians themselves, "while critical and suspicious of the British, [they] appear for the most part to be holding aloof in the belief that repeated British mistakes, coupled with none on their part, will infallibly orient the sentiment of these distressed countries toward Moscow." MacVeagh regarded such a shift as entirely possible because of the "low ebb to which British prestige has fallen. . . ." He concluded his report with the recommendation that, "in view of the great dangers for the future peace of the whole world, including ourselves, which the Balkan region continues to present as a cross-roads of empire, we should maintain and even intensify our present salutory efforts to associate the Russians together with the British in all Balkan planning and activity of whatever character, from the ground up and in complete openness and confidence. . . ."[102]

Preparing to leave Cairo for liberated Athens MacVeagh reviewed once more for the President the problems of the Balkan region generally, and of Greece in particular. Writing on October 15 he observed that the presence of Soviet forces in most of eastern Europe might lead to the "virtual if not nominal annexation to the Soviet Union of an imperial domain of some hundred million souls." Coming to the prospects facing Greece, he wrote:

She is not, strictly speaking, on the Russian periphery, and I have no doubt that the realistic Stalin recognizes the realism of Britain's strategic interest in her position in the Aegean Sea. Nevertheless, subversive social forces are continuing to operate powerfully in Greece today, and are receiving the open sympathy of Moscow, if not its active support. I therefore still feel that, however

[102] *Ibid.*, MRP, Naval Aide's File A-14: "International Agreements, 1942-1945." For the text of this undated memorandum from Mac-Veagh to the Department of State (covering note dated Aug. 28, 1944) see Appendix D.

the Russian Government may formally keep hands off, the Greece of the future is going to be very different from the Greece we have known in the past. . . .

Observing that in recent decades the split into royalists versus Venizelists had dominated all other issues, he continued:

Greece is now clearly conscious of issues which never troubled King Constantine or Venizelos, and Greek revolutions are likely, from now on, to wear, at least to some degree, a social aspect. This makes the question of the King's return a good deal less vital, except to him and his family, than it would have been in times gone by, when the dynasty was of real influence in the country. Russia, probably playing a deeper game, doesn't seem to care whether he returns or not, and even Britain appears to realize that beneath and behind the window-dressing which he represents, the new growth of class-consciousness and proletarianism has altered the whole aspect of the problem of retaining British control. These forces have already raised their heads once—in the recent Greek mutiny in the Middle East—and Russia may be well content with the strength they then revealed. Again, she has only to watch while the trends of the time work for her—while forces which the bolshevik revolution set in motion years ago exploit postwar conditions for the spread of Russian influence. As the Soviet Minister said to me here one day (he was speaking of Egypt, but the parallel is clear), "They are terribly afraid of me here lest I engage in subversive activity. But I intend doing nothing of the sort. I don't have to. Conditions in the country itself will do all that is necessary."

Aware that, "in the typical American view of foreign affairs," the Balkan countries represented "very small potatoes," MacVeagh nevertheless expressed the conviction that "eventually what goes on in the Balkans and the Near East generally will have to be recognized as of prime importance to us. . . ." Britain will no longer be able to exert her traditionally powerful influence: "I doubt if in any other part of the world it can appear so clearly as here,— along its principal artery,—that militarily speaking the British empire is anachronistic, perfect for the eighteenth century, impossible for the twentieth. Every day brings its evidence of weakness and dispersion, of consequent opportunism, and dependence on America's nucleated strength." For the United States the significance of Britain's decline was enormous: "No one, I feel, can keep his eyes and ears open here and fail to believe that the future maintenance of the Empire depends on how far England consents to frame her foreign policy in agreement with Washington, and how far we in our turn realize where that Empire, so important to our own security, is most immediately menaced. . . ."[103]

Ambassador MacVeagh's closely reasoned efforts to arouse in Washington concern for the fate of the Balkans and the Middle East remained ineffective. While eventually willing to participate in the organization and supplying of relief, the United States would not involve itself in political affairs. General Marshall made this policy clear in a formal statement to the British government in July 1944.[104] Furthermore, whereas the President, at Churchill's urging, had formally approved (on August 26) British plans for the handling of the Greek situation, there was to be mounting apprehension in American diplomatic circles concerning what many continued to regard as the overbearing tactics of the Foreign Office. Information reaching the Department of State continued to support the view that because of his association with the Metaxas regime and his evasive pro-

[103] *Ibid.*, PSF, "Greece: L. MacVeagh." Letter to the President dated Oct. 15, 1944.
[104] Macmillan, p. 476.

nouncements in more recent years, King George was very unpopular and that any attempt to restore him to his throne without a plebiscite would be resisted by most Greeks and would lead to violence. Thus in September 1944 oss sources in Cairo speculated that the return of the King would very probably cause the immediate resignation of the EAM Ministers, thus destroying the coalition government and plunging the country into civil war.[105]

While some American officials were uneasy about British political motives in Greece, others became increasingly convinced that London underestimated the magnitude of its task and the grave risks resulting from it. On the one hand, the British government was making no attempt to conceal its hostility toward the EAM-KKE alliance, and had in fact cut off the flow of arms and supplies to ELAS for fear that they would be used to seize control of the country as soon as the Germans had retreated. At the same time the British authorities were preparing to establish their presence only in Athens, and even there with a force too small to be an effective deterrent to violence. Thus they were declaring political war on an adversary whose strength they were not able to meet with adequate military forces. On the other hand, there is good reason to believe that their concern for the growing strength and prestige of ELAS led the British to permit the Germans to withdraw from Greece unmolested. According to a German source, there were moments when the German Command had the impression that the evacuation of its troops from the Greek islands to the mainland was taking place under the protection of British guns. This peculiar situation encouraged certain circles in Berlin to believe that an accommodation with the West was still possible, enabling the Germans to concentrate on the Soviet armies.[106]

Whatever the information at hand and the views prevail-

[105] DSR, 868.001G291/9-2544.
[106] Quoted in Pyromaglou, Kartalis, p. 547.

ing at various diplomatic levels, the policy of the United States remained one of allowing London a free hand in Greek affairs while seeking to avoid being identified with British aims. When, at Churchill's request, the Greek government had been brought to Italy, an American diplomat in Cairo reported that the effect of such a move was to make the Greeks appear as an "appendage" to the British. He therefore questioned the wisdom of having the United States Embassy accompany the government to its new location—a step which the British Ambassador considered "absolutely essential"—lest this be interpreted as American approval of the whole affair.[107] The Department of State decided to keep the Embassy in Cairo for the time being, invoking "technical problems" and the "political considerations involved."[108] Aware of the implications of this decision the Greek government, through its Ambassador in Washington, sought to have it reversed, arguing that it might hamper contact between Greece and the United States in the critical days ahead. He was told, however, that since the United States government had not been consulted about the move from Cairo to Salerno, and as the Greek Cabinet itself had confirmed the decision only at the very last moment, it would not be practical to transfer the American Ambassador to Italy. He would, of course, be authorized to travel to Italy as often as might be needed to maintain adequate liaison.[109]

On September 30, a British memorandum informed the

[107] *DSR*, 868.01/8-2944.

[108] *Ibid.*, 868.01/8-2944.

[109] *Ibid.*, 868.01/9-1244. Curiously, Macmillan had recorded in his diary on August 27, 1944: "The P.M. was very pleased with the President's reply about Greece, agreeing to all his proposals, including the use of American aeroplanes to carry British troops to Athens *and to the immediate move of the Greek Government from Cairo to Naples*" (Macmillan, p. 477; emphasis mine). However, neither the Churchill telegram of August 17 to the President, nor Roosevelt's reply of August 26 approving British plans for Greece makes mention of the transfer of the Greek government to Italy.

Department of State that an Anglo-Soviet understanding regarding the Balkans was already in effect. Specifically, it was disclosed that British authorities had advised Moscow of the intention to send British troops to Greece and had requested that no Russian troops enter the territory of that country. The Soviet government had raised no objection to these plans and had agreed to keep its forces out of Greece. Commenting on this arrangement a senior American diplomat thought it encouraging that the Russians had referred to "theaters of military operations," thus apparently heeding Washington's insistence that the agreement be limited to wartime considerations alone. However, the same official expressed serious doubt that the British were prepared to employ sufficient means to cope with the explosive situation in Greece, particularly as the Germans appeared to slow down their withdrawal from the area. "If the half-starved Greeks were forced to endure another unsuccessful campaign," he observed, "or even to undergo a long drawn-out liberation with the consequent further destruction of property and disruption of the present vital trickle of relief supplies, it seems questionable to me whether they would even survive."[110]

The American official was not overstating the case. Indeed, Macmillan himself discovered that plans to rush relief supplies to Greece were alarmingly inadequate. Although food and basic commodities appeared to be available, there were no facilities for transporting them quickly and efficiently. He lamented on October 4: ". . . everything is 'on order' and 'expected in December.' (What would happen if the Germans left Greece too soon, the planners don't seem to have thought of.) But 'on order' means that the order has been registered with the vast machinery of Washington . . . and 'expected in December' means that if there were any ships and the ships were allocated to the job and did leave

[110] *DSR*, 868.01/9-2844.

America in October they would probably reach Alexandria in December. . . ."[111]

Later a new and even more frustrating obstacle was to be encountered. In Greece, heavily damaged ports and transport facilities, together with a breakdown in administration, would cause endless delays in the unloading and distribution of those desperately needed supplies reaching the country. This situation would add much to the turmoil and recriminations that are a major background factor in the crisis of December 1944.

But in the excitement of the impending liberation, worries about such administrative details were easily swept away. On October 8 Churchill and Eden, on their way to Moscow, stopped briefly at Caserta. The impressive conference that was quickly convened devoted considerable attention to Greek affairs. Assured by now that there would be no Soviet or American meddling, the British leaders appeared quite confident that Greece's problems would lend themselves to a satisfactory and even to an early solution. And they sought to communicate their optimism to others, but especially to the members of the Greek government. Churchill expressed his own exuberance by subjecting Papandreou to what a high-ranking British observer characterized as "a monologue which was chiefly confined to the merits of monarchy."[112] Macmillan later recalled that Foreign Secretary Eden, ". . . very distressed at the obvious ill effect on Papandreou of Winston's royalist sermon . . . asked me to do what I could to smooth things over."[113] In trying to do so Macmillan found the Greek Prime Minister "both

[111] Macmillan, p. 481, who adds the following detail: "One of the many absurdities is the position about clothing. The American Red Cross have 600,000 garments which they want to *give* to the Greeks. UNRRA says goods must be *sold*, not *given*. So the American Red Cross are threatening to *give* them to the French, who (being sensible people) have contracted out of UNRRA altogether."

[112] *Ibid.*, p. 482.   [113] *Ibid.*

voluble and interesting," and rather upset that Churchill would only talk to him about the matter of the monarchy. For Papandreou, the great divisions in Greece were "not as between republican and monarchist, but as between revolutionary and evolutionary. It would therefore be tragic to divide the moderate forces on what was really an obsolete debate. . . ." On the other hand, he had no illusions about the Communists, whom he recognized as a revolutionary force and not a political party. He added: "For the moment, because this suited Moscow, EAM were serving [in] the Government, but he knew that the moment that it was thought more advantageous, the order would be given to leave the Government and make as much trouble as possible. . . ."[114] Nevertheless, Papandreou expressed confidence in his ability to cope with the difficult days ahead. As soon as he got to Athens he intended to "reorganize" his Cabinet, presumably to neutralize EAM's influence, and to promulgate the decrees necessary to maintain a firm hold over the country. Contrary to an earlier agreement, and as the Liberals seemed to fear, he apparently no longer planned to have his government resign upon returning to Greece. The real difficulty, as he saw it, was the need to provide a constitutional basis for his actions in the absence of an elected parliament. "How was this to be done," he pressed Macmillan, "if the King was in England?" At the same time, he feared that "if the King were to come to Greece the Government would immediately collapse and EAM would seize power by revolution." The apparent dilemma could only be resolved by the establishment of a regency council of respected political figures, which might well include personal friends of the King. He was obviously thinking of himself rather than the Archbishop as a candidate for the office of regent. Once his government had been firmly established in Athens, Papandreou expected that the matter of the mon-

---

[114] *Ibid.*, pp. 483-84: Papandreou, *I Apeleftherosis*, pp. 178-81.

archy could be brought to a satisfactory conclusion through a plebiscite. Although Macmillan was persuaded by all this, King George and Churchill were not: there was to be no regency until after the bloodshed of the Second Round. Nevertheless, Papandreou was confident that whatever the future of the monarchy, Greece would always be on Britain's side, a "fortress" standing guard over the "Imperial route."[115]

And so it was that on the morning of October 18, the Government of National Unity, headed by George Papandreou and accompanied by Macmillan, Leeper, and the American chargé d'affaires (Ambassador MacVeagh reached Athens on October 27) arrived in the Greek capital and joined in the frenzied celebrations already in progress.

[115] Macmillan, p. 484. Once in Athens Papandreou solved the problem of constitutional validation of new decrees by requesting the approval of the King (still in London), who would then authorize the Prime Minister to affix the royal signature to such new legislation.

AFTER LIBERATION

IN A VERITABLE marathon of public speaking and with a delivery that soon confirmed him as the country's champion orator Prime Minister Papandreou sought to imbue his compatriots with his own seemingly boundless optimism. His message was as simple as it was persuasive: Greece's heroic and universally acclaimed contribution to the allied cause, a contribution made at a time when victory was far from certain, entitled her to a position of honor and influence in the postwar councils. The allies had not only promised to help with generous relief and long-term assistance, but may at long last be expected to satisfy national aspirations and territorial claims. Thus the country's speedy recovery was assured and her future bright.

On October 18 the government resigned and five days later a new one was sworn in, again under the premiership of George Papandreou. Moreover, of the initially 23 portfolios, 14 went to the Prime Minister's personal choices and to Populists, 2 to Liberals, 1 to an independent, and 6 (later 7) to EAM. Thus there appeared to be a swing to the right, typified by the fact that in the official ceremonies celebrating the country's liberation the resistance organizations were completely ignored. Nevertheless, on October 25 the American Embassy reported that the general response to Papandreou's public utterances was very favorable and that EAM's rank and file continued to give him their enthusiastic support.[1]

---

[1] *DSR*, 868.01/10-2544. For the text of the Prime Minister's principal speech upon liberation see Papandreou, *I Apeleftherosis*, pp. 185-98.

But if circumstances called for a show of confidence the nation's immediate problems could no longer be ignored or their solution assigned to yet another allied commission. For Papandreou's Government of National Unity the moment of truth was fast approaching.

The country's devastation was almost beyond description. During the war, and in addition to more than half a million dead, almost 1,700 villages had been destroyed, roads, railroads, bridges, transportation and telecommunications equipment blown up, more than two-thirds of the merchant marine lost, livestock decimated, and about one-third of the forest area burnt. At the time of liberation wheat production was almost half the pre-war levels, while the tobacco and fruit industries were virtually ruined. The bulk of the population was weakened by prolonged near-starvation, and medical supplies and services had been reduced to dangerously low levels. Thus a massive relief program would have to be introduced immediately if more starvation and widespread suffering were to be averted in the coming winter. Provision would have to be made for the many thousands who had been left homeless and uprooted. A runaway inflation had to be checked immediately and the national economy propped up so as to encourage the resumption of production and restore faith in the state's monetary and fiscal policies. Massive unemployment on the one hand and a hydra-like civil service on the other would have to be brought under control. A nation which for four years had regarded government authority as the instrument of foreign tyranny and traitorous collaboration now had to be made conscious once again of the need for respect for the law and for orderly conduct. This at a time when thousands of weapons were in the hands of unruly and fiercely individualistic civilians. All state agencies, but especially those connected with national security and public order, tainted by their association with foreign occupation, would have to be purged and made trustworthy in the eyes of an impatient,

133

suspicious, and revenge-seeking public. Collaborators and all those who had taken advantage of the war years to settle personal scores and to increase their power and wealth would need to be properly charged, tried, and punished in a way that would not only satisfy an aroused nation but would also reestablish the court system as impartial. Organized guerrilla bands would have to be disarmed and dissolved and their members returned to constructive, peacetime activity. And for all these formidable measures to be carried out with any degree of success, a strong, bold, unified central authority would be absolutely essential. In October 1944 this task fell to the yet-to-be-tested Government of National Unity.

On the very day of his arrival in Athens (October 18) Macmillan recorded in his diary that the large crowds, "whether Communist or bourgeois, seemed very pro-Ally and particularly pro-British." Influenced by the nervousness characteristic of both Leeper's and Papandreou's state of mind, and expecting the worst from the extreme Left, he thought that serious trouble had barely been averted: "Had there been any longer delay between the departure of the Germans and the arrival of the Greek Government; or had the Government arrived without the disembarkation of substantial numbers of British troops and Air Force at the same time, I think EAM would have seized power. This *coup d'état* would perhaps have not been bloody, but it would have been successful. . . ." However, even with the Communists thus restrained, the prospects were far from encouraging. At a meeting of British officials Macmillan summarized his fears: "Unless Papandreou deals *at once* with the *currency* situation, there will be a most serious crisis and a collapse of the Government." At the same time, "Unless some way can be found to disarm ELAS forces (and all other guerrilla forces) in the territories evacuated by the Germans and to start a Greek National Army into which the better guerrilla elements should be incorporated, there will be a most dangerous situation leading inevitably to civil war." And finally, "Unless relief supplies can be rapidly landed and backed up by a better delivery programme than we have any assurance of to date, we shall cause a great disappointment to the population which will react against the legitimate Government. . . ." His colleagues in Athens did not question the correctness of his diagnosis: the difficulty lay, he lamented later, in having the necessary measures implemented, particularly when "Washington was suspicious and hostile, [and] London was deeply concerned with many other problems. . . ."[2]

Back in Italy for consultations Macmillan confided to American diplomats that he was quite disturbed about the political situation in Greece. He offered the opinion that if Papandreou managed to remain in power for another five days, presumably to get recovery measures under way, he might yet enjoy a long term in office. The most pressing issues facing him, according to Macmillian, were a "chaotic" inflation and the early establishment of a regular army which would absorb some of the ELAS units, allowing for the disarming of all remaining bands.[3]

Although early in the war Greece had been assigned to Britain's sphere of operational responsibility, and while London had subsidized the government-in-exile, plans to facilitate wartime relief and to prepare for postwar recovery had been from the outset an Anglo-American undertaking. In June 1942 King George and Prime Minister Tsouderos had visited the United States and had appealed for financial assistance as well as for political endorsement. De-

[2] Macmillan, pp. 488-89. On the other hand, reviewing these events in 1962 for a British audience, Woodhouse asserted once more that had the Communists wished to seize control of Athens in the period between the German withdrawal and the arrival of the government they would have succeeded and no available force could have expelled them (quoted in Pyromaglou, *Kartalis*, p. 616).
[3] *DSR*, 868.00/10-2044.

spite a widely shared anti-monarchy sentiment in official circles, President Roosevelt had treated the King with sympathy and had directed that funds be made available to the Greek government. Furthermore, the United States and Britain sponsored the chartering by the Swedish Red Cross of vessels which began bringing relief supplies to occupied Greece after February 1943.[4] In the early months of 1944 agreement had been reached for what was termed "combined Anglo-American military responsibility in civil affairs matters" in Greece, to be discharged until the United Nations Relief and Rehabilitation Administration (UNRRA) could begin to function in that country.[5]

While proceeding with these arrangements, the American government had sought to make it clear to all concerned that its own responsibility to Greece was to be very limited and that the activities of American military personnel were to be confined strictly to relief measures. In mid-August, commenting on a British draft proposal for allied cooperation in Greece, the Department of State had advised the American Ambassador in London that "The War Department is unwilling to be committed or appear to be committed to responsibilities which it is not able to assume under its present directives." On the other hand, the British proposal, "though ostensibly limited to relief by the preamble, contains clauses which provide for action considerably beyond the field in which the United States military is prepared to operate." Furthermore, the War Department was "concerned with the use of the term 'Allied' in the draft, since the very limited American participation made opera-

[4] Memorandum of July 23, 1942 by Under Secretary of State Sumner Welles and fn 71 in FR (1942), 800. For the "Swedish Scheme for Greek Relief" see FR (1943), 167-77. On the matter of American financial assistance to the Greek government-in-exile see also Department of State memorandum to the President dated April 26, 1943, in Roosevelt Papers, Official File 206: Greece, 1933-1945, OF 206A Misc. 1933-1939, Box 1.

[5] FR (1944), 179-80.

tions in Greece 'combined' only as regards the actual distribution of civilian relief and rehabilitation supplies in the
narrow sense, e.g. the United States military is not prepared
to engage in maintenance of law and order even though
such operations should be necessary to make relief distribution possible. At the same time, it appreciates that the British military must have sufficient authority available to permit it, if need arises, to cope with local disorders or even
with enemy resistance. The additional factor regarding
command of the Greek forces is likewise one which does not
concern the United States. . . ."[6]

The following month the Greek government received official notice of "the desire of the United States Government
to participate, for the initial period after liberation, in the
military program for the relief and rehabilitation of
Greece." For this purpose, "The United States Army has
been authorized to participate in conjunction with the
United Kingdom in the military program of essential relief
and rehabilitation activities essential to relief in liberated
Greek areas, within the limits of such supply and shipping
as may be made available for the purpose." The note stipu-
lated that American activities were to be confined to relief
services, including welfare, public health, and sanitation;
the provision of relief supplies; the emergency restoration
of public utilities, agriculture, and transportation "as may
be essential to relief," and assistance to displaced persons

[6] *Ibid.*, 187. At the same time, agencies of the American government studying the problems which occupied Europe would face upon
liberation appeared fully aware of the dangers ahead. A memorandum entitled "The Economic Consequences of Liberation," using
Greece as a case in point, concluded that unless the problem of
immediate and adequate supplies could be effectively solved, the result would be "disillusionment, unemployment, want, unrest, civil
disturbance and impotent government" (Papers of Harry L. Hopkins,
Roosevelt Library, folder "Supplies for Liberated Areas"). Regarding
the critical problem of transportation facilities in the Mediterranean in
view of the pressing demands of the Pacific theater, see *Hopkins
Papers*, Book 10, "Additions to Supplies for Liberated Areas."

and refugees. These activities were to be carried out by a "combined" military staff which would include a "limited number" of American officers. The financial responsibility of the United States was to be "its agreed share of the cost of civilian supplies furnished to Greece," as well as the services of the military personnel. A separate agreement at a later date was to settle the matter of the ultimate payment for these services to Greece.[7]

With these clearly stated limitations, and with lingering trepidation over possible political complications, the United States joined Britain in the task of providing emergency assistance to war-torn Greece. The prepared plans went into effect the moment the allied personnel which had accompanied the Papandreou Cabinet established themselves in Athens. But preparing plans in Washington, London, and Cairo was one thing; carrying them out in a devastated country was to prove an altogether different matter.

Within days, and while the Greek government appeared to be enjoying a most favorable reception, the dangers of the actual situation became quickly apparent to the British officials in Athens. The heightening currency crisis was recognized as the principal source of trouble. On October 21, during his brief trip to Caserta, Macmillan recorded that "The final stage of inflation has been reached, when the value of the drachma has practically—indeed completely—disappeared. This means that all the shops put up their shutters, and buying and selling stops, with consequent hardship, misery and despair. . . ." The Greek government had requested another 200,000 gold sovereigns, "But of course these will just go down the drain in a few days."[8]

---

[7] *FR* (1944), 193.

[8] Macmillan, p. 490. On the same day Macmillan heard Churchill's own account of his just-concluded visit to Moscow: "*On Yugoslavia,* the talks resulted in a really useful declaration and there seems a good chance that Tito and Subasic will come to terms. (But the F.O. and Winston *must* abandon the King). On the Control Commissions for Bulgaria, Roumania and Hungary there was a lot of very

Returning from the Moscow conference in mid-October Foreign Secretary Eden traveled to Athens accompanied by Lord Moyne, Minister of State for the Middle East, for a first-hand look. He found Prime Minister Papandreou "surprisingly confident, and probably rather over-optimistic." Eden recorded on October 25: "I am not too sanguine myself about the political situation, *but it is the financial problem that dominates all. Unless we can get that right all our efforts will have been wasted....*" He also reported his observations to Churchill:

> The political situation on the surface at least is fairly satisfactory, but it yet remains to be seen how far the authority of the Government can be established beyond Athens. Papandreou . . . showed confidence in his ability to handle the situation and he clearly has considerable popular backing. On the other hand, EAM is active and we should be unwise in my judgement to underestimate its strength. . . .
>
> Most immediately urgent question, however, is runaway inflation which is so serious as to resemble the situation of Germany after the last war. As you know, I do not pretend to understand these things but we have tried tonight, with the help of expert advisers on the spot, to see what we can do to deal with the problem. *Unless we can deal with it, Papandreou or any other representative of the Government will be swept away and anarchy will take its place....*[9]

At the urgent request of his Foreign Secretary, Churchill dispatched to Athens Sir David Waley, Under-Secretary of the Treasury, to tackle the problems of inflation and cur-

---

stiff argument and we got the worst of it. Greece was satisfactory. Altogether, the results were well worth the visit and the P.M. seemed more hopeful about the future than I have ever known him" (*ibid.*, p. 491).

[9] Eden, III, 566-67. Emphasis mine.

rency. In the meantime Eden attempted to examine the situation for himself. On October 26 he drove to the port of Piraeus where practical problems were everywhere in evidence: "Port position far from satisfactory," he recorded. "Daily clearance at present only one thousand four hundred tons which includes military supplies. . . . But we must do better than that. . . ." Nor was the human element better: "I fear that one of the troubles of this campaign, which is really a political and not a military campaign, is that most of the staff are the leavings of other commands. . . ." Indeed, the only encouraging factor seemed to be the attitude of the Greeks themselves: ". . . we found the streets packed with people. . . . They clapped frenziedly and were so dense as eventually to bring the car to a standstill. Battley (my detective) was very worried because the town has still plenty of German agents and any one of them could have lobbed a grenade or emptied a pistol into the car. . . . I confess that at that time my one anxiety was lest the car would crush or run over someone. It was an amazing experience. 'C'est du delire,' P [Papandreou] said, while Walter Moyne's comment was: 'It is good that there is one country where we are so popular.' "[10]

Eden's second report from Athens, dated October 27, provides a valuable synopsis of the Greek political scene as viewed from the British Embassy:

> We have had a further day of discussion and action on supply and monetary problems. As a result I feel happier about the former. . . . The monetary business is devilish. . . . I find the political situation extremely difficult to assess. There are so many uncertain factors, not least being the mercurial character of these people. Moreover we have only seen Athens. One thing is certain, that at present the only factor that really unites all the Greeks is their devotion to Britain, to whom they look perhaps rather too much for guidance and salvation.

[10] *Ibid.*, 567-68.

As regards the strength of EAM, their present importance lies in the fact that they are the only really organized party, but I still doubt whether in Athens at any rate they have any deep hold on loyal people. This does not mean that they could not or would not stage a *coup d'état* if the Government's hold on the country were weakened. . . .

Eden had agreed to meet with the EAM Ministers and had found that their "professions of loyalty to the Government of National Unity and their assurances of their intentions to work with us could not have been more profuse." Nevertheless, he confided to Churchill, ". . . I have no doubt that if we had not made our position pretty clear to Bear we would have had a good deal of trouble with them." As for the monarchy, about which Churchill was so anxious to hear,

> The King's position is difficult to pronounce upon because he is just never mentioned. This should not necessarily be taken as a comment wholly unfavourable to his prospects. On the contrary there are many who think that by the line he is following he is beginning to gain ground. . . . I am sure that advice given to him up to date has been sound in his own interests, for if he were to come at this moment when EAM is the only armed force in the country except for our own troops and three thousand Athens police, we should soon have civil war.

It would seem from the above that in the Foreign Secretary's own assessment, it had been the Soviet Union's noninvolvement and the King's absence abroad that explained EAM's failure thus far to resort to arms. However, the future remained far from certain:

> Papandreou has issued a decree calling on four classes from twenty-six to twenty-nine. . . . We hope to deliver to him within six weeks enough uniforms and equipment to allow him to have about thirty thousand men under arms. Agreement has been reached with EAM Ministers

141

that ELAS are to be demobilized. When that has happened and there is a National Army instead of an EAM Army, the political position may undergo something of a transformation. At the moment EAM are bullies in the background, who but for our presence would certainly come to the fore. If we can tide over the next six weeks, we should have considerably reduced the menace to the state.[11]

Before leaving Athens Eden asked Macmillan to return immediately to Greece and coordinate British efforts to deal with the economic crisis. A special committee of political and economic advisers was established at the British Embassy. In Macmillan's words, "We dispatched an enormous number of telegrams calling for cruisers, coffee, gold sovereigns, oil seeds, aeroplanes, and various other commodities which were believed to be useful in a monetary crisis. . . ."[12] Despite this flurry of activity, however, Eden advised Churchill on October 30 that "there is nothing more the family friends can do for the moment . . . but I am by no means confident that this little country will be able to regain stability without other and maybe terrible upheavals. It is so desperately poor in all natural resources and the Germans have so well planned their work of dislocation and destruction."[13]

In their increasingly more strenuous attempts to help the government in Athens deal with the worsening economic situation, the British made it plain that they would welcome a more active American role. However, in their view, Ambassador MacVeagh seemed to display a "rather detached interest."[14] Indeed, MacVeagh considered that initially the proper course for him to follow was "not to put myself forward, but to let the British hold the stage, in order to make it fully clear here from the start that, as the President said, 'we are not involved.'" He recorded in his diary on Novem-

11 *Ibid.*, 568-70.
13 Eden, III, 570.
12 Macmillan, p. 493.
14 Macmillan, p. 593.

ber 2, "Now I think I have let our cousins get out far enough ahead to permit me to take a normal course. . . ." He confined himself to the dispatch of almost daily reports, based mostly on information obtained through oss and British channels, which graphically portrayed the situation throughout the country. Thus on October 24 he relayed the opinion that in the Greek capital, full of hungry idlers, serious turmoil could be averted only if the currency was stabilized, factories resumed regular operation, unemployment was reduced drastically, and the unloading of relief supplies was stepped up. Although Papandreou's prestige was still high, he seemed to encounter increasing resistance in his efforts to strengthen the government's hold over the situation. Public sentiment appeared to remain unfavorable to the King's return.[15] The next day MacVeagh reported that morale in the capital was declining due to the general feeling that the government would not last more than a few weeks unless the food and economic situations were to improve dramatically. Prices now were worse than they had been before liberation, and thousands were on the verge of starvation. Though public security remained good, the maintenance of law was mostly in the hands of the gendarmerie and city police, many of whom had until recently belonged to the hated Security Battalions. According to oss reports, the eam leadership could be expected to cooperate with Papandreou only as long as British troops remained in the country. An elas division in civilian clothes was believed to be in Athens, and eam showed signs of intending to maintain and even strengthen its various organizations inherited from the occupation years. MacVeagh concluded: "All reports now reaching the Embassy agree that in combating dangers of immediate situation the Government would do well to concentrate chiefly on bringing in food and bringing down prices."[16]

[15] *DSR*, 868.00/10-2444.
[16] *DSR*, 868.01/10-2544. On October 28 MacVeagh recorded in his diary that high level Greek officials appeared to expect the British

In a long report dated October 30 the American Embassy summed up the situation as follows:

> . . . transportation facilities are far worse than expected . . . and trucks existing or imported are quite insufficient to transport supplies from the ports to the rural districts or from the latter to the cities. In addition, all authorities here agree that currency and supply problems are critical and closely related. The printing presses continue to print drachmas daily, in astronomic denominations, to cover the Greek Government's expenses. These consist mainly of Government salaries and allowances to Government servants and to employees of industries and private concerns for the purchase, on the free market, of food and other essentials which, as they decrease in quantity, rise in price. Even prices expressed in gold are increasing daily. Official opinion appears prevalent that the Government cannot continue to exist unless this situation is rectified within a fortnight, but no complete plan has yet been suggested to cope with it. . . .

Severe shortages of food and other essentials appeared to be at the heart of the problem:

> Financial circles in Athens, while considerably perturbed over the alleged Communist tendencies of the Government, the general lack of order throughout the country, the increasing demands of labor and the apparent weakness of the authorities, believe the currency chaos is entirely due to the lack of supplies. . . . They point out that the people have become gold-minded and the shortage of commodities on the market is making even gold lose

---

and Americans to rectify Greece's current economic problems. He made it clear to them that such expectations were not well founded, although he conceded that American assistance would be required if chaos were to be averted. However, he felt that time was running out for the government and that the situation was becoming "riper and riper" from the Communist point of view.

its value so that gradually the only means of exchange will be by barter. They recommend that since the currency situation is so tied up with the shortage of supplies every effort be made to increase the importation and distribution of the latter.

Ambassador MacVeagh's lengthy report struck a clear note of urgency:

It is the opinion of this Embassy that if the present situation is to be brought under control, a full and coordinated plan must be urgently and carefully worked out, widely publicized and every part put into operation at the same time. . . . Every effort should also be made to give the population at least the employment existing under German occupation. . . . Further delay in devising and implementing a program of this nature can only result in a mounting need on the part of the Greek Government (if such can continue to exist) for foreign financial assistance to cover its ever increasing expenses.[17]

At the urgent request of the British government the Department of State attached to the Athens Embassy a financial adviser and an economic and supply administrator, but thought it unnecessary to dispatch an adviser for civil and political matters also as the British wanted, "since US Army participation in civil affairs activities is limited."[18] Further-

[17] *FR* (1944), 199-201. "Economy of Greece completely broken down . . ." MacVeagh wrote in his diary on October 29. Unless great quantities of supplies reached Greece immediately, the starvation of 1941-42 might be repeated, necessitating the dispatch of more allied troops to maintain order. As there were no signs that matters would improve, ". . . I foresee a worsening of situation which will bring actual uprisings and bloodshed both in Athens and in the country districts. . . ."

[18] *FR* (1944), 205-6. The British government had requested that an American financial expert be appointed to an Anglo-American economic committee for Greece. MacVeagh had advised against such a measure, recommending instead that the expert in question come as an attaché to the American Embassy (entry in MacVeagh Diary dated Oct. 29, 1944).

more, American officials were perturbed to discover that their British colleagues were not as scrupulous in keeping out of Greek affairs. "The Americans," an exasperated Macmillan recorded, "participate for relief and rehabilitation but *not* for politics or military operations. Naturally, it is not too easy to draw the line, and they are equally offended by being asked in or left out. . . . In our effort to get some revenue for the Greek Government, we had broken the laws of the Medes and Persians."[19] In their turn American officials in Athens were angered when the British Embassy, annoyed by American criticism, excluded from its press conferences American correspondents with the excuse that the topics to be discussed were beyond their comprehension!

The advice of the British Treasury experts on the monetary crisis was formally presented to Papandreou and his Finance Minister, EAM's Professor Svolos, on November 3. In response to Svolos' request for more supplies and a loan Macmillan stated "rather firmly" that he would not ask his government for further assistance "unless it was quite clear that they would carry out all the things necessary, not only to make the stabilization but to preserve it." The Greeks were given a stern lecture on the need to balance their budget with other than inflationary methods, to tax and save by reducing salary expenditures, and to introduce internal loans. Papandreou agreed to try and seemed "clearly grateful" that the British had been so blunt with the leftist Svolos.[20]

Despite official endorsement of such corrective measures, positive results were not forthcoming. British diplomatic sources in Athens offered the view that whereas the political situation at the end of October was better than anticipated, political and military efforts would collapse "if the monetary situation which during the last few weeks deteriorated in alarming degree, cannot be met." On Novem-

[19] Macmillan, pp. 494-95.   [20] *Ibid.*

ber 1 an American official in Athens, conveying the above comment, observed: "I cannot too strongly emphasize . . . that the economy of the country has been completely broken down by what it has gone through, that its people are in feverish condition of undernourished excitement on the verge of another winter. . . . Unless therefore the terrible experience of 1941-1942 is to be repeated, and a situation created here demanding the despatch of more troops to keep order, together with relief on a scale beyond anything yet contemplated, energetic action must be taken now to increase supplies and accelerate their distribution."[21]

Still the economy continued to bedevil the experts. On November 7 Macmillan recorded with dismay that "things had slipped a little," and that "the usual Greek confusion reigns." The trouble, he thought, was that "no one stays 'put' for long. Waley gets them to agree to a scheme at the end of a long day's talk. But during the night they have lots of new and bright ideas, and so by the next morning he is back where he started."[22] Although a new currency was in fact announced on November 9—one new drachma for 50,000,000,000 old—the measure appeared to have little immediate effect on the situation. Macmillan, who would soon have to devote his attention to Italian problems, would remain apprehensive: "At present everyone sells gold in the morning and drachmas in the evening! If they are driven to print notes every week to pay their employees and fail to draw in equivalent notes . . . a fresh inflation will occur in a few months' time, leading to a fresh collapse."[23]

Through November the economic crisis continued unchecked. Despite allied efforts, supplies trickling into the country could do precious little to improve the diet of the

---

[21] *DSR*, 868.00/10-3144; *ibid.*, 868.00/11-144; *FR* (1944), 199-201. On November 5 British sources in Athens expressed the belief that "the bulk of people in the Greek capital still preoccupied with food and financial questions and politics is of secondary importance . . ." (*DSR*, 868.00/11-544).

[22] Macmillan, p. 495.   [23] *Ibid.*, p. 496.

vast majority of Greeks. The new currency simplified book-keeping practices by removing from circulation astronomical denominations, but the freshly printed drachmae brought no more comforts than the old. The causes of hardship and misery for the many appeared destined to become permanent features of the nation's economy. Moreover, the failure of the economy to respond quickly and positively to the remedies applied, and the rapidly declining public confidence in the government, caused a steady deterioration of the political situation. Public order, at best precarious since liberation, soon became the government's major concern, hindering efforts to improve economic conditions. A vicious circle was thus created, with a severe economic crisis unleashing political tensions which in turn would make it impossible for the government to deal effectively with the economy. And although the Papandreou government would be attacked from all sides, the Left emerged as its severest critic, denouncing it for its obvious inability to cure the system's glaring economic and social ills. Inevitably the question of the disarming of ELAS became the issue that symbolized the split between a British supported ineffective government and an increasingly bellicose Left.

Despite lingering speculation that the Left was intent on seizing power by force—and, later, endless theorizing as to why no such move had materialized—the EAM leadership appeared content to pursue its objectives by political, not military means. There is little doubt that initially EAM had been prepared to have ELAS disarmed and demobilized, and the resistance bands replaced by a new national army. Prime Minister Papandreou confided to an American diplomat in late October that he was personally satisfied with assurances on this matter which he had received from the EAM leadership.[24] According to another official report dated October 28, ELAS was behaving "with moderation" and was

[24] DSR, 868.01/10-2744.

supporting the Papandreou government.[25] On November 5 British sources in Athens reported once again that the EAM Ministers continued to express their loyalty to Papandreou and the British, and that the "Correct attitude of the Russians leaves no alternative to the Communists as they realize that the Soviet Government does not intend to play an independent part in Greek politics. Papandreou's line has been to accept this attitude and gradually to put it to test on concrete questions as they come up. . . ."[26]

Despite their initial moderation and cooperative attitude, EAM leaders were induced by the course of events following liberation to demand that certain important conditions be met before ELAS troops surrendered their weapons. These demands were motivated by a rising sense of uncertainty about the country's political future—and the role of the Left in that future—and by a feeling that prevailing conditions were favorable for a more determined political program of action for which the presence of ELAS could be a decisive psychological asset. In short, EAM's small share in the Papandreou Cabinet was no longer sufficient compensation for supporting the government.

That the Communist leaders were contemplating a protracted *political* struggle, and that they were far from confident of its outcome, is graphically revealed by a secret directive of KKE's Central Committee to the EAM Central Committee, dated October 23, 1944. Lamenting that "Our policy lacks direction, and if we had paid more attention to this we could have increased our influence over the masses," the KKE leaders urged that a number of steps be taken to correct this unhappy situation. First, to improve EAM's public image, its Central Committee must call upon the British Ambassador and take him on a tour of its offices, "where we must prepare a good reception, which will be given publicity in our press." Similarly, the Chief of the Soviet Mili-

[25] *Ibid.,* 868.01/10-2844.   [26] *Ibid.,* 868.00/11-544.

tary Mission, Colonel Popov, must be given a reception at the Headquarters of ELAS' First Army Corps, and the event must receive full coverage in the Communist press. Also, the Soviet government should be requested to improve the quality of its Greek radio programs which were "very poor" in contrast to the "excellent" broadcasts in French. Elaborating on the pressing issue of favorable publicity, KKE complained that Prime Minister Papandreou's telegram to Marshal Stalin, thanking him for Soviet assistance in liberating Macedonia (from the Bulgarians) was not exploited editorially in the Communist press: "This was a case in which we could have gained a real political victory." Moreover, "Our newspapers (especially *Rizospastis*) must be real newspapers, with photographs, reportage, and professional reporters, as there is a danger of losing the support of the *middle class*. This must be implemented urgently because readers who become accustomed to a newspaper do not readily change. . . ."

On the crucial issue of the attitudes of organized labor the KKE leaders showed remarkable understanding for patently un-Marxist prejudices: "The General Confederation of Workers of Greece must become a Confederation of Workers and Clerks, and the Workers Center a Workers and Clerks Center, because it is only natural that the bank clerks belonging to it may object to being members of purely labor bodies. Reaction on this point is doing us much harm. . . ." The only portion of this directive which may be regarded as "subversive" in intent reads as follows:

We have influence over many political personalities, and we have many members who are lawyers, bank employees, civil servants, etc. Thus there is no reason why we should not place some of them in official or semi-official government posts, in order to control the administration, which today is in the hands of fascists. We consider it essential to set up a department which will classify our members according to their abilities and qualifications, so that when vacancies appear it will be easy to provide the proper members.[27]

Whatever else might be said about the program of action the KKE leaders wished to embark upon, it was hardly the stuff of which armed revolutions are made.

As already mentioned, a few days after its arrival in Athens the Cabinet was reshuffled in an effort to make the coalition more workable and more responsive to the wishes of the Prime Minister. Despite its high hopes for an improvement of its position in the government after liberation —because of its indisputable if not popular superiority in the country—EAM found itself with 6 (later 7) of the Cabinet's initial 23 seats. A move to unseat Papandreou "from within" failed when Sofoulis, aging leader of the Liberal Party, refused to head an EAM-dominated Cabinet. The Left, rapidly becoming disillusioned with Papandreou and convinced that it was not getting its fair share of political influence, allowed the KKE to continue serving as its bellicose spokesman.

A factor that helped intensify the prevailing feeling of insecurity was frequent shooting incidents in Athens and elsewhere between ELAS men and right-wing bands such as the royalist "X." Although at first mostly the work of hotheads on both sides acting on their own, they dramatized the need to control and eventually disarm all such remnants of the war years. For the leftists the problem was not so much the danger of hostile bands, which were no match for ELAS, but the attitude of the regular security organizations such as the city police and the gendarmerie, the same forces

---

[27] Directive from the KKE Central Committee to the EAM Central Committee dated Oct. 23, 1944, in the records of the KKE Central Committee seized by the British Counter Intelligence Service in Athens in the early days of the fighting there (December 1944). Originals in the files of the British Embassy, Athens. Hereafter cited as *Captured K.K.E. Docs.* Emphasis mine.

that the occupation authorities had employed to hunt down all those involved in the resistance movement, especially leftists. As long as these security forces remained unpurged and in the service of the Papandreou government, EAM would regard them with strong suspicion, fearing that they might be used to impose upon the country political solutions favoring the Right and the monarchy, which in turn would attempt to destroy the entire Left, as the Metaxas regime had almost succeeded in doing. To the impartial observer such a possibility may have appeared remote; yet for many leftists the fear was quite real.

Aware of the problem and sensitive to charges that it was unwilling to punish collaborators, the government sought the answer in the rapid formation of new and politically untainted security forces. But in the midst of so many problems plaguing Papandreou, this was far from easy to do. "A new National Guard," wrote Macmillan in his diary on November 7, "is to spring into being on 20 November (like Athena from the head of Zeus). No one has ordered uniforms or equipment for these 10,000-20,000 men (I suppose they expect it to appear in the same way from General Wilson's tummy)."[28] Pending the establishment of such a force, two Indian brigades, originally sent to Greece to rest, and the brigade of British paratroopers which had arrived at the time of liberation, a total of about 8,000 men, were retained in or near the capital. Moreover, despite strong objections from the EAM Ministers, these forces were soon joined by the 4,000-strong "Mountain" (or "Rimini") Third Brigade which had been formed after the mutinies in the Middle East and the removal and detention of all leftist elements in the Greek forces there. Somewhat later the "Sacred" Battalion also reached Athens. There can be no doubt that these units were brought in by Prime Minister Papandreou and the British in order to balance the strength of the armed leftist organizations in the country. Not surprisingly

[28] Macmillan, p. 495.

the Left regarded this development as a drastic change in the political situation and a serious threat to its future.

EAM was not the only source of criticism for the move to use the Greek Brigade as a political counterweight. Colonel Woodhouse, British Commander of the Allied Military Mission to Greece, who knew the political climate in Greece far better than most British officials, "categorically advised against" bringing the Brigade to Greece at this time, "where it served no military purpose comparable to the need for it in Italy." Subsequently he characterized the move as "provocative, even if unintentionally," and viewed it as "the most important single factor contributing to the loss of faith by EAM/ELAS" in Papandreou and his supporters.[29] According to an American observer, "in leftist circles it was rumored that the Brigade had come from the battle in Italy in order to put down EAM and bring the King back by force. . . ." The same source continues:

> That the Brigade would have been able to bring the King back by force seems . . . highly doubtful. King George was living in London, and he would scarcely have been able to leave without the knowledge and permission of the British Government. And the British, though they tended to favor the King's cause, would certainly not have allowed him to be installed on his throne by force of arms. It is, however, perfectly true that a Government, supported militarily by the . . . Brigade, would have been able to put into effect measures favoring the King's return. It is even conceivable, though hardly probable, that a plebiscite could have been so administered within two or three months as to nullify EAM's popular strength and bring a majority in favor of the King. . . .[30]

[29] Woodhouse, p. 215 and fn.

[30] McNeill, pp. 155-56. MacVeagh recorded in his diary on Nov. 3, 1944 that the Mountain Brigade, whose political orientation was regarded by General Scobie as "very rightist," had been brought home "to control and discourage the Communist influence in the country."

153

Some years later, realizing the importance of the issue, Ambassador Leeper inserted in his published memoirs a strong defense of the decision to bring the Greek Brigade home at that particular moment. "It was a perfectly natural thing," he wrote, "that the Greek Prime Minister, seeing that he had no Greek armed forces whose loyalty to the Government could be relied upon, should wish to bring back this highly trained body of men at such a critical time. . . ." As for the Brigade's well known hostility toward EAM, ". . . that was the fault of EAM and did not make the brigade any less representative of Greek national feeling." Leeper further recalled:

> When Papandreou proposed to his colleagues that the brigade should return to Athens, the EAM Ministers objected strongly. They described the brigade as a volunteer force on a par with the guerilla forces, and that if the latter were to be disbanded, so too should the brigade. Faced with this opposition, Papandreou turned to General Scobie for advice. He was bound to do so for two reasons: (a) By the Caserta Agreement all Greek armed forces came under General Scobie's orders; (b) As the British troops were the only ones in Athens to support the Government in case of trouble, it was right that the Prime Minister should ask the British General whether he wished to have the brigade or not. The reference to the British was a perfectly proper proceeding.

Ambassador Leeper himself had played an important role in settling the matter:

> The number of British troops despatched to Greece had been reduced to a minimum in order not to weaken the Italian front. Though only a layman myself, I had never thought the numbers adequate in case of major trouble. We were running a risk, but war is necessarily full of risks and it was for the highest military authorities to de-

cide how much could be spared for Greece. When therefore this problem was put to me, I had no hesitation in supporting General Scobie's view that the brigade should come to Athens. The British Government held the same opinion and Papandreou, thus reinforced, rejected EAM's protests.

Perhaps with Woodhouse's objections in mind, Leeper concluded:

> This decision has been described as provocative to EAM and one of the factors which contributed to EAM's suspicions and subsequent conduct. I do not accept this. Even if that particular question had never arisen, EAM's attempt to seize power would have been made just the same. It was made primarily because they thought the British very thin on the ground and for political reasons unlikely to come into action. I would say that EAM acted as they did, not because of the presence of the Greek Brigade in Athens, but in spite of it. In any case, they knew that the brigade would be under General Scobie's orders, and if they did not think the General would use British troops, they would hardly expect him to bring the brigade alone into action. . . .[31]

On the other hand, it should be pointed out that the Caserta Agreement to which Leeper makes reference had accorded EDES and ELAS the same standing as the Mountain Brigade, having recognized them all as component parts of an allied command. Furthermore, his last point obviously overlooks the argument that whereas the British authorities might hesitate to employ British troops in suppressing disorders in Greece, allowing the Greek government to use Greek military units for that purpose might be a different matter altogether. In this regard it is interesting that when at Scobie's urgent request the use of tear gas against ELAS

[31] Leeper, pp. 94-95.

was considered in the first days of the fighting in Athens, British military authorities advised that, if approved by the Supreme Allied Command, it should be issued to the Greek police and troops, but not to the British. Ultimately the War Office ruled against the use of gas in Greece.[32] Moreover, that Papandreou was not prepared to completely dismiss EAM's protestations is evidenced by his decision to give the men of the Mountain Brigade "generous leave."[33] However, this decision was not carried out.

In retrospect there is good reason to believe that EAM's worst fears regarding the political consequences of the Brigade's arrival were grossly exaggerated. Papandreou was not in the least anxious to facilitate the King's return: he was much more preoccupied with his own strength and the stability of his coalition. Nevertheless, the fact remains that after liberation and until the Brigade reached Athens on November 9 there had been no indications that EAM was preparing to resort to force to obtain its goals. During those weeks there was no change in the disposition of the ELAS forces across the country, with the bulk of them remaining away from Attica. The shift in EAM's preoccupation is clearly reflected in KKE's secret directives to Communist echelons throughout the mainland. Thus, for example, on November 6 a telegram from the Party's Central Committee in Athens requested subordinate commands: "As the Government intends to appoint administrators, prefects, sub-prefects, please send by radio a list of suitable persons for each category. We should have the names at once."[34] Significantly, two days earlier a telegram from an ELAS command in Western Macedonia had brought the KKE's Central Committee alarming news about Slavic-speaking bands

[32] DSR, 868.00/12-744.
[33] Woodhouse, p. 215.
[34] Telegram of Nov. 6, 1944 from the KKE Athens to KKE Headquarters in Macedonia, Epirus, Thessaly, Sterea, Crete, and Mitylene, signed by George Siantos, Secretary of the KKE Central Committee. Captured K.K.E. Docs.

which had been repulsed by force after penetrating into Greek territory north of Florina. At that time, Tito's well-known lieutenant in Macedonia, Svetozar "Tempo" Vuk-manovic, had angrily declared to a KKE representative: "I am very much afraid that the KKE together with the British, will find themselves up against the New Yugoslavia and the Soviet Union. The detachment which arrived will be armed by us and sent south; if ELAS tries to prevent this they will defend themselves. If you attack them we will send assistance." Urgently requesting instructions in anticipation of similar incidents, the ELAS officer had called the situation in his region "always critical" and added: "disturbance of our relations with the Yugoslavs will damage our cause."[35] Thus for the time being EAM found itself waging a two-front battle: against domestic adversaries in Athens as well as against Tito's hard-liners in the north. The moment was hardly propitious for an armed attack upon the Papandreou government.

However, on November 9, the day the Brigade reached Athens, a secret KKE message to subordinate commands dealt with entirely different matters, revealing a dramatic change in orientation away from the problems of infiltrating government bureaucracies and of resisting Yugoslav pressures in Greek Macedonia. It read:

Reaction aims to create conditions favorable to a coup and dictatorship. Watch. ELAS should remain at their position until prerequisites for a normal development of the situation are secured. Will disband only when the forces from Egypt are disarmed and a new army is formed under the command of men enjoying the confidence of

[35] Telegram of Nov. 4, 1944 from Kapetan Leonidas, HQ Macedonia, 75/a & b, to John Ioannidis, member of the KKE Central Committee and influential figure in the EAM and ELAS commands (*ibid*). KKE's reply to this message has not been preserved. Regarding the tension between the Greek Communists and Tito's partisans at this time see Evangelos Kofos, *Nationalism and Communism in Macedonia* (Thessaloniki, 1964), pp. 123-28.

the fighting people. Civil Guard [*Politophylaki*] should remain in charge until National Guard [*Ethnophylaki*] corresponding to the people's will is formed. Gendarmerie should be dissolved. See that a democratic front is created against the danger of monarchy. Geros.[36]

To deal with the mounting problems of internal security and to eliminate ELAS as a potential threat to the government, Papandreou had obtained (on November 2) British support for a stage-by-stage program of action. According to it, on November 20 a conscription class was to be called up to form a National Guard (*Ethnophylaki*) which would replace the existing gendarmerie. On November 27, this new force was also to take over the duties of EAM's Civil Guard (*Politophylaki*), which would then be disbanded. On December 1 all guerrilla troops were to be dissolved, a process to be completed by December 10, when a new national army was to be formed from four conscription classes.[37] According to the British Ambassador, in making these plans Papandreou had no "illusions" about the sinister intentions of the Communists but "wished to do everything in his power to prevent a clash with them which would bring with it civil war. He hoped that they would also shrink from it and that apart from a small hard core of Communists, there would be sufficient division in the ranks of EAM to avert war, or at any rate if a clash had to come at some time, it should not happen until the Government had a proper force behind it. Papandreou's plans for dealing with the establishment of order were designed to put to the test by stages the sincerity of EAM's spirit of co-operation inside the Government."[38] As the KKE directive quoted

[36] Telegram of Nov. 9, 1944 from KKE Athens to KKE Headquarters in Thessaly and Sterea. *Captured K.K.E. Docs.* "Geros" (old man) was one of Siantos' *noms de guerre.* The Politophylaki (Civil Guard) was an EAM-controlled, lightly armed auxiliary of ELAS, and a leftover of the occupation.

[37] Papandreou, pp. 204-5. [38] Leeper, 91.

above indicates, after November 9 the problem arose as to just how Papandreou's timetable for disarming the guerrillas was to be complied with without precipitating an explosion.

At first the signs were encouraging. On November 4, after a visit to Athens, a senior American military official reported that Papandreou had impressed him as the only man capable of taking positive action. The disarming of guerrilla bands might be facilitated with the granting of a small compensation to the men, some of whom would be recruited into the new national army.[39] Four days later an American diplomatic source reported from London that according to British spokesmen, the incorporation of both ELAS and EDES into the new army was being considered, "but it remains to be seen whether these elements will be quietly absorbed or will follow the French pattern . . ." of refusing to be disarmed.[40]

On the day following the arrival of the Mountain Brigade Papandreou expressed to Ambassador MacVeagh his continued confidence in the government's ability to deal with the nation's problems. He expected that the most critical moment for his efforts to reestablish a stable government in a demoralized country, "by political means only and without force to impose it," would come in the first days of December when the guerrilla bands were scheduled to be disbanded. Papandreou said that most of the opposition to his program came from the Liberal Party, but "while his careful and gradual methods of tranquilizing and organizing would appear to have the support of EAM and the Communists at present, all depends on getting the people back to work." He requested American support in obtaining needed supplies and credits abroad with which to combat

[39] The same official reported that the financial situation remained "chaotic" and the Greek government had "failed completely to cope with it" (DSR, 868.00/11-544).
[40] Ibid., 868.00/11-844.

159

the existing unemployment. On the issue of those who had collaborated with the enemy Papandreou thought that there would have to be some executions. He recognized the need to show "severity with justice"; otherwise the Communists would "certainly attempt direct action not only with the likelihood that much injustice will be done but with fatal results" for the prestige of the government. He speculated that fear of Communism might already be reviving royalist support, particularly in the country's southern provinces.[41]

Within days, however, the atmosphere in the capital began to change. During November 10-14, in a move apparently calculated to neutralize the effect of the Mountain Brigade's presence in the capital, small ELAS units in Attica and beyond were moved closer to the city. According to reports of the British Counter Intelligence Service which reached Leeper on November 15, at a recent conference of ELAS commanders a decision had been taken to spread Communist propaganda among the men of the British forces, while the Greek people would be told that Britain was sure to renege on her commitment to continue the shipment of relief supplies. The Greek government would then be asked to make certain important concessions to EAM or have them imposed upon it by the ELAS forces converging on Athens. "EAM," wrote the British Ambassador when apprised of these reports, "had already made tentative plans for a *coup d'état*, but it was not yet clear whether they were to present demands first or act first."[42] Yet when the same intelligence reports were shown to Ambassador MacVeagh, his conclusions were materially different from Leeper's. He recorded in his diary (entry dated November 15) that he did not think it likely that the Communists would risk everything in battle against the combined strength of the British and the Greek government forces. They might, however, attempt to frighten the government into certain con-

[41] FR (1944), 138.   [42] Leeper, p. 92.

cessions, or provoke the Right into action which would permit them to emerge as the nucleus of a broad democratic movement.

It is beyond doubt that by mid-November ELAS was beginning to build up its strength around the capital. The purpose of the move, however, is far from clear. Available information on this point is sketchy. One cannot, of course, discount the possibility that the British Ambassador's interpretation (rather than MacVeagh's) was accurate and that the Communists had in fact decided to stage an armed coup. Rumors supporting such a hypothesis abounded in Athens. It is much more likely, however, that the movement of ELAS forces (whose command and major strength continued to be located in central and northern Greece) was motivated by fear, also widespread in the city, that the impending coup would come from the Right, with the use of the Mountain Brigade. That the fears regarding a rightist coup cannot be dismissed as a case of Communist autosuggestion is evidenced by the fact that they were viewed with genuine concern by impartial observers, including the American Ambassador who warned Papandreou against condoning such a development.[43] Moreover, that EAM had not opted for a coup is strongly suggested by events in the second half of November, which continued fluid and spasmodic, as well as by a secret order dated November 20 from KKE's Central Committee to the notorious Aris. The ELAS commander was sternly advised that his "suggestions" to other ELAS leaders, and the recent conference of commanders (very probably the same meeting mentioned in the British intelligence reports of November 15) were deemed "unwise" and that such activity on his part "at the present moment creates confusion and very risky misunderstandings. . . ." Aris was also ordered to stop communicating directly with the British authorities in Athens; instead,

[43] The same advice would soon be given to Papandreou's successsor, Prime Minister Nikolaos Plastiras (*DSR*, 868.00/7-2345).

161

ELAS's General Sarafis should comply with General Scobie's request to present himself to the government for consultations.[44]

Strong circumstantial evidence indicates, therefore, that in mid-November the Communist leadership continued to keep its options open, exploring opportunities as they developed and preparing to respond to threats as they appeared. It apparently still hoped to exert a powerful influence upon the country's socio-political system by the sheer weight of is presence. It was also much exercised over the arrival in the capital of the Mountain Brigade, which it viewed as the military arm of the Right. Nevertheless, whatever KKE's reasoning, the movement of ELAS forces closer to the capital was bound to have a dangerously unsettling effect on an already precarious balance. It also brought General Scobie to the forefront. Alarmed by the ELAS activity and the lack of adequate government troops, he responded in a military manner to the problem at hand: on November 16 he issued orders forbidding armed men to come to Athens and warning EAM that any hostile act against British troops would result in severe countermeasures, including the imposition of martial law.[45] Declaring Athens off-limits to ELAS men could, of course, mean any number of things and, predictably, the Left imagined the worst. EAM immediately challenged Scobie's authority in issuing such orders.[46] These protests were ignored. "It is possible, though not probable," noted the British Ambassador, "that we may have to use force. If we do not make it clear that we are prepared to do

[44] Telegram of Nov. 20, 1944 from KKE Athens to Aris at ELAS Headquarters, Larissa. *Captured K.K.E. Docs.* The message, signed by "Geros," does not identify Aris' "suggestions," which might well have been for a show of force in Athens. The same message also ordered ELAS's General Markos Vafiadis to "go at once to his post."

[45] Leeper, pp. 92-93.

[46] *FR* (1944), 139-40. According to one account which reached American sources, the EAM leaders refused to comply with Scobie's orders until the precise nature of his authority in Greece had been clearly defined (*ibid.*; also *E.A.M. White Book*, p. 34).

so, matters will go from bad to worse. The Communists are feeling their way in order to test our resolution."[47]

To further demonstrate the government's resolve, two British Spitfire squadrons and one Greek squadron of Baltimores (36 planes in all) arrived on November 17 at the Athens airfield near Kalamaki and were greeted personally by Papandreou amid much fanfare. While inspecting these units the Prime Minister confided to Ambassador Leeper that the EAM Ministers had apparently decided not to break away from the government at this time, which Papandreou had told them they would have to do unless they were prepared to collaborate with him more closely in the future.[48] Reporting on the arrival of the Greek airmen the American Ambassador observed that they were "notably Rightist in sentiment" and, consequently, "The presence of these conservative troops here under British command may give promise of better order in Athens for the time being, but may also serve to strengthen EAM's nation-wide claim to represent Greek ideals of liberty and freedom from foreign control."[49] The following day General Ventiris was appointed Commander-in-Chief, with Generals Spiliotopoulos and Liosis as his deputies. The republican General Othonaios who had briefly occupied the office of Commander-in-Chief was compelled to step down when he protested political interference from the Right in army matters. Thus the Supreme Military Council was now in the hands of declared royalists, and the guerrilla organizations found themselves completely and unceremoniously removed from all military decision-making. In this, ELAS and EDES appeared to share the same inglorious fate.

Clearly the situation in Athens had taken a dangerous turn for the worse. British diplomatic circles speculated once again on November 17 that EAM might stage a coup

[47] Leeper, p. 93.
[48] Entry in MacVeagh Diary dated Nov. 17, 1944.
[49] FR (1944), 140.

before early December, when ELAS would have to be disarmed.[50] At the same time, however, a careful examination of the Communist press in the Greek capital strengthens the view that the reports of the British Counter Intelligence Service regarding KKE's propaganda campaign and pressure tactics were unfounded. Not only was there no attempt to cast an unfavorable light upon the British military authorities, but there was continued though often qualified support voiced for the Papandreou government. On November 15, in a widely publicized interview with Reuter's, Party Secretary Siantos declared that "we desire domestic order and tranquility so that the country can, with United Nations assistance, move gradually on the road to recovery. . . ." On the issue of the future of ELAS he was cautious and flexible: "All the Greek volunteer armed forces without exception, formed at home and abroad, should be disbanded, and a new national army established through the normal call-up of several age groups." However, in an obvious reference to the security forces in Athens, he continued: "To satisfy the popular demand for a democratic rebirth of Greece, this new army should, as the Prime Minister himself declared in his policy statements, be previously rid of all those elements which have desecrated the liberties of the people and collaborated with the enemy."[51] On the other hand,

[50] *DSR*, 868.00/11-1744.

[51] *Rizospastis*, Nov. 16, 1944. The same issue contained this statement: "Following the dissolution of the Communist International, the KKE is not, and does not need to be, in contact with the Communist Parties of other countries. As a true Marxist Party, with the experience of twenty-six years, it is capable of regulating its own policies and of acting independently for the solution of all Greek problems, using as a guide the protection of the fundamental interests of the Greek people." On a different matter, on November 18 Sarafis, ELAS's C-in-C, found it necessary to telegraph from Northern Greece to ELAS 1st Army Corps: "Reference 564 11-11-44 of Military Governor of Attica. Please ask Soviet Military Mission whether all Russians should be sent to Athens, no matter what part of Greece they happen to be in" (*Captured K.K.E. Docs.*; no reply has been preserved).

while giving prominence to Siantos' words, *Rizospastis* also informed the Party faithful that the matter of purging the civil service of collaborators was now being seriously considered by the government. Moreover, on November 19 *Rizospastis* reported that food rations were being increased and dutifully repeated the government's assurances that fears regarding a further rise in prices were totally unfounded.

On November 21 *Rizospastis*, anxious to report even the most innocuous sign of Soviet sympathy for the cause of Communism in Greece, reproduced a lengthy *Pravda* editorial concerning the political risks involved in having wartime resistance groups dissolved upon liberation by the forces of conservatism. Significantly, however, the Soviet writer had made absolutely no mention of Greece in developing his thesis. Elsewhere, in a speech celebrating KKE's 26th anniversary, Siantos again summed up the Party's aims as follows: "We are struggling for the independence and territorial integrity of the country! For the solution of the economic problems in accordance with the interests of the people. For an early and free plebiscite. For the arrest of all traitors!" Returning once again to the key question of the armed bands, he was more outspoken than before, developing a harder and more alarmist line:

We believe that the first basic prerequisite for the implementation of the Government's program is the proper settlement of the military question. . . . They demand that ELAS and the Civil Guard be dissolved. Yet at the same time the [right-wing] reaction, whose ultimate aim is a dictatorship, is strengthening its own armed bands. It is doing all it can to prepare for battle thousands from the Security Battalions. It is trying through devious means to drag the Mountain Brigade and the Sacred Battalion into a civil war, against the liberties and rights of the peo-

165

ple. . . . We agree to have all volunteer units which were organized at home and abroad demobilized and replaced by a national army: an army formed by regular conscription, commanded by cadres purged of traitors and fascists. . . .[52]

At the same time the Communist press reported with approval and child-like pride the formation by the government of a workers' unemployment compensation program (for which "the Minister of Labor, Comrade Porfyrogenis" was applauded), and the introduction of measures to end black market profiteering. On November 22 *Rizospastis* publicized the arrival of large quantities of supplies and printed the texts of encouraging messages from Ambassador Leeper and General Scobie to the Greek Prime Minister on the food situation. Indeed, optimistic accounts about the problems of relief, and about the role of the British in helping the nation's economy recover, continued until the end of November. Thus throughout that month there was clearly no discernible attempt to inflame public fears and generate suspicions concerning the British or Papandreou, or to psychologically prepare KKE's followers for any form of illegal military action. This fact is further substantiated by an oss report on the mood of the EAM leadership during November 1944, based on a review of EAM's official organ, *Nea Ellada*. Although "radical in tone," EAM's public position was found to endorse "orderly and disciplined support of the Papandreou Government, in order to frustrate royalist and reactionary plans to provoke foreign intervention." In the area of socio-economic policy it favored the preservation of private enterprise, under broad state regulation. What struck the oss analyst as particularly significant was the fact that in foreign affairs EAM's line was purely and intensely nationalistic, arguing for close relations with all

[52] *Rizospastis*, Nov. 21, 1944.

three major allies, for the satisfaction of national claims including union with Cyprus, and for a policy of peace and reconciliation toward Greece's neighbors to the north.[53]

On the other hand EAM intensified the political struggle in the hope of achieving its goals through the medium of the government. When this appeared to be failing, as Papandreou showed little concern for the demands of the Left, there was an attempt to discredit the government into submission. For this reason EAM sought to focus public attention on the failure of the authorities to deal swiftly with those accused of treason and collaboration with the enemy. "Who could have imagined," wrote *Rizospastis'* editors on November 22, "that the horrible . . . executioners of the people would continue to remain practically free? . . . Who could have anticipated that the hated Gendarmerie would not have been dissolved by now, despite the categorical statements of the Prime Minister? Infinitely fewer traitors and collaborators of every kind have been apprehended in Greece than in any other liberated country of Europe. *And none has been tried. . . .*"

At first the Left's direct criticism of the government remained muffled. The rightist "reaction," in an effort to assist all such "traitors," "tries to overthrow the National Government, because that will bring chaos and will rescue the traitors from the axe of Popular Nemesis. . . . Because that will make possible a coup by the dark reactionary circles to return Mr. Glücksborg by force and not by an honest popular plebiscite. . . ." For *Rizospastis*, the pressing question remained: "What does the National Government say about this? . . . What are the Prime Minister's plans? What is still left of his policy declarations? When will the fifth column surrender its weapons? And it is not merely the 'activist'

[53] OSS report "Political and Economic Outlook of the EAM on the Eve of the Greek Crisis (December 1944)," Jan. 5, 1945. Reproduced as Appendix F.

fifth column, but the political and the ideological as well. . . ."[54]

The moderate and liberal elements in and around the government were not insensitive to the charge that official efforts to punish collaborators were less than vigorous. However, their dilemma could not easily be resolved. If the real wartime traitors were to be properly identified and prosecuted, the process would have to be slow, meticulous, and judicious; it would also be sure to arouse further the suspicions of the outraged Left. If on the other hand the popular demand for an immediate purge and punishment was to be satisfied, the security forces would have to be rendered ineffective, leaving ELAS the only native military force of any consequence. This would have had the effect of surrendering the country to EAM's terror tactics and suspected political ambitions. However much the moderates in the Papandreou Cabinet might wish to placate the natural urge for the punishment of the guilty, they were most reluctant to face EAM without some counterweight for ELAS. As a result, and although there were some arrests among the most conspicious of the collaborators, no serious attempt was made to remove wartime collaborators from the city police and the gendarmerie. Furthermore, largely because of the poor quality of the security forces, the British authorities charged with the responsibility of maintaining order in the capital let it be known that they would not permit the demobilization of the Mountain Brigade.[55] In this decision they were enthusiastically supported by the right-wing Supreme Military Council. Accordingly, in the impending crisis, the Mountain Brigade assumed an importance that was symbolic as well as practical. While the government temporized on the matter of the collaborators in the security forces, the issue of demobilizing the resistance bands and other armed units at the same time that the Mountain Brigade were retained in government service became the

[54] *Rizospastis*, Nov. 22, 1944.   [55] McNeill, p. 158.

bottleneck to all progress toward stability and pacification. The Left would refuse to see ELAS disbanded until those it considered collaborators had been punished, the security forces purged, and the "monarchists"—including the Brigade—were also disarmed; the others would insist that ELAS be dissolved as a prelude to all else. Each side was convinced of the evil intentions of the other; each side believed that it enjoyed popular sympathy and support in its cause. Working at cross purposes they made compromise impossible.

On November 22 Prime Minister Papandreou attempted to break the developing impasse by declaring that "all volunteer units" would soon be demobilized. Although the distinct impression was created that he had meant this formula to apply to the Brigade as well, he did not make it sufficiently clear that such was his intention. This ambiguity served to further sharpen the division and suspicion between Left and Right.[56] Two days later a new National Guard was called to service, as a first step toward the creation of security forces which would be both reliable and acceptable to all political factions. However, the selection of officers for this new body became instantly a matter of violent controversy, thus preventing it from becoming an effective force for some time to come.

A new directive from Siantos, dated November 22, to all KKE commands of the mainland, dramatizes the lack of clear and forceful policy which continued to characterize the Party's leaders, as well as their anxiety lest these organizations lose their effectiveness in the difficult times ahead. Still, the government's plans for the creation of a National Guard were not to be sabotaged:

All members of the Party of 1936 class must be the first to join the temporary National Guard. Also, all members

[56] *Ibid.*, pp. 157-58. See also Richard Capell, *Simiomata. A Greek Note Book: 1944-1945* (London, n.d.), p. 121. Also Pyromaglou, *Kartalis*, p. 498.

of ELAS and of the Civil Guard ["Politophylaki"]. Communists and EAMites must organize themselves securely within the National Guard. Members of this body should be perfectly free to read any paper and discuss politics. This need not interfere with carrying out their duties in a model way. Members of ELAS and of the Civil Guard of 1936 class must hand in their weapons to ELAS before they join the National Guard. Remaining members of Civil Guard, after handing over duties to the National Guard, must join ELAS with all their arms and equipment. We will keep you informed of any change in the situation.[57]

Similarly, on November 24, Aris at ELAS General Headquarters was ordered to facilitate the recruitment of ELAS men of the 1936 class into the new National Guard. Reserve officers and men of both ELAS and of the wartime Civil Guard which was now being replaced were expected to be "the first to present themselves" for induction. However, before joining the National Guard all men of the Civil Guard were directed to surrender their weapons to the nearest ELAS command.[58] At the same time, the Central Committee of EAM directed ELAS troops to join the country's official Veterans Associations, "but to do so in such a way that they would not lose their military cohesion and their fighting value, should the occasion arise *after the demobilization of active* ELAS, in accordance with the Party's policy regarding the evolution of the situation in the immediate future. . . ." The directive emphasized that even the most recent ELAS recruits were to apply for membership in such Veterans Associations.[59] Clearly, while preparing to see the regular ELAS demobilized, the Communist leadership hoped

[57] Telegram of Nov. 22, 1944, from "Geros" to KKE commands in Peloponnesus, Sterea, Macedonia, Epirus. *Captured K.K.E. Docs.*
[58] Telegram of Nov. 24, 1944, from "Geros" to ELAS General Headquarters for Aris. *Ibid.*
[59] Telegram, n.d., no destination preserved, from ELAS General Headquarters. Emphasis mine. *Ibid.*

to preserve as much of its military potential as possible for the uncertain days ahead.

On November 26 General Scobie convened a meeting to consider the matter of disarming the guerrilla organizations. According to Sarafis' account, Scobie requested that the commanders of ELAS and EDES countersign an order declaring the disbandment of both guerrilla forces on December 10. While EDES's representative assured Scobie that Zervas (who was not present) would comply, Sarafis replied that he would need some time to study the matter. At a new session in the evening hours of the same day, Zervas, now in attendance, confirmed that the proposed order was acceptable to him. Sarafis, however, argued that disbandment of the resistance organizations was a domestic matter which could be decided by a formal decree of the national government and not by Scobie's own orders. Thereupon Scobie produced a letter from Papandreou in which the Prime Minister endorsed the proposed order. When Sarafis insisted that Papandreou's personal message did not constitute a government decree Scobie accused the ELAS chief of disobeying superior authority. To this Sarafis responded that he was prepared to carry out Scobie's orders but only as they pertained to military action against the enemy. As for the disarming of resistance organizations, such action exceeded Scobie's authority and could be decreed only by the government. In the ensuing heated exchange Scobie angrily announced that unless his proposed order were authorized by the next day, he would leave Greece. On November 27, at a third and last session, Scobie announced that the government had been unable to agree to issue the demobilization decree but again requested Zervas and Sarafis to sign his order. Once again Sarafis refused to comply and the same day he left for the ELAS General Headquarters at Lamia.[60]

[60] Sarafis, pp. 442-47. Also W. Byford-Jones, *The Greek Trilogy* (London, 1945), pp. 124-28. Also Leften S. Stavrianos, "The Im-

171

Despite the obvious failure of Scobie's efforts it appeared for a brief moment that the deadlock over the demobilization of the guerrilla bands might be broken. At Papandreou's urging the leading EAM Ministers, Zevgos, Svolos, and Tsirimokos, prepared a compromise formula which was submitted to the entire Cabinet on November 28. According to government sources the proposed arrangement provided for the creation of a national army of which the nucleus would consist of two brigades of *equal* numerical strength: the first composed of the Mountain Brigade, the Sacred Battalion, and one EDES unit, and the second a purely ELAS force.[61] All other bands and units, including those still in the Middle East, would be demobilized by December 10. According to the same sources, this ingenious proposal was discussed and accepted by the Cabinet.[62] However, the same afternoon and again the following day (November 29) the three EAM Ministers withdrew their consent, accused Papandreou of bad faith, and demanded once again the demobilization of the Mountain Brigade and Sacred Battalion, as well as all existing units of ELAS and EDES, before the new army could be formed.[63] As before, these demands were rejected: Papandreou and the British authorities would not negotiate the fate of the Mountain Brigade.

Following the crisis of December the Communist contention was that whereas under the agreement of November 28 the Mountain Brigade and Sacred Battalion were to be included in the total strength of the two brigades to be formed, Papandreou deviously planned to keep them outside the arrangement altogether, merely placing them "on leave." Such a move would have resulted in the formation

---

mediate Origins of the Battle of Athens," *American Slavic and East European Review*, VIII (1949), 247-48.

[61] Papandreou, pp. 209-10; Macmillan, p. 498; McNeill, p. 158. For the Communist view see *E.A.M. White Book*, pp. 23-24.

[62] Papandreou, p. 207; Leeper, p. 97; McNeill, p. 158.

[63] Papandreou, pp. 209-10; Macmillan, p. 499; Kousoulas, pp. 201-2.

of two forces of equal strength, with the Mountain Brigade and Sacred Battalion providing Papandreou with decisive superiority over the extreme Left. In support of this charge Communist sources quoted the Greek Prime Minister as having declared that ". . . until our regular army is organized, and in order to continue the participation of Greece in the common allied struggle, *besides the Mountain Brigade and the Sacred Battalion* there will also be organized from the forces of national resistance a Brigade of ELAS and a proportionate unit of EDES. . . ."[64]

It is entirely possible, of course, that Papandreou had intended all along to implement the agreement of November 28 faithfully and fully, and that the statement attributed to him by the Left had been the product of misunderstanding, or of deliberate distortion, aimed at scuttling all chances for a workable compromise. On the other hand, there is every indication that the November 28 formula, while treated as a government secret, had caused great confusion even in well-informed and well-meaning minds. Thus MacVeagh recorded in his diary (entry dated November 30) that Papandreou was attempting to "palliate" the Communists "by giving them a brigade of ELAS, to parallel the Mountain Brigade, but of course there would be an EDES formation too, and the air force, and the Sacred Regiment [*sic*]—so the Rightists would predominate on the whole. Suspicions are understandable! . . ."

In retrospect one can only speculate on the reasons which prompted the EAM Ministers to go back on their word. The Communist explanation has already been reviewed: at present it does not appear possible to substantiate it fully, or to refute it on the basis of concrete evidence. In fact, the motives and plans of the Communist leadership throughout this critical period will not be adequately revealed until

---

[64] *E.A.M. White Book*, p. 24. This source does not identify the circumstances under which Prime Minister Papandreou's alleged statement was made, or where and when it was first published.

and unless the decision-makers of EAM and KKE who are still alive today decide to write their version of history instead of crude propaganda tracts. One important study, relying on the recollections and personal records of an ELAS divisional commander, arrives at a very different conclusion. According to this scholarly account, a message received on the evening on November 27 from Marshal Tito had encouraged the Greek Communists to seize the capital by force. The Yugoslavs are said to have offered "moral" support for such a bold move, while Stalin himself may have approved it but would not authorize open Soviet assistance. Thus the explanation for EAM's abandonment of the demobilization formula is to be found in the Communist Party's deliberate decision on the night of November 27 to seize power "through armed action." It is further alleged that this decision was forced upon the EAM Central Committee by the Communist leadership at a meeting on November 30, over the objections and protests of the Popular Democratic Union (ELD) representatives. A formal resolution was passed denouncing the demobilization scheme, using as a pretext Papandreou's continued refusal to dissolve the Mountain Brigade and the Sacred Battalion.[65] Following the same reasoning and relying on this earlier study Macmillan has written that EAM's rejection of the demobilization agreement of November 28 indicated clearly that "the decision had been taken by the Communist leaders to make a direct bid for power."[66]

Despite the simple logic of this explanation, the issue of intent remains obscured. Did the Communist Party definitely decide by November 27-28 to resort to a coup and therefore deliberately scuttled the demobilization agreement, falsely accused Papandreou of deceit, while using the whole affair as the convenient pretext for armed insurrection? Or did the Communist leaders, in their increasing mis-

[65] Kousoulas, pp. 200-4.   [66] Macmillan, p. 499.

174

trust of Papandreou and fear of the Right, continue to regard the dissolution of the Mountain Brigade and Sacred Battalion as the *sine qua non* for the disarming of ELAS, even after the three EAM Ministers had submitted their compromise formula? In the absence of conclusive evidence, and in view of the bloody events of December, the question remains open to various and conflicting answers. One might thus conclude that the Communists acted as they did not really in response to fears, however unfounded, of being outmaneuvered by their political opponents, but because they had finally become persuaded that the time had come to resort to arms for the purpose of seizing control of the country and imposing their brand of "popular democracy." Nevertheless, the second possibility, which would imply in addition to mounting mistrust and confusion regarding the demobilization formula and Papandreou's intentions, at least a momentary but crucial gulf between the EAM Ministers and the Communist Party's political and military masters, remains entirely real, however disturbing to those who have already decided the matter otherwise. Even with the Mountain Brigade and Sacred Battalion included in the arrangement, the suggested compromise—with all its appearance of fairness—would have been disadvantageous for ELAS which, although larger than the other units combined, was definitely inferior to the two Greek government units in both fire-power and discipline.[67] Moreover, unlike the

---

[67] McNeill, p. 158. On November 27 a Foreign Office spokesman in London speculated that there would not be any "trouble" over the disarming of ELAS but conceded at the same time that "Greeks are hot headed and there was a possibility that ELAS might make difficulties. . . ." He believed that EAM was "well aware" that the incorporation of ELAS into the new national army would diminish EAM's strength, and that the ELAS command was also very much disturbed because of its "unpopularity" and "fears that if disarmed it will be the object of reprisals on the part of those persons or relatives on whom they have practiced their merciless activities . . ." (*DSR*, 868.00/11-2744).

government forces which were concentrated in the capital, ELAS was widely scattered across the country.[68] From the Communist point of view, therefore, the resulting balance would have been highly unfavorable, as it would have brought to an end the virtual monopoly of military power which ELAS and its auxiliaries had enjoyed at the time of liberation outside the capital. Any intimation that the Mountain Brigade and Sacred Battalion might be left outside the pact rendered the compromise totally untenable. Thus, in the final analysis the agreement would have proven workable only if it had been based upon sufficient trust and on the unshakable conviction that, whatever else might happen, there would not be a resort to arms. Perhaps the three EAM Ministers thought that such was the case, thereby disregarding the realities of the purely military situation. However, their Communist allies and above all the ELAS command did not share their optimism regarding the chances for a peaceful outcome: in November the principal military figures on each side expected their opponents to use force. Under the circumstances, to reduce their military

[68] At the outbreak of the December 1944 hostilities in Athens the approximate strength of the various *land* forces *in all of Greece* was as shown below. Of these, the government troops were virtually all stationed in or near Athens, while no more than one-fifth of the ELAS strength was in the Attica region. The bands of EDES were in northwestern Greece.

Government forces and supporters:
Greek:

Mountain Brigade	4,000
Sacred Battalion	500
City Police	3,000
"X"	1,000

British:

3 Infantry Brigs. (Indian)	9,000
Airborne Brigade	2,000
Armored Brigade	1,000
Battal. Inf. Reg. (Leicestershire)	1,000

Guerrillas:

ELAS	50,000
EDES	10,000

strength appeared to be the height of folly. The demobilization scheme was, therefore, not acceptable to the KKE-ELAS leaders as long as the Mountain Brigade remained intact and in Athens.

Interestingly enough, one obvious solution, that of returning the Brigade to the Italian front in exchange for a politically neutral British unit of the same strength—an arrangement which the Left appeared to accept through its official attitude regarding the presence of British forces in Greece, and a move which would have weakened neither the allied forces in Italy nor the security forces in Athens—was not considered. Nor would Papandreou send the Mountain Brigade to guard the frontiers which remained open to frequent intrusions from the north. Such solutions, which the Right and the army's high command opposed with vigor, required the cooperation of the British government, and Churchill would undoubtedly have rejected them out of hand. Indeed, the British Prime Minister had already written Foreign Secretary Eden on November 7 that, "having paid the price we have to Russia for freedom of action in Greece, we should not hesitate to use British troops to support the Royal Hellenic Government under M. Papandreou. This implies that British troops should certainly intervene to check acts of lawlessness. Surely M. Papandreou can close down EAM newspapers if they call a newspaper strike." The military situation in Athens was bound to improve with the arrival there of the Mountain Brigade which "will not hesitate to shoot when necessary. . . ." However, Churchill added, "We need another eight or ten thousand foot-soldiers to hold the capital and Salonika for the present Government. Later on we must consider extending the Greek authority. I fully expect a clash with EAM and we must not shrink from it, provided the ground is well chosen."[69]

Thus it is clear that after his understanding with the

[69] Churchill, vi, 286-87.

Soviet government on Balkan affairs Churchill was in no mood to compromise and had no patience for what he regarded as the obstructionist tactics of the Greek Left. In his directives to his representatives in Athens he allowed no room for negotiation or indeed for anything other than the complete capitulation of Papandreou's critics. Encouraged by such powerful support, Papandreou became even less interested in the preservation of his cooperation with the Left. Increasingly, whenever pressed for an answer to EAM's specific demands and complaints, his reply would be that the British would not allow him to act otherwise.

One must conclude that in the last days of November neither side was willing to place its trust in genuine negotiations; each side was determined to preserve for itself a position of demonstrable strength. This made violence extremely likely. What made it virtually inevitable was the fact that the British government, while displaying an increasing impatience with the Greek Left, had made inadequate provision for a clear military superiority which would have compelled the Left to acquiesce to the demobilization of ELAS even while the Mountain Brigade remained.

The secret directives of the Communist leadership to subordinate commands in the mainland during the crucial period of November 28-30 shed further light upon the prevailing situation. They reveal repeated attempts by the KKE Central Committee to justify to the rank-and-file Party members its stand on the question of the disarming of ELAS and convey orders to prepare for action which might become necessary at any moment. Yet they contain no decision to seize the initiative and there is no attempt to organize and coordinate anything remotely resembling a concerted attack upon the government and its supporters. Thus on November 28 Siantos issued the following general directive:

The Prime Minister insists on the disbandment of ELAS and has refused to disband the Mountain Brigade and

178

Sacred Battalion. This is unacceptable. Situation is critical. Watch and be ready to repulse any danger. British and Greek opposition demand disbandment of Peoples' Army by 10th December. At the same time they insist on retaining Greek armed bodies organized by Greek fascists in the Middle East with the argument that they constitute an allied force. They intend to impose a fascist dictatorship with the aid of the above fascist bodies and the secret armed forces of fascists in Athens after ELAS has been disbanded. Trusting our organized popular forces, a large portion of which are armed, we have made it a condition for the disbandment of ELAS that all armed forces of the opposition, including the Gendarmerie, should be disbanded simultaneously. The British have refused this *and are pressing the opposition to start a civil war* which may begin at any time. We are ready to take up the challenge.[70]

Later in the day (November 28) Aris at ELAS General Headquarters radioed the KKE Central Committee in Athens:

All movements of officers and men of Gendarmerie should be forbidden. Allied Mission demanded persistently and by repeated orders of General Scobie that all officers and men of the Gendarmerie in Thessaly go to Athens. Yesterday they passed through Livadia. Total number 200. Probably General Scobie and the Allied Mission will demand the moving of Gendarmerie from other places. Please let us know if we should refuse.[71]

There is no evidence that the KKE leadership ordered ELAS to block the movement of gendarme units to Athens.

[70] Telegram of Nov. 28, 1944, from "Geros" to KKE commands in Macedonia, Thessaly, Sterea, Epirus, Peloponnesus. *Captured K.K.E. Docs.* Emphasis in the original.
[71] Telegram of Nov. 28, 1944, from Aris at ELAS General Headquarters to Siantos, KKE Athens. *Ibid.*

However, on November 29 the Party's Central Committee advised subordinate commands in Macedonia, Epirus, Thessaly, Sterea, and Peloponnesus:

> Situation extremely critical. Opposition is ready to start civil war by insisting on retention of Mountain Brigade and Sacred Battalion, and on disbandment of ELAS. Enlighten the public. Take all measures to face any eventuality. Justice is on our side. Have faith in our policy and our forces. Victory is ours.[72]

A few hours later came the first clear order for a military move, which suggests once more that the initiative was expected to come from the other side:

> Situation continues to be extremely critical. Opposition insists on retaining Mountain Brigade and Sacred Battalion, and on disbanding ELAS. Opposition ready to start war against us. Issue necessary orders and take suitable arrangements vis-à-vis Zervas forces. Inform [me?] regarding situation and steps considered necessary with regard to the Civil Guard. Watch. Justice is on our side. Have faith in our forces.[73]

Significantly, on *November 30*, two days after the collapse of the demobilization agreement (and, according to

[72] Telegram of Nov. 29, 1944, from "Geros" to KKE commands in Macedonia, Thessaly, Sterea, Epirus, Peloponnesus. *Ibid.*

[73] Telegram of Nov. 29, 1944, from "Geros" to ELAS General Headquarters. *Ibid.* The same collection of messages contains the following two orders from Major General Emmanuel Mantakas of the ELAS Central Committee in Athens to the ELAS General Headquarters, dated Nov. 30, 1944: (1) "It is necessary to send explosives and mines for probable fighting in build-up areas, preferably through the 2nd Division. It it likewise considered advisable that six organized demolition squads go to the 1st Army Corps. The men of these should be sent in small groups, under the guise of going on leave, in the shortest possible time. The despatch of W/T sets requested, together with suitable personnel, should also be expedited." (2) "Please send 15 automatic weapons with their ammunition which were intended for Crete to 2nd Division, where they are badly needed."

some accounts, after the date on which the presumed decision to seize power by force was made), the KKE Central Committee issued the following directive to the ELAS Headquarters:

> Scobie has printed an order and proclamation concerning demobilization of ELAS on December 10. No similar Government order has been signed by the Council of Ministers. *This is dependent on political agreement which has not as yet been reached. Until the situation is cleared up no demobilization of ELAS should take place. On the contrary, you must be ready to repel any attack which may develop.* We will keep you informed of developments in the situation. Under present conditions it is impossible for the Civil Guard to hand over its duties to the newly formed National Guard.[74]

It is impossible to see how such an order could have been issued *after* a decision had been taken to employ ELAS in battle to capture the capital.

Publicly the Communist position was presented once again by the editors of *Rizospastis*. On November 28 they directed their fire at Zervas who had recently arrived in the capital to take part in the meetings arranged by Scobie. The EDES leader was called a "lackey of Glücksborg" and a "mercenary" who puts in an appearance "in all anomalous situations that smell of a coup and of dictatorship."[75] The same issue drew attention to Papandreou's alleged charge that the old political parties were leading the country to civil war. The Prime Minister was quoted as having declared:

[74] Telegram of Nov. 30, 1944, from "Geros" to ELAS General Headquarters. *Ibid.* Emphasis mine.

[75] *Rizospastis*, Nov. 28, 1944. The editorial refers to an article on Zervas written by James H. Powers for *American Mercury* of August 1944, in which the resistance leader had been labeled a mercenary. According to Kousoulas on the evening of November 27 Siantos had prepared another editorial which, however, was shelved because of that night's decision to seize power by force (Kousoulas, pp. 200-201).

Fully conscious of our responsibilities, we are struggling to avert a civil war. Struggling to avert a civil war we are grateful to those who lend support to our efforts. . . . A civil war would become the tomb of Greece. . . . We are being condemned for our excessive willingness to give in during this stage of the negotiations. We prefer this charge to history's condemnation that we were proven inadequate in this historic hour, and we failed to avert a civil war. . . .

Two days later (November 30) under the ominous heading "Who Wants Civil War?" *Rizospastis* charged that the "reactionary Right" was bringing the country closer to "the storm of civil war" and that the disagreement over the "military question, which constitutes the heart of all the onerous problems that the country faces, has come to the fore in its full intensity." The two opposing views on this question were summarized once again:

We demand the dissolution of all volunteer bodies, of ELAS, EDES, the Mountain Brigade, the Sacred Battalion, and the other sinister creatures in the Middle East. We demand that the evil Gendarmerie be sent home, until the Supreme Military Council has ruled for each man and each officer whether or not he is to be transferred over to the National Guard. We demand that, by December 10, the principal leaders of the national betrayal . . . be tried. The Reaction demands in essence that only ELAS be dissolved, since from it only one brigade will remain. Half of EDES would be retained, since it too will form one brigade, thus 3,000 men of its present 6,000 will stay on. The entire Mountain Brigade and the entire so-called Sacred Battalion would be retained. It demands that the Gendarmerie be retained "off duty" until its fate has been decided in the indefinite future. It promises a lukewarm "speeding up of the enforcement of the Law on Penalities for collaboration. . . ."

Thus in contrasting its case to that of the rightist "Reaction," the Communist leadership, taking advantage of the prevailing confusion and uncertainty, insisted that the establishment of the proposed two new brigades would have resulted in unequal strength for the two sides, with ELAS being outnumbered. Turning to the government, *Rizospastis* continued the attack, trying to answer the charge that the Left had gone back on its word in the demobilization scheme:

> ... we categorically ask Mr. Papandreou and all his Ministers of the Right: Didn't the Government's policy statements explicitly promise that all volunteer bodies will be dissolved and that the national army of the future will be based on regular conscription? Who, therefore, has "reneged"? How many days have gone by since the Prime Minister signed the agreement to send the Mountain Brigade on indefinite leave? How many days have gone by since it was officially declared that the Gendarmerie was being dissolved and disarmed? Who, therefore, has "reversed" his position?

Despite the invective and ignoring the demobilization formula of November 28, the same *Rizospastis* issue (November 30) insisted that the door to a compromise settlement was still ajar: the men of ELAS "agree to be demobilized ... but demand, and with them the entire Greek people, that the ground first be cleared of the danger of a fifth column and of a dictatorship. ..." Chiding its adversaries by suggesting that the terrain of Athens was too level and unchallenging for the "Mountain" Brigade, the Communist organ concluded:

> Do you want ELAS dissolved on December 10? It will be dissolved, but so must also be all volunteer bodies. This has been the basis upon which the National Government was founded. ... If, Gentlemen of the Reaction, you do

183

not wish to have all volunteer bodies dissolved, if you do not wish to disarm the nationally bankrupt Gendarmerie, if you do not wish to have the big-time collaborators tried immediately, then it means that you take the Greek people for fools. *You demand their weapons so that you may turn them over to their executioners.* . . . We know that you threaten the Greek people and their national forces with civil war on the "fateful day" of December 10, or even sooner. We know that . . . you are preparing for this civil war. The Greek people and their national organizations await you calmly. . . .

These rhetorical exercises would be repeated again on December 1, in an editorial in *Rizospastis* entitled "The 'Intransigence' of the KKE." Once again the Communist Party organ would accuse its opponents of plotting to use force to enslave the masses and assert that ELAS would stand guard over the nation's freedom.

In the last days of November, while the political situation deteriorated as no compromise over the demobilization issue appeared forthcoming, tension in the Greek capital became almost unbearable. Rumors about impending violence were being spread by the Left and by the Right, and by those caught in the middle. Convinced that a stern warning was essential to discourage those who might be plotting to seize power by force, General Scobie, after consulting Prime Minister Papandreou, issued a statement on December 1, declaring in part:

> I am determined as far as it lies within my power to make a success of the tasks assigned to me by my Government. I am convinced that in many parts of the country there is no freedom of speech, no freedom of the press, and that terrorism and victimisation still exist. I stand firm behind the present constitutional Government until the Greek state can be established with a legally armed force and free elections can be held. I will protect you and your

184

Government against any attempt at a coup d'etat or act of violence which is unconstitutional.[76]

This statement, in which the Left was being castigated for its strong-arm tactics in the areas under its control, was immediately followed by another from the British government. The British Prime Minister wished to make it clear that "General Scobie's message to the Greek people stressing the need for unity and emphasising our full support of the present Greek Government was made with the knowledge and entire approval of His Majesty's Government."[77] Obviously with backing from London and ignoring the failure of his talks with Sarafis on November 26-27, Scobie publicly ordered the Commanders of ELAS and EDES to make certain that their forces were dissolved by December 10. As before, Zervas immediately announced his intention to comply.

General Scobie's power move was intended to serve as the masterful blow that would cut the gordian knot of the demobilization issue. It was based on the assumption that such a public pronouncement would bring pressure to bear directly upon the men of ELAS who might thus choose to disband rather than disobey the command of the government and its British General. However, it proved counterproductive: under orders from their superiors, ELAS troops remained at their posts. Moreover, EAM immediately launched a countermove, publicly challenging the right of a British officer to intervene in such a "high-handed" manner in the country's internal affairs.[78] To further complicate

[76] Leeper, p. 99.   [77] *Ibid.*

[78] The Communist argument remained that under the Caserta Agreement General Scobie's powers were derived solely from the authority the Greek government had explicitly vested in him. In the absence of such detailed authorization he had no right to act. On the other hand, Kousoulas suggests that "Because of a rather unfortunate translation which conveyed an irritating air of arrogance . . . [Scobie's] proclamation served as excellent material for arousing the 'filotimo' of the rank and file of ELAS. The Communist agitators took care that full use was made of it" (Kousoulas, pp. 204-5).

matters, the Cabinet had not been able to issue a formal decree on the demobilization arrangement before the EAM Ministers withdrew their support. Although for Scobie this was a minor technicality for which the stubborn EAM Ministers were entirely to blame, the Left was able to claim once more that Scobie's order of December 1 was illegal because it had been issued without proper authorization from the Greek government. To rectify the situation and silence this argument once and for all the Cabinet was summoned to sign a decree authorizing the demobilization measures requested by Scobie. The EAM Ministers refused to attend such a meeting. According to one account, the text of this decree was then dispatched to the EAM Ministers "on the understanding that failure to sign the document would be tantamount to resignation from the Government."[79] In the early morning hours of December 2 the EAM Ministers resigned. At the same time the Central Committee of ELAS was reactivated and its reserves in Athens and Piraeus were ordered to mobilize; active units nearby were directed to approach the city.[80] They were to *"avoid any provocation* and try to persuade the British to stay our of the conflict," but to *"defend themselves* by all means, upholding their military honor by the use of arms," should the British resort to "forcible intervention."[81] As a result of these cautious instructions a strange situation soon developed: five days after the fighting had started in the capital an ELAS team at Marathon engaged a group of South African sappers in a spirited game of soccer.[82] Clearly, most ELAS commanders had no intention of initiating trouble with the British.

[79] *Ibid.*, p. 205.
[80] *Ibid.*, 207. The 6 who resigned were: Svolos, Zevgos, Porfyrogenis, Tsirimokos, Angelopoulos, and Askoutsis. General Sarigiannis, who as Under Secretary for the Army had recently raised the Left's representation in the Cabinet to 7, did not resign (published texts of resignation statements in *E.A.M. White Book*, pp. 36-37; of EAM decisions of Dec. 1 and 2 in *ibid.*, pp. 38-39).
[81] Kousoulas, p. 208. Emphasis mine. Also Capell, p. 127.
[82] Capell, p. 121.

The resignation of the EAM Ministers, a move which may be viewed with the wisdom of hindsight as a serious error on their part because it deprived them of important leverage over Papandreou, freed the Left of any lingering inhibitions regarding the existing political order. The Communist leadership decided to anticipate the approaching December 10 deadline imposed by Scobie's public statement with a mass demonstration which would either force Papandreou to accept EAM's conditions for demobilization or bring down the remainder of his government. Thus the EAM/KKE forces chose to openly challenge Papandreou's government, a government which Churchill had solemnly committed himself to support and which, by December 3, was in a state of near-panic. All the powerful ingredients for a terrible explosion were now present. The spark that set it off came almost immediately.

On Saturday, December 2, and with its representatives now withdrawn from the Cabinet, EAM declared a general strike for Monday the 4th. For full dramatic effect it also called for a mass demonstration on Constitution Square, to take place at 11 A.M. Sunday the 3rd. EAM's auxiliary organizations in and around the capital immediately went to work, determined to produce the greatest show of popular strength Athens had ever seen. Considering that many among the working classes were in the habit of taking their Sunday morning stroll around Constitution Square, EAM's task promised to be relatively easy.

At first the rump Cabinet, which EAM duly petitioned for the required permission for public assembly, agreed to allow the demonstration. However, Saturday evening (December 2) the Cabinet met at the Foreign Ministry and considered the matter again, in view of alarming predictions that the crowd was going to be unusually large and very probably unruly. When Papandreou solicited the opinions of those present, the Chief of the City Police, Colonel Evert, replied somewhat casually: "Let them demonstrate!"

For a moment Papandreou appeared ready to accept Evert's suggestion. However, his Minister of Press and Information reminded him that the time of the proposed demonstration coincided with an address which Ambassador Leeper was scheduled to deliver at the Parnassos Club, Athens' prestigious literary society, located very near Constitution Square. The Prime Minister, who was also expected to attend the Parnassos affair, now hesitated: the gathering of so many dignitaries might prove a tempting target for the demonstrators, turning Leeper's lecture into a humiliation for the authorities. "Can EAM be persuaded to postpone the meeting?" he inquired. Evert replied that he did not believe EAM would agree. In that case, Papandreou declared, "We shall forbid it!"[83] At his urging the Cabinet rescinded its permission for the demonstration and advised the EAM leaders accordingly.

EAM angrily denounced the new ruling as an oppressive measure and in its turn declared that it was now much too late to call off the activities planned for the following morning. Whether in fact EAM could have notified its workers during the night of December 2 that the demonstration had been canceled, assuming it wished to abide by the government's orders, remains a mute question. During the occupation its communications network, while primitive and not always reliable, had performed small miracles and very probably could have done so again. But EAM had no intention of backing down at the last minute. On the contrary, the size of the turn-out was to be dramatic proof that it could defy the Papandreou government with impunity.

Early Sunday morning, uncertain of EAM's intentions, the government took steps to implement its ban and prevent a crowd from gathering on Constitution Square. All the principal arteries leading to it were cordoned off by policemen and the police guards of public buildings in the area, including the Police Headquarters on the corner of Kifissia

[83] *Ibid.*

188

Boulevard and University Street—a tall structure overlooking the Square—were augmented and issued carbines. Though orders were to fire blanks, and that only as a last resort, some of the men apparently continued to carry live ammunition.[84]

The men of the Athens police were nervous, and with good reason. For them the impending mass demonstration was not aimed at the "government" so much as it was directed against them personally. Pathetic leftovers of the occupation regime trying to perform their duty while smeared (very often unfairly) with the charge of collaboration, they knew well the violent hatred which the Left harbored for them. In the weeks following liberation there had been isolated instances where policemen had been the targets of attack by Leftist extremists. Some cases had all the markings of a family vendetta; but the political overtones were unmistakable. Now the same men had been ordered to face EAM's hordes and to defend themselves with blanks. Demoralized, poorly trained, and with no experience in the control of large crowds, they nervously stood across the street pavement fearing for their very lives.

Long before 11 A.M. on Sunday, crowds began to move toward the center of Athens. Some had walked from their homes; others, from outlying suburbs and villages, had been driven to the city's outskirts by the few trucks which EAM had impressed into a makeshift shuttle service. The

[84] The events of December 3 were witnessed and subsequently widely reported by scores of foreign correspondents as well as British and American officers who had a ringside view from their own windows and balconies at the Grande Bretagne and King George Hotels which overlook the Square and, in the case of the former, faced the Police Headquarters building. Because it has been asserted that these journalists were duped by leftist propaganda and were therefore unfair in their reporting I have chosen not to rely on their despatches. The following account is based on McNeill (pp. 165-71), Leeper (pp. 100-105), OSS reports, Ambassador MacVeagh's diary, and on a report prepared by the Greek government for distribution among allied governments.

vast majority were teenagers and women: it subsequently developed that ELAS had already mobilized its Attica reservists and they were reporting to their units outside the city limits. There were leftist marching-songs and fists of defiance waved at every sign of authority. The mood of the crowd combined exhilaration with anger. It became ugly when the demonstrators discovered that their way to the Square was being blocked by the police. As ranks thickened, pushing and shoving began, accompanied by a barrage of verbal abuse directed at the police. Soon swinging police clubs and demonstrators' fists and sticks were taking their toll of bloody noses and cracked skulls. A number of wounded policemen were carried to the Police Headquarters, in full view of the dozen or more frightened guards in the building's entrance on Kifissia Boulevard.

For a while the lines held. A few blocks up on Kifissia Boulevard and very near the Prime Minister's apartment the crowd attacked the police cordon and, according to some reports, fired several shots. The police responded with blanks and the crowd hastily retreated. According to eyewitness accounts, there were no injuries.[85]

The squad guarding the Police Headquarters moved to

[85] According to the Greek government report two hand grenades were thrown against the police, killing a passing civilian and seriously wounding a policeman. MacVeagh, who witnessed the scene from his office window across the street, wrote in his diary that he saw no weapons in the hands of the demonstrators, mentioned no grenades or casualties, and confirmed that the police were firing blanks "for the most part." He reports hearing "bombs" further up on Kifissia Boulevard and down toward Constitution Square, and speculates that they may have been thrown by the demonstrators, although he could not be sure. McNeill, at the time Assistant Military Attaché of the United States Embassy in Athens with the rank of captain, also reports that this episode produced no casualties (McNeill, p. 169). It is difficult to see how the explosion of two grenades in an extremely crowded street could have resulted in the light casualties mentioned in the government report. The government's "Official News Bulletin" for December 5, 1944, mentioned a grenade attack and shots having been fired outside the Premier's residence but had nothing to say concerning casualties.

190

the opposite sidewalk of Kifissia Boulevard and took shelter behind the stone wall separating the street from the narrow ramp of the Old Palace above. From that position they could survey the entire upper level of the Square facing the marble-paved area before the monument to the Unknown Soldier. Suddenly, at about 10:45, on the far side, the police cordon at Syngrou Boulevard broke and a screaming mob of several hundred began charging across the Square heading straight for the squad guarding the Police Headquarters. The policemen, in a state of near-panic, appeared momentarily paralyzed. At this precise moment, according to virtually all eyewitness reports, a man in military clothes not belonging to the police came running out of the Police Headquarters gate and, reaching the line of policemen, shouted to them to "Shoot the bastards!" and began firing an automatic weapon into the advancing crowd. The policemen lowered their own weapons and opened fire. Frantically the howling wave of demonstrators wheeled around and ran for cover, leaving behind about a dozen dead or seriously wounded.[86]

[86] The government report reads: "The members of the police, although mistreated by the demonstrators, acting in accordance with orders, showed great patience. The first shots were fired by armed demonstrators, who were also supplied with hand grenades. A police sergeant was killed, and three policemen wounded. Most of the ten dead demonstrators, as was proven by the coroner's inquest, were killed by hand grenades, of which no use was made by the police. Be it noted that of those killed, only one was a woman, and of the sixty-six wounded, only two were children." In his memoirs Macmillan follows Kousoulas' account regarding the mysterious man in military uniform who initiated the shooting, and adds: ". . . there was strong reason to believe that the fatal shots were in fact fired by a Communist *agent provocateur*" (Macmillan, p. 499). McNeill argues: "That so few were hurt can only be explained by supposing that most of the policemen fired blanks. Perhaps only one man—perhaps the man who had run out at the last minute and started the shooting—fired to kill. A single carbine could easily have done all the execution of that morning. If all of the police had fired live rounds, not fifteen but at least a hundred would have been hit, for the crowd was close and entirely unprotected" (McNeill, p. 169).

191

The shooting stopped as quickly as it had broken out. After some hesitation, a few demonstrators, arms waving to indicate their intentions, returned to carry away the dead and wounded. The bulk of the crowd continued to cower along the edges of the Square, kept at bay by the occasional firing of a shot from the direction of the Police Headquarters.

A little after 11 A.M. another wave of demonstrators, apparently unaware of what had happened, surged across the Square, having broken the police line at Hermes Street. This time there was no shooting as the policemen fled into the courtyard of the Police Headquarters and locked themselves in, behind the tall, spear-like steel fence. Elsewhere policemen simply abandoned their posts and fled. Some were attacked and killed before they could find shelter. For the next several hours a huge crowd packed the Square and all nearby areas, venting its frustration and hatred by shouting anti-government slogans and waving fists in the direction of the police. According to McNeill's detailed account:

> Around the spots on the pavement where their fellows had been slaughtered, little borders of flowers and twigs were erected, and hundreds of persons bent down to dip their handkerchiefs in the blood which lay fresh on the pavement. These were made into banners, which were paraded through the crowd while their bearers exhorted all around them to touch the blood-stained rag and swear vengeance against the men who had made the slaughter.

> It was the greatest demonstration that Athens had ever seen. Perhaps sixty thousand persons jammed the Square, and other thousands stood outside. The excitement was indescribable and the anger which exuded from the crowd seemed almost palpable. A tiny wizened woman, dressed in widow's weeds, came up in front of the Police Headquarters, a wooden stick in her hand, and remained

there for half an hour, the very image of wrath. She hurled threats and spat out curses, gesticulating with her whole body. She must have struck a chord of fear in the heart of any policemen who heard or saw her. Young girls, scarcely more than fourteen years old, paraded with the hems of their skirts dipped in blood from the pools on the street. Some boys raised an American Army officer, who had tried to walk through the crowd, up on their shoulders and carried him more than forty yards before he kicked his way free. The crowd made a definite effort to distinguish between the American and British policy. They shouted "Roosevelt, Roosevelt," constantly, and carried vast numbers of American flags. There were also many Greek flags, a few Russian, but no British. Banners in English exhorted British soldiers not to interfere in Greek affairs, and reproached General Scobie and Ambassador Leeper for what they had done.[87]

At about 2 P.M. a company of British paratroopers reached Constitution Square, as the crowd quickly opened a narrow path for their vehicles to pass through. Calmly but firmly they formed a line, one man deep, and slowly walked the length of the Square, shepherding the demonstrators ahead of them. In about twenty minutes the Square was empty except for the few British soldiers who remained behind to keep an eye on the situation.

However, according to the report prepared for the Greek authorities for distribution among allied governments, in other parts of the city the bloody events continued to unfold:

In the afternoon of the same day armed members of the EAM began assaulting various sections of the city, committing acts of terrorism and vandalism, abducting and kill-

[87] *Ibid.*, pp. 170-71. McNeill's account of the events of December 3 was pronounced "painstakingly impartial" by the British commander of the Allied Military Mission (Woodhouse, p. 214).

ing members of nationalistic organizations and other citizens. . . . They entered homes of peaceful citizens in no way connected with politics and fired against unarmed and defenseless men, women and children. . . . There were countless acts of vandalism during the night of December 3-4. The followers of EAM simultaneously attacked police stations, liquidating on the spot many of the policemen, whom they found alive after capturing the stations.

In the face of this organized attack, the Greek Government and the British Command found themselves unprepared. For two days, December 4 and 5, the Official State was subjected to attack but did not counterattack. The Mountain Brigade remained at its barracks; so did the gendarmerie. Greek sailors were attacked by groups of terrorists, who had been preparing for many weeks for this purpose and had been entrenched in houses around the Greek Admiralty. Indicative of the prior preparation of the revolt is the fact that although the strike had been set for December 4, the Gas Company ceased functioning two hours before the mass meeting. . . .[88]

[88] Report presented to the Department of State by the Greek Embassy in Washington. On the other hand, a British Foreign Office spokesman attributed the shooting to the nervousness of the Athens police (DSR, 868.00/11-11-2744; telegram dated Dec. 4, 1944). The number of casualties remains uncertain. The report of the Greek government gives the figure of 10 dead and 26 wounded among the demonstrators; McNeill writes of "at least" 7 dead. Surprisingly, the Department of State informed the President that in the incidents of December 3 the Greek police had "killed twenty-one and wounded one hundred and fifty of the demonstrators" (FR [1944], 148). Information in the Department files does not substantiate this higher figure which was most probably obtained from journalistic sources. On December 4 The New York Times reported the casualties as at least 10 dead and 61 wounded. The following day the figures were raised to 21 dead, 140 wounded. In the debate in the House of Commons on December 8 the casualties were given as 15 dead and 148 wounded. Obviously, in view of the panic and confusion, no accurate count was possible.

The savage fighting that lasted until the truce of February 12, 1945 (the Varkiza Agreement), the atrocities committed by the Communists, the suffering and horror of the people of Athens, and the magnificent spirit of the British soldiers caught in a treacherous war not of their making, are all part of the Second Round but cannot be related here. Nor are the military measures which repelled ELAS and forced it to capitulate within the scope of this study. What remains to be examined in the following chapter is the political struggle which preceded the Varkiza Agreement and led to the establishment of a regency under Archbishop Damascinos. It might thus be appropriate to end the present portion of the narrative examining the causes of the Second Round with certain key passages from a letter that the American Ambassador in Athens addressed to the President on December 8, giving his views as to what was happening in the Greek capital. "As I have feared for many months," MacVeagh wrote, ". . . the disciplinary British and the unruly Greeks have at last come to blows. Moreover, in trying to do what they aim to do here, namely, to 'keep order' and 'protect constitutional government' with the small force at their disposal, the British would appear to have got a bear by the tail. . . ." Acknowledging that the crisis may have been aggravated by German and Communist propaganda, and that "primal and ugly Balkan passions have risen again to the surface here," he sought to draw the President's attention to "other factors which are of greater importance and bode worse for the future":

> There can be no question that thousands of the ELAS and EAM are genuinely convinced,—misled, if you will, but convinced,—that they are fighting for liberty and independence, like their ancestors, and in this they are fanatical. They believe that Mr. Papandreou and the British, who set him up as Prime Minister and are supporting him through thick and thin, even to the point of not letting

him resign, intend to force the King back on the people together with the dictatorship for which they hold him personally responsible. Nothing the British say to the contrary in regard to this belief will these "patriots" even take seriously, and unfortunately little that the British actually do belies it. As Professor Svolos, the head of the EAM, said to me the other day most aptly and moderately, "The British *must* give the Greeks at least the impression that they are free people." But this they have not been either deft enough or understanding enough to do, and I greatly fear that the opportunity which their attitude gives the communists (and just now the Germans too) to spread the idea among the Greeks that in opposing the British they are standing for freedom, opens the door to trouble which will not be terminated by "restoring order" or "defending constitutional government" but will last for years, with wide-spread bitterness and enduring disturbance, perhaps affecting British relationships with the people of all the Near Eastern countries. . . .

MacVeagh thought that the crisis might have been at least momentarily averted had Churchill allowed an immediate change in the Greek government, as suggested by Leeper, believing that "a political new deal might have provided a palliative for the moment." Moreover, "at bottom, the handling of this fanatically freedom-loving country (which has never yet taken dictation quietly) as if it were composed of nations under the British Raj, is what is the trouble, and Mr. Churchill's recent prohibition against the Greeks attempting a political solution at this time, if a blunder, is only the latest of a long line of blunders during the entire course of the present war." In the Ambassador's view, the suspicions and fears dividing the Greek world were extremely powerful, even if not always well-founded:

Not only the old royalists, but now also not a few of the old liberals who have vested interests (the intelligentsia are mostly leftists) are quite as convinced as the guerrillas of the correctness of their own point of view; and the rightist view is, of course, that behind the guerrillas' libertarian program lies an intention to impose a communist dictatorship. Many people are now wanting the King back not because they like royalism but because they fear communism. But the truth is that neither pure royalism nor pure communism has many followers in Greece today, while each enjoys accretions of strength, none the less dangerous for being fundamentally fictitious, from suspicions which are rife and growing among democrats with possessions, on the one hand, and among democrats without possessions but hungry, homeless and armed on the other. Mr. Svolos sadly commented to me, "At the bottom of the whole thing lies the King question." Dozens of old Athenian friends have similarly told me, "Communism is the fundamental issue." But the Greeks will never be quiet under any dictatorship, or suspicion of dictatorship, from either right or left. . . .

To remove these fears and suspicions which made political compromise impossible, a truly impartial agency was essential. The Greeks themselves, and now the British, were too involved in the affair to be able to play such a role. Consequently, only an international commission composed of British, Russians, and Americans could possibly be accepted as impartial by all concerned. The British Ambassador, with whom MacVeagh had discussed the matter, appeared to welcome the idea and was communicating it to his government. If London could be persuaded to initiate such a proposal it would be face-saving as well as a way of extricating itself from a most dangerous situation.

Aware that his own superiors had not welcomed his earlier suggestions for greater American responsibility and for an international commission for Greece, MacVeagh returned once again to his central theme:

Let me repeat that fundamentally it is mutual suspicion that is the trouble in Greece today. It has led to the present fighting, and will lead to more, no matter how successful Mr. Churchill's undoubtedly benevolent severity may prove for the time being. Disarm such suspicion on both sides, however, and there is enough soundness left in the Greeks, despite all they have gone through, to warrant some hope that they may settle back to their relatively harmless normal state of political instability with the passage of time, the restoration of communications and the provision of food and shelter. Otherwise, communism will continue to exploit its present marvelous opportunities for still further collapsing the social order and creating a "Greek problem" to plague Britain, and us in the background, perhaps for many years to come. Of course, I realize that to set up an International Commission is a serious affair, presenting many difficulties. But I give you the suggestion advisedly, believing that the problem to be solved is also serious. . . .[89]

On the same day (December 8) and writing much along the same lines to a colleague in the Department, MacVeagh concluded:

You know, I don't think all this would have happened— the house is shaking with explosions at the moment—if my suggestion of last winter for an American command here had been taken. We would have disarmed and reformed the guerrillas, because there would have been no suspicions as to our motives like those connected with British insistence on maintaining the Mountain Brigade. But *dis aliter visum*! Now the British are paying for many follies, and we who are "not involved" will also pay, in the loss of prestige and good will which the Western Powers

[89] MacVeagh letter to the President, dated Dec. 8, 1944, *Roosevelt Papers*, PSF, "Greece: L. MacVeagh."

are going to suffer from Mr. Churchill's policies in Greece and Yugoslavia.[90]

Reviewing the immediate background of the crisis it is apparent that if the Communists had already decided on November 28 to employ armed force to seize control of the capital, the bloody events of December 3 would have no particular significance except perhaps as the opening skirmish of a war already declared. Thus, according to one student of this period, "If these particular incidents had not occurred some others could have served just as well. What matters is that five days earlier the Communist leadership had decided to plunge the country into civil war."[91] And Macmillan, citing the above study, agrees: "Wherever the truth may lie, it is certain that the events of Sunday 3 December, although perhaps a convenient date for historians to mark the beginning of the December Revolution, were not its cause. The Communist rebellion was not provoked by an unfortunate clash during a political demonstration. It was the result of a definite decision taken by the Communist leaders, . . . at least five days before."[92] The evidence now available to the historian does suggest that at the end of November the situation in the Greek capital was highly explosive and the threat of violence very real. Yet, however narrow and difficult, the avenues of negotiation and compromise had not been entirely closed, and neither side wished to see the country's future depend on the outcome of street-fighting and murder. It was the bloodshed on Constitution Square that served to break the fragile thread of reason, plunging the capital into the fratricide of the Second Round.

[90] *DSR*, 868.00/12-2044.   [91] Kousoulas, p. 207.
[92] Macmillan, pp. 499-500.

THE STRUGGLE FOR ATHENS

THE FLARE-UP of December 3 delivered the deathblow to the Government of National Unity, which had already been severely truncated by the departure of the EAM Ministers. On December 4, recognizing that the bloodshed at Constitution Square had rendered his own position untenable, Prime Minister Papandreou announced his intention to step down immediately and apparently agreed that the 84-year-old Themistoclis Sofoulis, leader of the Liberal Party, should head a new coalition. This move, clearly designed to prevent the further polarization of the Greek political world and to avert a civil war, was welcomed by all factions, despite sharp disagreement on the ever-crucial matter of EAM's share of Cabinet seats.[1] It was also thought unavoidable by Ambassadors MacVeagh and Leeper, and the latter advised the Foreign Office accordingly.[2]

But there was to be no last-minute reprieve from the impending holocaust. In London Prime Minister Churchill who, upon hearing of the latest crisis in Athens, had assumed personal direction of Greek affairs,[3] immediately brushed aside all advice that Papandreou was now a clear liability and that new leadership was desperately needed in Athens. He was convinced that the time had come for a decisive showdown with the Greek Left. In the small hours

---

[1] McNeill, p. 172; Papandreou, pp. 228-30.

[2] FR (1944), 142. MacVeagh Diary, entry dated Dec. 5, 1944. And two days later: "The Papandreou government should resign—it was made and imported by the British—and the King should be definitely barred out of the country until the plebiscite is held. . . ."

[3] Churchill, VI, 288; Macmillan, p. 500.

of December 5 he sent General Scobie the by-now famous order:

> You are responsible for maintaining order in Athens and for neutralizing or destroying all EAM-ELAS bands approaching the city. You may make any regulations you like for the strict control of the streets or for the rounding up of any number of truculent persons. Naturally ELAS will try to put women and children in the van where shooting may occur. You must be clever about this and avoid mistakes. But do not hesitate to fire at any armed male in Athens who assails the British authority or Greek authority with which we are working. It would be well of course if your commands were reinforced by the authority *of some Greek Government,* and Papandreou is being told by Leeper to stop and help. *Do not hesitate to act as if you were in a conquered city where a local rebellion is in progress.*
>
> With regard to ELAS bands approaching from the outside, you should surely be able with your armour to give some of these a lesson which will make others unlikely to try. You may count upon my support in all reasonable and sensible action taken on this basis. *We have to hold and dominate Athens. It would be a great thing for you to succeed in this without bloodshed if possible, but also with bloodshed if necessary.*[4]

Subsequently, and for the benefit of the inquisitive historian, Churchill sought to soften the impact of his directive to Scobie which, he admitted, had been "somewhat strident in tone." His purpose had been to give Scobie a "strong lead" with a sternly worded command which would "not only encourage him to decisive action, but gave him the certain assurance that I should be with him in any well con-

---

[4] Churchill, vi, 289. Emphasis in the original, except in first instance.

ceived action he might take, whatever the consequences might be." He felt gravely concerned about the Greek situation and was determined that "there should be no room for doubts or hedging." In what one might call a Freudian slip, Churchill thought the problem in Athens was analogous to that faced by Arthur Balfour in the 1880's when, confronted with a rebellious Ireland, the British statesman had sent through open telegraphic channels the order: "Don't hesitate to shoot." Although the bold action had caused a storm of protest in the House of Commons, it had "certainly prevented any loss of life. . . ."[5]

Whatever the explanation for his action, the significance of Churchill's reaction to the events of December 3 cannot be overstated. Through his order to General Scobie he had committed Britain's prestige and power to the bolstering of a government which had proven itself ineffective beyond salvation to all in Athens, and which the entire Left—and not simply the Communists—suspected, however unjustly, of planning to return the King without an honest attempt to ascertain the nation's wishes on the subject. To his troubled ambassador in Athens, whose advice regarding Papandreou's premiership he had just chosen to ignore, Churchill sent (on December 5) equally stern instructions, making it quite clear that Scobie had been granted commanding authority for the duration of the crisis:

> This is no time to dabble in Greek politics or to imagine that Greek politicians of varying shades can affect the situation. You should not worry about Greek Government compositions. The matter is one of life and death.
> You must urge Papandreou to stand to his duty, and

[5] *Ibid.*, 289-90. In view of this reasoning it is interesting to recall that his order to Scobie, rather than being sent through the open telegraph, was in fact in code and highly classified. When its contents were "leaked" by American military channels and appeared in Drew Pearson's syndicated column on December 12, the British Ambassador in Washington conveyed to the Department of State Churchill's indignation over the matter (*DSR*, 868.00/12-1244).

assure him he will be supported by all our forces if he does so. The day has long gone past when any particular group of Greek politicians can influence this mob rising. His only chance is to come through with us.

I have put the whole question of the defense of Athens and maintenance of law and order in the hands of General Scobie, and have assured him that he will be supported in the use of whatever force is necessary. Henceforth you and Papandreou will conform to his directions in all matters affecting public order and security. You should both support Scobie in every possible way, and you should suggest to him any means which occur to you of making his action more vigorous and decisive.[6]

Leeper had the unpleasant task of informing Sofoulis that Churchill had vetoed a change in the person of the Prime Minister. As for Papandreou, he telegraphed the King in London that, following Churchill's directive, he would remain in office and, incredibly, added: "Governmental crisis no longer exists. . . ."[7]

Churchill's determination to confront the Greek Left with armed force made him the target of persistent and often vicious attack in most of the British and American press. Leading papers such as the *Manchester Guardian, Daily Chronicle,* and *The Times* were to remain hostile to the government's handling of Greek affairs. Ambassador Leeper was particularly upset by the press reports emanating from Athens.[8] In London a critic of the government in the House of Commons demanded to know whether Churchill claimed "the right to appoint Prime Ministers of Allied States as he might appoint a few Parliamentary Private Secretaries, or as Hitler appoints gauleiters in the different countries which come under his sway." Speculating that Britain might be motivated by a desire for military

[6] Churchill, vi, 290.   [7] Papandreou, p. 232.
[8] Leeper, pp. 101-2.

bases in Greece, as had been reported in the press,[9] the same Labor M.P. melodramatically proclaimed: "I would rather this right hand of mine were burnt off at the wrist, leaving a blackened and twisted stump, than sign an order to the British army to fire on the workers of Greece. . . ."[10]

In the full and noisy debate in the House of Commons on December 8, sparked by a Labor-sponsored amendment to the traditional vote of confidence in response to the King's speech, Churchill proved himself a master dialectician. The amendment had sought to express ". . . regret that the Gracious Speech contains no assurance that His Majesty's forces will not be used to disarm the friends of democracy in Greece and other parts of Europe, or to suppress those popular movements which have valorously assisted in the defeat of the enemy and upon whose success we must rely for future friendly cooperation in Europe."[11] Deliberately submerging the Greek crisis into the ocean of general European problems, Churchill was able to fend off and divide his critics. As Macmillan rightly observed following the defeat of the Labor move to censure, "The framers of the amendment made a great tactical error in making it so wide. If they had narrowed it to Greece, the P.M. would not have been able to develop the general argument, and here Belgium, Holland . . . etc. were of great assistance to him in expounding his theme."[12]

Churchill's "theme" was quite involved. He first lectured his detractors on the meaning and character of true democracy which, as he chose to put it, "is no harlot to be picked up in the street by a man with a tommy gun":

> . . . let me present to the House the charge which is made against us. It is that we are using His Majesty's Forces to disarm the friends of democracy in Greece and in other

[9] E.g., *New York Times*, Dec. 3, 1944.
[10] Great Britain, *Parliamentary Debates* (Commons) 406, (1944-45), 915-16.
[11] *Ibid.*, 908.   [12] Macmillan, p. 501.

parts of Europe, and to suppress those popular movements which have valorously assisted in the defeat of the
enemy. . . . The question however arises. . . . Who are the
friends of democracy, and also how is the word "democracy" to be interpreted? My idea of it is that the plain,
humble, common man, just the ordinary man who keeps
a wife and family, who goes off to fight for his country
when it is in trouble, and goes to the poll at the appropriate time, puts his cross on the ballot paper showing the
candidate he wishes to be elected to Parliament—that is
the foundation of democracy. . . . But this man, or woman, should do this without fear, and without any form of
intimidation or victimisation. He marks his ballot paper
in strict secrecy, and then elected representatives meet
and together decide what government, or even, in times
of stress, what form of government they wish to have in
their country. If that is democracy I salute it. I espouse
it. I would work for it. . . . But I feel quite different about
a swindle democracy, a democracy which calls itself
democracy because it is Left Wing. It takes all sorts to
make a democracy, not only Left Wing, or even Communist. I do not expect a party or a body to call themselves
democrats because they are stretching further and further
into the most extreme forms of revolution. I do not accept
a party as necessarily representing democracy because
it becomes more violent as it becomes less numerous. . . .
The last thing which resembles democracy is mob law,
with bands of gangsters, armed with deadly weapons,
forcing their way into great cities, seizing the police stations and key points of government, endeavouring to introduce a totalitarian regime with an iron hand, and
clamouring . . . to shoot everyone . . . who is politically in-
convenient as part of a purge of those who are said to
have—and very often have not—sought to collaborate
with the Germans during the occupation. . . . That is the
antithesis of democracy. . . .

Turning once again to the more specific charges against his Greek policy, Churchill pressed his counterattack: "If what is called in this Amendment the action of 'the friends of democracy' is to be interpreted as carefully planned *coups d'état* by murder gangs and by the iron rule of ruffians seeking to climb into the seats of power, without a vote ever having been cast in their favour—if that is to masquerade as democracy I think the House will unite in condemning it as mockery. . . ." The fact that Papandreou had become Prime Minister by British *fiat* and not following popular elections did not appear to bother Churchill. Moreover, reference to a modern-day "white man's burden" was certain to appeal to those in his audience proud of Britain's *mission civilizatrice*:

> . . . I say we march along an onerous and painful path. Poor old England! Perhaps I ought to say "Poor old Britain." We have to assume the burden of most thankless tasks and in undertaking them to be scoffed at, criticised and opposed from every quarter; but at least we know where we are making for, know the end of the road, know what is our objective. It is that these countries shall be freed from the German armed power and under conditions of normal tranquillity shall have a free universal vote to decide the Government of their country—except a Fascist regime—and whether that Government shall be of the Left or of the Right. . . .

Churchill's attack on the political enemy in the Greek situation was barely qualified, suggesting that a Fascist regime was not the only one he would not tolerate:

> ELAS is a mixed body and it would be unfair to stigmatise them all as being entirely self-seeking in their aims and actions. Nevertheless, during the years of Greek captivity I must say that ELAS devoted far more attention to beating up and destroying the representatives of the EDES. . . .

For the past two years ELAS have devoted themselves principally to preparations for seizing power. We may, some of us, have underrated the extremes to which those preparations have been carried or the many privations and cruelties which have been inflicted on the village populations in the areas over which they prevail. . . . ELAS did not hesitate on occasion to help the Germans to catch and kill the supporters of EDES. . . . From the depredations and ravages of ELAS there was, however, as we can now see, a fairly well organized plot or plan by which ELAS should march down upon Athens and seize it by armed force and establish a reign of terror under the plea that they were purging collaborationists. How much the Germans knew about this before they left I cannot tell, but a number of them have been left behind and are fighting in ELAS ranks. . . .

This, therefore, is the way in which the British Prime Minister had chosen to interpret what had occurred in Greece in the summer and fall of 1944. In his long and detailed arguments he managed to avoid completely the issue of the monarchy's role in Greek politics, and the charge that the King, whom Churchill had supported at every turn, had condoned the Metaxas dictatorship. Furthermore, Britain's interests in Greece were noble and entirely beyond reproach:

His Majesty's Government felt that having regard to the sacrifices that they have made at the time of the German invasion of Greece, and to the long affection which has grown between the Greek and British people since their liberation in the last century, and having regard also to the decisions and agreements of our principal Allies, we should see what we could do to give these unfortunate people a fair chance of extricating themselves from their misery and starting on a clear road again. That is the only wish and ambition which we had . . . for our entry into Greece and for the action forced upon us there. . . .

207

As for the matter of the Greek Prime Minister, Churchill argued that it would have been "silly or futile or dangerous" to change leaders while the fighting was going on in Athens, and made a pointed reference to Sofoulis' advanced age. He concluded with a proud declaration: "If I am blamed for this action I will gladly accept my dismissal at the hands of the House; but if I am not so dismissed—make no mistake about it—we shall persist in this policy of clearing Athens and the Athens region of all who are rebels to the authority of the constitutional Government of Greece. . . ."[13]

After the vote, in which the Labor amendment was defeated by 279 to 30, with most Labor and some Conservative Members abstaining, Macmillan found Churchill "very exhausted and in rather a petulant mood," and recorded: "The debate had obviously tired him very much and I think he realized the dangers inherent in the Greek policy on which we are now embarked. He has won the debate but not the Battle of Athens."[14] For his part, Churchill sought to make it clear to all concerned that he was indeed determined to see his policy prevail. "I do not yield to passing clamour," he telegraphed Leeper on December 9, "and will always stand with those who execute their instructions with courage and precision. In Athens as everywhere else our maxim is 'No peace without victory.' "[15]

He clearly liked the sound of his last phrase, which he had obviously borrowed from his thinking on a war much greater than the fighting in the streets of Athens. On the same day (December 9) he sent a note to Macmillan urg-

[13] *Parliamentary Debates* (Commons) 406, (1944-45), 908-1020.

[14] Macmillan, pp. 503-4. Harold Nicolson, who also took part in the debate, later recalled: "Winston was in one of his boyish moods, and allowed himself to be interrupted all the time. In fact, he seemed to me to be in rather higher spirits than the occasion warranted. I don't think he quite caught the mood of the House, which at its best was one of distressed perplexity, and at its worst one of sheer red fury" (Harold Nicolson, *Diaries and Letters*, Vol. II, *The War Years, 1939-1945* [New York, 1967], 416).

[15] Churchill, VI, 296.

ing him to remember "always that our maxim is 'no peace without victory.' "[16] And to Harry Hopkins, in a move calculated to elicit from the President a public endorsement of British action in Greece, he wrote:

I hope you will tell our great friend that the establishment of law and order in and around Athens is essential to all future measures of magnanimity and consolation towards Greece. After this has been established will be the time for talking. My guiding principle is "No peace without victory." It is a great disappointment to me to have been set upon in this way by ELAS when we came loaded with good gifts and anxious only to form a united Greece which could establish its own destiny. But we have been set upon, and we intend to defend ourselves. I consider we have a right to the President's support in the policy we are following. If it can be said in the streets of Athens that the United States are against us, then more British blood will be shed and much more Greek. It grieves me very much to see signs of our drifting apart at a time when unity becomes ever more important, as danger recedes and faction arises.[17]

In the debate in Parliament the British government had implied broadly that it had acted in Greece with the knowledge and approval of the Americans. Subsequently Church-

[16] Macmillan, p. 504.

[17] Churchill, VI, 297. He also reminded Hopkins that, as regards Greece, "our action was fully approved" by the United States at the Quebec Conference. In a bit of bravado, he added: "For you personally. Do not be misled by our majority yesterday. I could have had another eighty by sending out a three-line whip instead of only two. On Fridays, with the bad communications prevailing here, Members long to get away for the week-end. Who would not?" This was the debate which according to a prestigious publication, "shook the British Government more severely than it had been shaken at any time since its formation . . ." (Arnold Toynbee and Veronica M. Toynbee, eds., *The Realignment of Europe* [*Survey of International Affairs, 1939-1945*] [London, 1955], p. 396).

ill recorded that during the winter of 1944 and in the Greek crisis, "in the main the President was with me. . . ."[18] Nevertheless, as he openly admitted to Hopkins in the statement just quoted, there could be no doubt that British policy in Athens had seriously strained Anglo-American relations. Nor was there any effort in Washington to conceal this fact. On December 3 the "Voice of America" broadcast a statement by Secretary of State Stettinius which the Left in Greece immediately and loudly welcomed as a clear sign of American sympathy for its cause. "The 'Voice of America' has the authorization to point out once more," the statement read, "that the United States policy has always been to refrain from any interference in the internal affairs of other nations. In conformity with this policy, the United States has scrupulously refrained from interfering in the affairs of other countries which have been liberated from the Germans." Moreover,

> The United States Government will continue to refrain from interference in the affairs of other countries. Unless the military security of the Allied armies is at stake, the United States will make no attempt to influence the composition of any government in any friendly country. The American people have naturally viewed with sympathy the aspirations of the resistance movements and the anti-Fascist elements in liberated countries. The American people know that these groups which fought so courageously against the Germans have no intention of hampering the present all-important military operations against Germany.[19]

In Athens, where the leftist press reported on December 4 that the American Ambassador had protested vigorously to his British colleague British "interference" in Greek

18 Churchill, vi, 296.
19 *FR* (1944), 148. *Rizospastis* gave Stettinius' statement full publicity on the same day, December 3.

affairs, MacVeagh issued a formal denial that he had taken such a step. He advised his superiors that "While doing all I can not to allow this Mission to become involved in internal affairs, I have also been careful so far as possible not to embarrass our British allies and my British colleague realizes this as well as the delicacy of the position involved."[20] Nevertheless, obvious signs of official American displeasure persisted. On December 5 another statement of Secretary Stettinius dealing with the controversy surrounding the composition of the Italian government emphasized that the United States had "reaffirmed to both the British and Italian Governments that we expect the Italians to work out their problems of government along democratic lines without influence from outside. This policy would apply to an even more pronounced degree with regard to Governments of the United Nations in their liberated territories." The last sentence of this much-publicized statement was widely and correctly interpreted as an intentional slap at the British for their Greek policy.[21]

Alarmed by the strong innuendo the Greek Ambassador in Washington called on the Department of State on December 6 and sought to persuade his hosts that the situation prevailing in his country was entirely different from that in Italy, particularly in so far as the use of armed force was concerned. He was given assurances that the American government was indeed aware of these differences, but was also told that the Secretary's words, to which the Greek government had taken exception, had merely reiterated the American policy of not wishing to see foreign intervention

[20] *FR* (1944), 143; MacVeagh Diary, entry dated Dec. 4, 1944.
[21] Churchill, vi, 296-97; Macmillan, p. 501; Nicolson, p. 416. There can be no doubt that Stettinius' words were in fact intended to serve as a warning to the British to refrain from dictating political solutions to the liberated countries (see Fleet Admiral William D. Leahy, *I Was There: The Personal Story of the Chief of Staff to Presidents Roosevelt and Truman Based on His Notes and Diaries Made at the Time* [New York, 1950], pp. 284-85).

in the domestic political affairs of liberated countries.[22] What the Greek diplomat could not know was that even as he was objecting to the implications of Stettinius' pronouncement, a new memorandum was being drafted for the Secretary of State by his advisers on Greek matters for the purpose of clearly and formally disassociating the United States from British action in Athens. Blaming EAM's refusal to allow the disarming of ELAS on the King's failure to give positive assurances that he would not return to Greece pending a plebiscite, the draft note asserted that British insistence on supporting Papandreou after the bloody events of December 3 would inevitably lead to far worse difficulties. Accordingly, the suggestion was offered that the President might urge Churchill to accept Papandreou's resignation, to permit EAM's participation in a new coalition, and to seek the early establishment of a regency. However, because of official British furor over Stettinius' statement of December 5, this memorandum was not shown to the Secretary, and the suggestions it contained were presented to the President in a much more tempered form.[23] On the other hand, the Secretary himself would not let the matter drop. In a press conference on December 7 he returned to the fray. Noting that two days earlier the British Prime Minister had told the House of Commons that "whether the Greek people form themselves into a monarchy or republic is for their decision. Whether they form a government of the right or left is for their decision. These are entirely matters for them," Stettinius declared: "With this statement, I am in full agreement. It is also our earnest hope that the people and authorities of Greece and our British Allies will work together in rebuilding that ravished country."[24]

Strong American resentment of British "interference" in Greece was manifested in other, more practical and direct

[22] *DSR*, 868.00/12-644.
[23] *Ibid.* Also *FR* (1944), 148-51.
[24] Department of State *Bulletin*, Dec. 10, 1944, 713.

ways. Immediately following Stettinius' statement of December 5, Admiral Ernest J. King, Chief of U.S. Naval Operations, had ordered the American Commander of the Mediterranean Fleet, Vice Admiral H. K. Hewitt, not to permit American vessels to be used in the shipment of supplies to the British forces in Greece. This order, which was in clear violation of the allied chain of command, had actually caused only momentary inconvenience to the British. American Navy officers on the scene, while wishing to remain uninvolved in the Greek crisis, easily recognized the predicament in which their British comrades had been placed by this highly irregular order. On December 9 and following consultations between the Departments of the Navy and State, they had already transferred the vessels in question, 7 LST's, to the British who were thus able to continue using them under their own flag.[25] Very probably unaware that practical minds had solved the problem, Churchill called Hopkins at the White House on December 9 and despite a very poor transatlantic connection managed to express his anger over the matter. Hopkins took the problem to Admiral William D. Leahy, Chief of Staff to the President, who persuaded Admiral King to withdraw the offending order. Hopkins then strongly urged the British Ambassador to dissuade Churchill from pursuing the matter further, and above all from protesting to the President directly, because "public opinion about the whole Greek business in this country was very bad and that we felt the British Government had messed the whole thing up pretty thoroughly."[26] Indeed, if Elliott Roosevelt's recollection is to be trusted, his father's first reaction to reports of the fighting in Athens had been an explosion of indignation: "How the British can dare such a thing! The lengths to

[25] *DSR*, 868.00/12-944. Also the Diaries of Henry L. Stimson, Yale University Library, entry dated Dec. 19, 1944.
[26] Robert E. Sherwood, *Roosevelt and Hopkins* (New York, 1950), pp. 840-41.

which they will go to hang on to the past! I wouldn't be surprised if Winston had simply made it clear he was backing the Greek Royalists! That would be only in character. But killing Greek guerrillas! Using British soldiers for such a job! . . ."[27]

Prudently, Churchill agreed to comply with Hopkins' advice to drop the matter. Through the American Ambassador in London he expressed to Hopkins his gratitude for his timely intercession and accepted his assurances that Admiral King's order had been issued without the President's knowledge.[28]

Hopkins' assessment of the mood of the American public was quite accurate. A memorandum from the Secretary of State dated December 30, 1944, on public opinion regarding recent European developments, informed the President that "American opinion was shocked by the spectacle of armed conflict between the British and Greeks, and strongly reacted against British action." Despite signs that the situation in Athens was improving, "suspicion remains that Churchill seeks to dominate the Greek Government against the will of the Greek people, and many reserve judgement pending the results of the negotiations."[29]

From his office in downtown Athens, within sight and

[27] Elliott Roosevelt, *As He Saw It* (New York, 1946), pp. 222-24. The President told his son that ". . . we are going to be able to bring pressure on the British to fall in line with our thinking in relation to the whole colonial question."

[28] Ambassador John G. Winant's letter to Hopkins, dated Dec. 11, 1944. *Hopkins Papers*, Book x: "Growing Crisis in Greece." Winant also conveyed Churchill's strong wish that the President would support him publicly on Greece. The Ambassador expressed the personal view that the President might urge all factions in Greece to lay down their arms and unite, promising at the same time that a referendum would determine the country's constitutional question. Winant thought the Russians would have to be consulted prior to any such moves, and expressed the fear that they might decide to intervene in Greece, despite the fact that so far they had scrupulously adhered to the Churchill-Stalin agreement on the Balkans.

[29] *Roosevelt Papers*, psf, "State—E. R. Stettinius," Box 35.

sound of the fighting, Ambassador MacVeagh continued to provide his government with a running commentary on the unfolding situation. "I am convinced," he reported on December 8, "that the greatest danger for the future in [the] present deplorable Greek situation . . . lies in the deep-seated mutual suspicions of groups in conflict." The basic issues were essentially simple: "Many thousands of patriotic Greeks now siding with the extreme Left are undoubtedly doing so because they suspect that behind the Government's action lies an intention to bring back the King and possibly also the hated Fascist dictatorship for which they hold him personally responsible, while many thousands of others equally patriotic are convinced that behind activities of the guerrillas lies a plot to establish a Communist dictatorship. . . ." In his view, these suspicions and fears "are probably too profound and too firmly sealed by the blood which has now been shed to be cured by any purely Greek initiative." Consequently, the only hope lay in international action:

> . . . I believe the danger of continued civil war here of indefinite duration and detriment to the peace of this whole region and the interests of the United Nations might still be avoided if after restoration of order in Athens the British were able and willing to announce formation of an international commission composed of British, Russian and American representatives to oversee the holding of a plebiscite on the regime and guarantee impartial settlement of other critical problems likely to cause trouble. This would give both sides equal assurance of fair play and also restore confidence in British intentions which is now so sadly if unjustly lacking throughout the Greek world.

Aware that his recommendation for an international commission for Greece would find precious few supporters in Washington MacVeagh sought to add weight to his argument by pointing out that his British colleague entertained similar ideas and was presenting them to his own government. On the other hand, he also sensed that the British were now determined to fight their way out of their predicament. He therefore concluded his report with a cautiously worded warning: "I feel certain," he wrote his superiors "that the present drastic foreign support being given to one side of local Greek quarrel in which so much genuine patriotic fervor and even fanaticism is enlisted in the other contains little if any hope of furnishing a durable solution unless it can be followed by some such clear proof of genuine impartial interest in the Greek people as a whole."[30] Similarly, in his numerous communications MacVeagh also repeatedly emphasized the need to avoid giving the impression in Greece that British activity there in any way carried Washington's endorsement. "Our policy of non-intervention," he wrote on December 9, "appears recognized by the guerrillas and no guards are necessary for Americans or their property which is lucky as the British have all they can do to protect themselves." Nevertheless, "the guerrillas are so anxious for our effective aid and the British so eager to give the impression that we side with them that there is no telling how long this happy but precarious situation may continue."[31]

Despite the obvious difficulties which such an international effort would surely face, MacVeagh felt quite strong-

[30] *FR* (1944), 145. MacVeagh's contacts with the Greek political world were excellent, and far more extensive than Leeper's. On several occasions Greek political figures would come to MacVeagh for an introduction to Leeper.

[31] *DSR*, 868.00/12-944. When a pro-government newspaper in Athens claimed that Stettinius had expressed himself in full agreement with British policy in Greece, MacVeagh telegraphed Washington for clarification but confidently assumed that the report was incorrect (*ibid*). A senior American Army officer urged his superiors on December 9 to have the War Department issue orders forbidding American personnel in Athens to transport British soldiers through the ELAS lines in their vehicles, under cover of the American flag (*ibid*., 868.00/12-1044).

ly that it should be undertaken. However, his immediate superiors in the Department were not convinced. A memorandum to the Secretary, dated December 18, referred to the proposal for an international commission as "somewhat questionable."[32] Similarly, Stettinius expressed no enthusiasm for the idea, but advised the President:

> It seems likely that Mr. Churchill would immediately veto Russian participation, as he appears acutely to fear Russian penetration into Greece, and I think we should refuse any possible counter-proposal to intervene on a purely Anglo-American basis. I should also have some hesitancy in participating in an international commission unless we are prepared to send some civil affairs troops into Greece so that we could actually be sure of what was going on. You may consider Ambassador MacVeagh's proposal impracticable, for the foregoing or other reasons. However, in communicating our reaction to his proposal, we might well ask the Ambassador to report whether he or the British there have any suggestions to submit as to any way in which we could be helpful.[33]

Taking a more firm stand, the American Ambassador in Italy had reported on December 11 that, in his view, the United States had two alternatives in Greece; to continue the shipment of supplies and the presence of American personnel in the hope of using both as leverage that might bring the British around to a policy more agreeable to Washington, or to discontinue its participation in relief operations in Greece and insist upon a policy of nonintervention in that country's internal affairs. The American official appeared to favor the second course, observing that the

---

[32] *Ibid.*, 868.00/12-1844. On the other hand, a Department memorandum dated December 22 expressed the view that, if requested to do so, the Department should be prepared to give sympathetic consideration to the question of American participation in the supervision of the plebiscite (*ibid.*, 868.00/12-2644).
[33] *FR* (1944), 150.

equitable distribution of supplies was not possible where conditions of chaos and anarchy prevailed. Relief operations might thus have to be suspended until the Greeks themselves had decided on their form of government and had reestablished law and order.[34]

In a lengthy and rather evasive communication to Churchill on December 13, Roosevelt chose to ignore the suggestion for an international commission for Greece. Instead, he offered little sympathy and much unwelcome advice. "I have been as deeply concerned as you have yourself," the President wrote, "in regard to the tragic difficulties you have encountered in Greece. I appreciate to the full the anxious and difficult alternatives with which you have been faced. I regard my role in this matter as that of a loyal friend and ally whose one desire is to be of any help possible in the circumstances." And, for good measure, he added: "You may be sure that in putting my thoughts before you I am constantly guided by the fact that nothing can in any way shake the unity and association between our two countries in the great tasks to which we have set our hands." Nevertheless, Roosevelt continued:

> As anxious as I am to be of the greatest help to you in this trying situation, there are limitations imposed in part by the traditional policies of the United States and in part by the mounting adverse reaction of public opinion in this country. No one will understand better than yourself that I, both personally and as head of State, am necessarily responsive to the state of public feeling. It is for these reasons that it has not been possible for this Government to take a stand along with you in the present course of events in Greece. Even to attempt to do so would bring only temporary value to you and would in the long run do injury to our basic relationships. I don't need to tell you how much I dislike this state of affairs as

[34] DSR, 868.00/12-1144.

between you and me. My one hope is to see it rectified so we can go along in this as in everything, shoulder to shoulder. I know that you, as the one on whom the responsibility rests, desire with all your heart a satisfactory solution to the Greek problem and particularly one that will bring peace to that ravished country. I will be with you wholeheartedly in any solution which takes into consideration the factors I have mentioned above. . . .

Thus, if the President had been angry at the British for "killing Greek guerrillas," his feelings were vented for the benefit of his son alone. To Churchill he continued: "With this in mind I am giving you at random some thoughts that have come to me in my anxious desire to be of help.":

. . . I of course lack full details and am at a great distance from the scene, but it has seemed to me that a basic reason—or excuse, perhaps—for the EAM attitude has been distrust regarding the intentions of King George. I wonder if Macmillan's efforts [in Athens] might not be greatly facilitated if the King himself would approve the establishment of a regency in Greece and would make a public declaration of his intention not to return unless called for by popular plebiscite. This might be particularly effective if accompanied by an assurance that elections will be held at some fixed date, no matter how far in the future, when the people would have full opportunity to express themselves. Meanwhile, might it not be possible to secure general agreement on the disarmament and dissolution of all the armed groups now in the country, including the Mountain Brigade and the Sacred Battalion, leaving your troops to preserve law and order alone until the Greek national forces can be reconstituted on a non-partisan basis and adequately equipped. . . .[35]

[35] *FR* (1944), 150-51. Reports from Italy which reached Washington on December 13 indicated that Field Marshal Alexander was considering the complete disarming of all Greek forces as a compromise solution (*ibid.*, 152).

Churchill's prompt response (on December 14) revealed little appreciation for the comradely but unsolicited advice from across the Atlantic. Observing that Washington's attitude on the Greek affair was compounding Britain's "difficulties and burdens," the Prime Minister made it very clear that there would be no compromise with the enemy. Choosing to read in Roosevelt's message a suggestion for withdrawal from Greece, he retorted: "You will realize how very serious it would be if we withdrew, as we easily could, and the result was a frightful massacre, and an extreme Left Wing regime under Communist inspiration installed itself, as it would, in Athens." Britain's government "of all parties" was simply "not prepared to act in a manner of dishonourable to our record and name." There was nothing left to do but fight back: "Stern fighting lies ahead, and even danger to our troops in the centre of Athens. . . ." On the issue of the much-debated regency, Churchill would only say that King George would not have it, and "Therefore an act of constitutional violence will be entailed if we finally decide upon this course." As for Archbishop Damascinos and his often-mentioned suitability for the office of Regent, "I know nothing . . . except that our people on the spot think he might stop a gap or bridge a gully."[36] In another cable, on December 17, Churchill added that Damascinos was also "obnoxious" to the Papandreou Cabinet and distrusted and feared by the King. Finally, regarding the suggested disarming of the Mountain Brigade and the Sacred Battalion, "who have fought so well at the side of British and American troops," such a move would not only "seriously weaken" British strength in Athens, but would also lead to their "massacre." Churchill would not let his friend off the hook: "We embarked upon it [British policy in Greece] with your full consent. . . . I have felt it much that you were unable to give a word of explanation for our action, but I understand your difficulties. . . ."[37]

[36] Churchill, vi, 301.   [37] Ibid., 303-4.

While the American government thus persisted in its feeble efforts to modify Britain's policy in Greece so as to patch up existing divisions and avert further bloodshed, Moscow's official attitude toward the entire affair remained one of gloomy disinterest. Throughout the Second Round the Soviet government made no detectable attempt to influence the origins, course, or outcome of the crisis. Without its own correspondents on the scene, *Pravda* confined itself to brief news items, often under the bland heading "The situation in Greece," based on press despatches from London and New York.[38] These were factual and without editorial comment, avoiding the clichés and invective with which Greece was to be pelted in the entire Communist press after 1945. To be sure, there were reports in Athens, often circulated by the KKE, that the Greek Communists had secured Soviet endorsement for a move to seize power by force, but the same sources frequently admitted that Moscow would not promise tangible support.[39] Churchill later wrote that Stalin "adhered strictly and faithfully to our agreement of October, and during all the long weeks of fighting the Communists in the streets of Athens, not one word of reproach came from *Pravda* or *Izvestia*."[40] On January 20, 1945, in the diplomatic talks which paved the way for the Yalta Conference, the Assistant Commissar for Foreign Affairs, Ivan Maiski, told the American Ambassador in Moscow, Averell W. Harriman, that although the British had not handled the Greek situation with their usual finesse, the Soviet Union would remain "completely neutral" in that crisis. Personally Maiski did not believe that Churchill was entirely fair when he sought to depict the EAM/ELAS faction as the devils and the other side as saints. In his view, both

[38] *Pravda*, Dec. 4, 7, 8, 10, 13, 14, 15, 19, 20, 21, 23, 24, 25, 1944.
[39] Kousoulas p. 201.
[40] Churchill, VI, 293. On December 15 Churchill wrote the Prime Minister of Canada that "Although Communists are at the root of the business, Stalin has not so far made any public reflection on our action" (*ibid.*, 305).

sides were at fault and it was unfair to blame the Left because it was opposed to the return of the King and of another Metaxas-type regime which would persecute it as in the past. The Greeks were primitive people, ready to use their knives quickly, and cruel to each other. Moreover, the EAM/ELAS camp had agreed to the appointment of the Damascinos Regent, a fact which indicated that they were not entirely unreasonable. But it was understandable that they would be reluctant to surrender their weapons as long as the other side remained armed, because they would then be helpless against persecution. Maiski concluded his remarks on the Greek problem by repeating that he was speaking his own mind, and that the Soviet government would remain neutral.[41]

A few days later, at Yalta, Stalin inquired rather casually about developments in Greece, but was quick to stress that he had "complete confidence in British policy" in that country. Churchill was thus prompted to thank Stalin "for not having taken too great an interest in Greek affairs."[42] According to the Bohlen minutes of the fifth plenary meeting at the Livadia Palace, on February 8, 1945, the exchange went as follows:

> Marshal Stalin then said . . . he would also like to know what was going on in Greece. He said that he had no intention of criticizing British policy there but he would merely like to know what was going on. The Prime Minister said that Greece would take a great deal of time to explain and he would reserve it for the next meeting. . . . The Prime Minister said that in regard to Greece he was hopeful peace would come on the basis of amnesties except for those who committed crimes against the laws of war. He doubted that a government of all the parties could be established since they hated each other so much.

[41] *Hopkins Papers*, Book x: "Background for Yalta."
[42] Edward R. Stettinius, *Roosevelt and the Russians: the Yalta Conference* (London, 1950), p. 21.

Marshal Stalin said that the Greeks had not become used to discussion and therefore they were cutting each other's throats. The Prime Minister concluded he would be glad to give information on Greece. He said that recently Sir Walter Citrine and five members of the trade unions had gone to Greece and they might have their report. He said that they had had a rather rough time in Greece and they were very much obliged to Marshal Stalin for not having taken too great an interest in Greek affairs. Marshal Stalin repeated that he had no intention of criticizing British actions there or interfering in Greece, but merely would like to know what was going on.[43]

Years later, Nikos Zahariadis, KKE's Secretary General, praising Stalin's contributions to the cause of Communism in Greece, could only cite as evidence a telegram of sympathy sent to the Party by the Soviet leader in May 1945.[44] Zahariadis' often-quoted words that "The existence of the Soviet Union and the People's Democracies in the Balkans and Eastern Europe constituted an extremely favorable, decisive factor for our passing into the Socialist revolution" may shed some light on the wishful thinking of the Greek Communist leadership but it reveals nothing about Soviet policy and actions. Moreover, they pertain to the "Third Round" of 1946-49, and to a quite different set of circum-

[43] Department of State, *Foreign Relations of the United States. Diplomatic Papers. The Conferences at Malta and Yalta, 1945* (Washington, D.C., 1955), pp. 781-82. According to the Matthew Minutes, Stalin had been speaking of the Yugoslavs when he said that they were "cutting each other's throats." When Churchill thanked him for his "help," Stalin replied: "On Greece I only wanted to know for information. We have no intention of intervening there in any way" (*ibid.*, 790-91; also Lord Moran, *Churchill. Taken from the Diaries of Lord Moran. The Struggle for Survival: 1940-1965* [Boston, 1966], p. 250). The published Soviet record of the Yalta Conference makes no mention of this Stalin-Churchill exchange on Greece (*The Tehran, Yalta and Potsdam Conferences-Documents* [Moscow, 1969]).

[44] Nikos Zahariadis, "Greetings (to the XIX Congress of the CPUSSR) from the Communist Party of Greece," *For a Lasting Peace, for a People's Democracy!*, Oct. 24, 1952.

stances.[45] Thus, despite persistent efforts to argue otherwise,[46] the only conclusion that is supported by available evidence as well as by a careful analysis of Moscow's aims during 1944 is that the Soviet Union had nothing to do with the Greek Second Round. At the same time, there can be no question that throughout that period of its turbulent history, the Greek Communist Party was Moscow-oriented, hoping for guidance and assistance from afar. It received precious little of either.

As for the Communist regimes to the north of Greece, still in their infancy, they facilitated the movement of ELAS units across their borders but offered no other assistance.[47] After Tito's expulsion from the Cominform and while re-

[45] Kousoulas, p. 224.

[46] Christoforos A. Naltsas, *To Makedonikon Zitima kai Sovietiki Politiki* (Thessaloniki, 1954), pp. 365-73; Franz Borkenau, *European Communism* (New York, 1953), pp. 430-33; Jan Librach, *The Rise of the Soviet Empire. A Study of Soviet Foreign Policy* (New York, 1964), pp. 183-89. In his argument Librach and others rely heavily on a secret letter from Markos Vafiadis to Nikos Zahariadis, dated February 10, 1948, which contains the following revealing passages: "You are familiar with Comrade Stalin's historic message of December 1944, which induced us to launch the popular uprising which had its well-known and tragic results leading to Varkiza, results due to the fact that when we appealed for help to Moscow, Comrade Stalin forgot all his promises and spoke of his diplomatic commitments. When Germany fell at last, Stalin saw that his hands were free and that he could turn to this corner of the earth called Greece, seeing that she was indispensable to him for the completion of his ambitious plans. . . ." This document, which in any event supports the thesis that there was no Soviet involvement in the Second Round, was reproduced in the *Giornale d'Italia* (May 12, 1948), in the *Greek Bulletin* of the Greek Embassy in London (July 1, 1948), in F. A. Voigt, *The Greek Sedition* (London, 1949), and in the Royal Institute of International Affairs, *Documents on International Affairs, 1947-1948* (London, 1952), the last publication indicating that the letter's authenticity might be in question. Despite the wide attention it has received this letter is, in fact, the work of Greek government propagandists designed to reveal the traitorous actions of EAM/ELAS and was based on rumors and stories collected from captured guerrillas by military interrogators.

[47] Woodhouse, pp. 218-19; Kofos, pp. 119-53.

viewing the events of December 1944, Zahariadis complained that the Yugoslav bands which had been cooperating with ELAS during the German occupation had been withdrawn into Yugoslavia as soon as the fighting had erupted in Athens. As for material aid which they had promised, the Yugoslavs gave "practically nothing."[48] Significantly, according to Tito's biographer, the arrival of British forces in Athens had created "quite a commotion" in Belgrade where it was thought that the British move was "equally aimed against the People's Liberation Movement in Yugoslavia."[49]

In Athens the outburst of December 3 had been followed by a momentary lull, while each side contemplated its next move. As already shown, Papandreou withdrew his resignation and continued to act as head of the government. However, Churchill's abrupt refusal to allow a change in the person of the Prime Minister was indicative of the most profound consequence of the events of December 3-4: real authority in Athens was now vested in the British military, with General Scobie anxious to carry out his orders rigidly and swiftly. There was to be no political activity in the Greek capital until the military situation had been cleared up to the satisfaction of the British Prime Minister, whose current motto was "No peace without victory." There could be no dealings with the "treacherous aggressors" of December 3, unless it was to accept their capitulation. "It is no use doing things like this by halves," Churchill insisted. "The mob violence by which the Communists sought to conquer the city and present themselves to the world as the Government demanded by the Greek people could only be met by firearms. . . ."[50]

Spurred on by Churchill, General Scobie had given ELAS until midnight December 6-7 to withdraw from the Athens-

---

[48] *For a Lasting Peace, for a People's Democracy!* June 30, 1950.
[49] Vladimir Dedijer, *Tito Speaks* (London, 1953), p. 238.
[50] Churchill, VI, 288.

Piraeus area and warned its men against further attacks upon police stations and government buildings. Faced with a short ultimatum the Communist leadership, now openly in command of EAM/ELAS, appeared to hesitate. The arrival of an ELAS brigade from the Peloponnese on December 5 and 6 may have played an important role in the ultimate decision to act. As British fighter planes and armored vehicles kept a close watch on the roads leading to the capital, this 2,000-man force was in fact the only ELAS reinforcement to reach the city and the backbone of the troops which were used in the fighting. Instead of concentrating on the battle for Athens, ELAS launched an attack against EDES positions in Epirus, as though settling old scores with Zervas' men was more important than overthrowing Papandreou. On December 6, and while making every effort to avoid an encounter with British troops, ELAS began to attack government buildings in the center of the capital. Hastily organized and poorly executed, the move failed, at least in part because British sentries were found guarding these buildings. Lacking orders to fire on them, most ELAS men decided against it.[51] Nevertheless, there could be no doubt that the aim of the extreme Left was to finish off the Papandreou "government." Despite serious divisions within the ELAS command, assaults on government installations and hostile organizations—and, eventually, on British units which placed themselves between the two warring factions—would continue in the capital until the second week of January, interspersed with offers to end the shooting and negotiate a settlement.[52] But it was now too late: London was determined to destroy the Communist-dominated Left. Informed of the first peace feelers, Churchill cabled Scobie on December 8:

There is much talk in the Press tonight of a peace offer by ELAS. Naturally we should be glad to have this matter

[51] McNeill, 175-76.
[52] Leeper, p. 117; E.A.M. White Book, pp. 44-55.

settled, but you should make quite sure, so far as your influence goes, that we do not give away for the sake of kindness what has been won or can still be won by our troops. It would seem to me that anything less satisfactory than the terms agreed upon before the revolt took place should not be accepted. Also it is difficult to see how EAM leaders, with their hands wet with Greek and British blood, should resume their places in the Cabinet. This might however be got over. The great thing is to proceed with caution and to consult us upon the terms when they are made. *The clear objective is the defeat of EAM. The ending of the fighting is subsidiary to this.* I am ordering large reinforcements. . . .[53]

With the help of additional troops rushed from Italy— which arrived in the nick of time on December 13—the British were able to stand their ground in the heart of Athens and along the shore, and slowly enlarged the area under their control. Thus, on December 11 Macmillan recorded in his diary:

At present, the British forces (and the Embassy) are besieged and beleaguered in the small central area of Athens. We hold about 5-10 out of 50 square miles of built-up area (Athens and Piraeus). The airfield at Tatoi is lost, and nearly 800 Air Force H.Q. and ground staff cut off in that suburb. Our airfield at Kalamaki is very insecure and the communications between it and the main body in Athens all under fire. We do *not* hold a port at all. . . . We are defending on the beaches at Phaleron Bay, but we have no real communication between the airfield and the beaches or between Athens and the beaches. In other words, we have no secure base anywhere from which to operate. . . .[54]

[53] Churchill, vi, 291. Emphasis mine. On December 11 Papandreou advised the King that "governmental cooperation with the Communist Party must now be definitely precluded" (Papandreou, p. 233).
[54] Macmillan, 505.

On the same day Field Marshal Alexander, hastily sent to Athens to study the military problems confronting Scobie, explained the situation to Ambassador Leeper in equally bleak terms:

> You are in a grave situation. Your seaport is cut off, your airport can only be reached by tank or armoured car, you are outnumbered, your dumps are surrounded and you have three days' ammunition. I can put that right in time, but it may take a fortnight. It will need two fighting divisions to come from Italy. The heavy stuff will have to be landed on the open beaches of Phaleron and December is not the best month for that. . . .[55]

But whereas the military situation would gradually improve, the political impasse appeared complete. "The political problem in Athens," lamented Macmillan on December 9, "is probably insoluble. . . ."[56] Since the policy of "No peace without victory" appeared to have little chance of success, what was needed was a dramatic political move which would establish a new and viable basis for compromise between the sharply polarized Greek factions. Such a compromise would reopen the channels of peaceful and positive competition for political influence, making fighting as unnecessary as it was repugnant to all. The British Ambassador in Athens had in mind just such a basis for compromise when, on December 10, he pressed his government for the immediate appointment of Damascinos Regent.[57]

[55] Leeper, pp. 114-15.   [56] Macmillan, p. 504.

[57] Leeper, p. 120; Churchill, vi, 298. The idea for a regency under the Archbishop was first revived by Dimitrios Maximos on December 3, in a talk with MacVeagh. The American Ambassador sent Maximos to Leeper with an appropriate introduction and the British Ambassador expressed great interest in the proposal. A month earlier (November 5) Leeper had confided to MacVeagh that the Papandreou government had "just let the regency question go by default, for lack of interest and because of the pressure of other affairs." According to Leeper, the King behaved as though he were simply on a voyage to

As Leeper was careful to point out, the suggestion that the Greek political situation be defused by openly and convincingly shelving the constitutional issue until passions had subsided was not new. And from the start, as early as 1943, such a suggestion had been linked with the person of the Archbishop of Athens, the only Greek who commanded the respect of enough of his compatriots. However, thus far King George had firmly opposed such an arrangement and in this he had been supported by Churchill who believed that the creation of a regency would benefit the Left and would diminish the King's chances of ever returning to his throne.

There is little doubt that in resisting pressures to endorse the regency idea Churchill had also been motivated by his strong antipathy for and suspicion of Damascinos. It has already been shown that when Roosevelt expressed support for the regency Churchill replied that he knew nothing about Damascinos, "except that . . . he might stop a gap or bridge a gully." Three days later, on December 17, Churchill wrote the President that "There is suspicion that the Archbishop is ambitious of obtaining chief political power, and that, supported by EAM, he will use it ruthlessly against existing Ministers. . . ."[58] On the same day he confided to Field Marshal Alexander in Italy that he had "heard mixed accounts of the Archbishop, who is said to be very much in touch with EAM and to have keen personal ambitions. . . ."[59] And again, on December 19: "The Cabinet feel it better to let the military operations to clear Athens and Attica run a while rather than embark all our fortunes on the character of the Archbishop. Have you looked up his full rec-

London which in no way affected his royal authority (MacVeagh Diary, entry dated Nov. 5, 1944). For a glimpse of the towering figure of Damascinos in occupied Athens see Jeanne Tsatsos, *The Sword's Fierce Edge* (Nashville, 1969).

[58] Churchill, vi, 303.   [59] *Ibid.*, 308.

ord . . . ?"[60] With his more intimate advisers Churchill was much more outspoken on the subject. Eden recorded on December 21; "Very difficult Cabinet on Greece. W. has his knife into the Archbishop and is convinced that he is both a quisling and a Communist. In fact, as Alec [Cadogan] puts it neatly, he has taken the place of de Gaulle. . . ." And again: "But W. clung to his opposition to Regency of Archbishop, or 'dictatorship,' as he insists on calling it."[61]

The British Prime Minister was destined to undergo a complete change of heart, displaying rare statesmanship and the ability to accept the inescapable with alacrity and grace. Admittedly not a man of moderation, he liked or disliked with equal enthusiasm and passion. Three days after the "difficult" Cabinet meeting on Greece, he left for Athens to see for himself, "and especially make the acquaintance of the Archbishop around whom so much was turning. . . ."[62] On December 26 he reported from the Greek capital that the prelate had "generally . . . impressed me with a good deal of confidence. He is a magnificent figure. . . ."[63] And on the 29th he wrote to the President: "I have seen the Archbishop several times, and he made a very good impression on me by the sense of power and decision which he conveyed as well as by his shrewd political judgements." Still, Churchill could not resist the luxury of minor doubts regarding his newly discovered friend. To Roosevelt he added: "You will not expect me to speak here of his *spiritual* qualities, for I really have not had sufficient opportunity to measure these. . . ."[64] For his part Eden speculated that Damascinos' bitter denunciation of the Communists for their atrocities during the fighting was one important factor in Churchill's sudden admiration for the Greek prelate.[65]

---

[60] *Ibid.*, 309, To Churchill's amazement, Damascinos' "record" included a brief career as a professional wrestler, before entering the priesthood!

[61] Eden, III, 578-79.

[62] Churchill, VI, 311.

[63] *Ibid.*, 314.

[64] *Ibid.*, 320. Emphasis mine.

[65] Eden, III, 580.

Ambassador Leeper's recommendation of December 10 for the early establishment of a regency under Damascinos received the immediate and strong support of Macmillan and Alexander, who sent a joint telegram to London advising its acceptance.[66] Still, opinions on this matter reaching London were far from uniform. Field Marshal Smuts, the self-appointed patron of the Greek monarchy, urged Churchill on December 14 to disregard Leeper's proposal, "as it may later be used as an argument against you for undue interference in the affairs of Greece." The South African continued to believe that King George "should return to discharge his proper constitutional functions" as soon as the Communists had been defeated.[67] To further complicate matters, Macmillan discovered to his dismay that Papandreou would not authorize a telegraphic message to the King recommending acceptance of the regency. The Greek politician now asserted that the entire political world of Greece opposed the idea because it would be viewed as a sign of weakness before Communist pressures, and insisted that "Communism must be absolutely crushed."[68] On December 15 Macmillan, Leeper and Scobie once again urged Papandreou to advise the King to accept a regency. They argued that the prevailing crisis necessitated a head of state other than the King, that the American government strongly favored the Archbishop's appointment, and that such a move would also improve the position of the British government vis-à-vis its critics at home and elsewhere. The Greek Prime Minister now expressed himself in agreement with the proposal, but suggested that the regency should consist of three persons including the Archbishop. Papandreou was obviously offering himself as a candidate for one of the three seats on the regency council. Other political

---

[66] Macmillan, p. 506, 514.   [67] Churchill, vi, 302.

[68] Macmillan, p. 509. Two other Greek politicians present at this meeting, and who shared Papandreou's views, were thought by Macmillan to be Populists or royalists.

figures in Athens voiced sharply conflicting opinions on the entire matter and took it upon themselves to communicate with the King directly in the hope of influencing his decision.[69] Meanwhile the fighting continued. Reporting on this confusion MacVeagh observed on December 16 that "both Leeper and Macmillan are much alarmed as well as disgusted at this recrudescence of political maneuvering at this critical time and believe—as I feel correctly—that passions can now be calmed only by the appointment of a single Chief of State enjoying the confidence of the people and by an act which will completely and clearly remove the King question from the present picture. They have, therefore, telegraphed Churchill that he should at all costs and today, if possible, persuade the King to appoint the Archbishop as sole Regent."[70]

Churchill, however, preferred to temporize. Instructed to produce from Athens a recommendation for the King that would be acceptable not only to the monarch but to the principal non-Communist factions the hapless Macmillan continued his round-robin of talks with Papandreou, Sofoulis, Kanellopoulos, Plastiras, Damascinos, and others. He was particularly anxious to persuade the Archbishop not to submit to various restrictions and conditions that were being pressed upon him from all sides.[71] Also, alarmed that the Greek government now expected the British troops to sweep the Communists out of every corner of the country, he dispatched General Scobie to warn Papandreou and his colleagues that the British "were *not* (repeat *not*) prepared to become the tool of a Right-wing reaction throughout

[69] *Ibid.*, pp. 511-12.   [70] *FR* (1944), 158.

[71] One such condition was that no EAM follower, no matter how inactive in the current crisis, should ever be allowed to enter civil service or the armed forces. Macmillan commented: "I told him [Damascinos] that the Government seemed to regard him not merely as a prelate of the Church, but as St. Peter himself. He replied, 'No, it is not Heaven that they want, it is the earth'" (Macmillan, p. 513).

Greece." His own mission was to assist in the achievement of a "settlement of conciliation and we would not allow ourselves to be dragged into a long war from one end of Greece to the other to exterminate the Communist Party." As Papandreou continued to speak of a complete victory over the Communists Macmillan sullenly recorded in his diary that the Greek Premier "may be right from his point of view and perhaps from the long-term view of Europe. But I don't think he has any idea of our military difficulties or of the dangers on his northern frontier. We don't wish to start the Third World War against Russia until we have finished the Second World War against Germany—and certainly not to please M. Papandreou. . . ."[72] Indeed, while doing his best to carry out Churchill's orders, Macmillan was troubled by what he saw in Greece. "I think," he wrote to Eden on December 21, "it is very easy to jump to false conclusions about Greek opinion. I am not quite certain that there is so much opposition to EAM/ELAS as many suppose. It is always difficult to tell political opinion, even in one's own country. . . . I am certain that there is a large amount of sympathy with EAM in Greece, that a moderate, reasonable, progressive policy could detach the vague, radical element from the hard, Communist core. The policy [which some] would like to follow will have the result of solidifying, not liquefying, EAM/ELAS forces."[73] Furthermore, according to an American source, Macmillan telegraphed Churchill that the Greek King "does not realize that Greece is a mass of violent internal hatred and that the country is on the brink of a bloody civil war. . . . King George ought to be told that this was his last chance to try to save the monarchy" by accepting the regency proposal; "otherwise any hope of doing so would be gone forever." Moreover, "if this matter should not be settled," Macmillan warned his chief, "there is great danger of the British Government and the

---

[72] *Ibid.*, p. 515.   [73] *Ibid.*, p. 518.

British people being accused of connivance with King George's selfish policy. . . ."[74]

The loud disagreement in Athens on the merits of the regency and on its possible composition, together with the mood in government circles there which Macmillan saw as "dangerous optimism," were bound to influence the course of events in London. When, on December 12, Churchill and Eden presented the regency proposal to King George, he rejected it categorically, arguing that "his people . . . would take the appointment of a Regent to mean that he was abandoning his cause and his duties." The scene was repeated two days later, and again on the 16th. According to Eden's account, the King continued to insist that "while he would feel bound to follow his Government's advice, the recommendations he was receiving from M. Papandreou and the other politicians were by no means all in favour of a regency."[75] Furthermore, the Foreign Secretary reported to Macmillan that not only was the King being "very obstinate," but Churchill was "unwilling to press him unduly."[76] On Churchill's recommendation the Cabinet decided to allow a few days to elapse "before pressing the King again."[77]

Explaining his own views to Field Marshal Alexander, who on December 15 had once more warned that the military situation in Greece called for a quick political settlement, Churchill reflected that "We have not yet decided whether or in what way to overcome the King's resistance. If this cannot be overcome there will be no constitutional foundation other than an act of violence, to which we must become parties." To compel him to act contrary to the advice of the Papandreou government would be tantamount to "punishing the King for obeying his constitutional oath and [we would] be ourselves setting up a dictator." Accordingly, Churchill had decided to "await further developments of the military situation before taking final and fate-

[74] FR (1944), 156-57.　　[75] Eden, III, 577.
[76] Macmillan, p. 521.　　[77] Eden, III, 577.

ful decisions." Churchill was still determined to obtain a military victory. To Alexander he added: "Personally I feel that our military predominance should be plainly established before we make terms, and in any case I should not like to make terms on grounds of weakness rather than of strength. Of course if you tell me it is impossible for us to be in control of Attica within a reasonable time the situation presents difficulties, but not such as should daunt us after all the others we have overcome. . . ."[78]

However impressive Churchill's concern for the letter of the Greek constitution (suspended in 1936 by the Metaxas regime with the King's consent), his actions fail to lend support to his words in this matter. While claiming that it would be improper to force the King to disregard Papandreou's advice on the question of the regency, he would not use his influence with the Greek government, whose dependence on British support was by now total, to accept a regency under Damascinos, which would have demolished the King's "constitutional" argument. On the contrary, on December 19 Churchill strongly reprimanded Macmillan in Athens "for having pressed [in favor of] the regency with arguments about the political position at home and Anglo-American relations instead of confining [himself] to purely Greek considerations."[79] For the same reason he was equally annoyed with Ambassador Leeper and referred to them both as his two "fuzzy wuzzies" in Athens.[80] Clearly the British Prime Minister continued to hope that the improvement of the military situation in the Greek capital and the defeat of the Left would render the regency an unnecessary measure and would pave the way for the King's return. When, on December 22, Churchill and Eden saw the Greek monarch once more, the Prime Minister not only communicated to him his support and sympathy, but reminded him that "Charles I had lost his head by fighting but had per-

---

[78] Churchill, vi, 308-9. [79] Macmillan, p. 515.
[80] Eden, iii, 579.

petuated crown and Church. . . ."[81] Although the particular historical example could not have been very heartening, it is hardly surprising that King George remained adamant in his rejection of a regency, despite definite indications that Prime Minister Papandreou was now beginning to see the merits of the proposal.[82]

This diplomatic logjam was to be broken by the restrained but clear warning of Field Marshal Alexander that Churchill and King George must not count on a military victory in Athens to rescue them from the suggested regency. As already quoted, on December 19 Churchill had informed Alexander that "the Cabinet feel it better to let the military operations to clear Athens and Attica run for a while rather than embark all our fortunes on the character of the Archbishop. . . ." Taking the by-now familiar line Churchill added: "it is a hard thing to ask me to throw over a constitutional king acting on the true advice of his Ministers, apart from British pressure, in order to install a dictator [Damascinos] who may very likely become the champion of the extreme Left. We are waiting here till the scene clears a little more, after which we shall give all the necessary directions."[83] Alexander's prompt reply (on December 21) made it painfully apparent that Churchill's optimism was simply not supported by the facts. ". . . I am most concerned," he cabled the Prime Minister, "that you should know exactly what the true situation is and what we can do and cannot do. This is my duty. . . ." Stressing that

[81] *Ibid.*

[82] *Ibid.* On December 22 Churchill also wrote to Field Marshal Smuts that the return of the Greek King would not by itself constitute a firm basis for British policies. "We must at all costs avoid giving the impression of forcing him on them by our bayonets." Complaining that Damascinos' regency was being promoted by "all Leftist forces and our people on the spot . . ." he added: "But if the powers of evil prevail in Greece, as is quite likely, we must be prepared for a quazi-Bolshevised Russian-led Balkans peninsula, and this may spread to Italy and Hungary . . ." (Churchill, vi, 311).

[83] *Ibid.*, 309.

available troop strength would permit the defeat of ELAS only in the Athens-Piraeus area—thus leaving most of the country in enemy hands—he emphasized that "the Greek problem cannot be solved by military measures. The answer must be found in the political field." Alexander would allow no room for doubt—or hope—in his chief's mind: "Finally, I think you know that you can always rely on me to do everything in my power to carry out your wishes, but I earnestly hope that you will be able to find a political solution to the Greek problem, as I am convinced that further military action after we have cleared the Athens-Piraeus area is beyond our present strength."[84]

Alexander's powerful statement, which represented the views of the British diplomatic and military community in Athens, was reinforced by Macmillan's personal letter to the Foreign Secretary, written on the same day (December 21):

> Both Alex. and I agree that there is no (repeat no) military solution of the Greek problem. It can only be solved by a political agreement. That is why we have battled so long and by so many means for the Archiepiscopal regency. I know the Prime Minister thought that I was over-anxious for this, but I assure you that Rex Leeper and I felt, and still feel, that it was the only way to get the thing loosened up at all. The King is obstinate and I gather now falls back on constitutional niceties. All I can say is, "Constitution my foot." He did not care two hoots about the Constitution when he made Metaxas dictator. As for the politicians . . . they beat anything I have yet seen in the Mediterranean. . . .[85]

[84] *Ibid.*, 310.
[85] Macmillan, p. 517. According to American diplomatic sources Macmillan telegraphed Churchill that "if the civil war continues much longer the Greeks may find it very difficult to win back Macedonia which is the 'happy hunting grounds' of various kinds of Slav insurgents whose infiltrations the British are unable to control and

Eden, who needed no prodding on this matter, presented his own views to Churchill on December 23, this time in writing:

It is hardly conceivable that Papandreou can continue in office after EAM have accepted Scobie's terms and preside over a broad-based Cabinet including EAM. We desire such a Cabinet for the post-armistice period and a new Prime Minister will presumably have to be found to head it. The King's idea appears to be that he could form such a new Government from London by telegraph. This hardly seems possible. Much negotiation is likely to be required on the spot and for this a trusted Regent could be of great service. If there is no Regent it looks as though our representative will have to do the job. I cannot see Papandreou organizing the Government that is to succeed him.

Eden reminded his chief that the issue of the King's return had been at the heart of the Greek crisis:

The principal EAM weapon throughout this business has been to pretend that it was our intention to impose the King upon his people. There is no doubt that despite all our protestations this has been pretty widely believed. The appointment of a Regent together with a statement by the King . . . to the effect that he will not return until after a plebiscite would, I believe, go far to remove this fear and to ease the tension when the armistice comes. If, on the other hand, the King continues to attempt to carry out Cabinet-making from here I fear that suspicion of him and his motives would be intensified and our difficulties correspondingly increased.[86]

---

which the Kremlin shows no apparent desire to control . . ." (*FR* [1944], 167).

[86] Eden, III, 579-80.

Churchill's response to these mounting and irrefutable arguments was, as Eden put it, "to reconnoitre for himself." On Christmas Eve, dragging along his Foreign Secretary and his personal physician, Lord Moran, he left for Athens.

In suddenly deciding on such an extraordinary move, Churchill was also mindful of increasing irritation with his Greek policy on the other side of the Atlantic, a development which he could ill afford. Complaining to a confidant that he was "powerless" to stop the spreading of Communism across eastern Europe, he cited "great stresses and quarrelling with America" as the principal reason for his frustration.[87] Warned by Hopkins about a loudly hostile public opinion in the United States over developments in Greece, "which throw into the public gaze our several difficulties," Churchill expressed himself "distressed and puzzled" over this remark and invited Hopkins' advice and comments "on any points on which you think we, or I personally, have been in error. . . ."[88] Despite such protestations, however, there was no mistaking the most pressing of these "difficulties." On the same day (December 17) Churchill telegraphed Roosevelt that neither the King nor Papandreou would accept Damascinos' regency. Therefore he proposed to await the outcome of the military operations scheduled for the next several days. He argued again that his Greek policy had been decided upon with the President's consent, and expressed disappointment that no public endorsement had been forthcoming from Washington.[89] Meanwhile, at the ambassadorial level, Leeper in Athens had solicited the support of his American colleague in having Damascinos' regency approved, as such a move would represent "the only reasonable hope of saving the Anglo-American (sic) position" in Greece. This despite the fact that Churchill himself was opposing the proposal! MacVeagh reported that the effort was "as well conceived as

[87] Churchill, vi, 311. [88] *Ibid.*, 302-3. [89] *Ibid.*, 303-4.

anything could be under the present circumstances in which compromise and moderation appear essential though the amnesty regarding which ELAS is reported to be particularly anxious and the reacceptance of the Communist Party into the Government are bound to be very unpopular with the extreme Right. . . ." To this observation Secretary Stettinius replied, on December 16, that the suggested solution was "the most promising proposal yet advanced and closely parallels Department's ideas already communicated to the British." MacVeagh was commended for his "correct reaffirmation of the Department's views," despite the serious disruption of communications between the Embassy and Washington, caused by the fighting in Athens. And on December 20, reporting that now only the Populist Party opposed Damascinos' regency, MacVeagh commented: "This group and the King's stubborn preference for the interests of the dynasty over all other considerations in this country seem threatening now to extend indefinitely the present deplorable struggle."[90]

Aware of the complete lack of support for his position in American government circles and probably recalling Roosevelt's earlier sympathetic reaction to his plight, King George attempted once again to enlist the President's help in resisting pressures to consent to a regency. In a letter which reached the White House on December 19 he appealed for assistance in "dispelling the misunderstanding which I find existing in the United States, to the detriment of the national policy which I am endeavoring, in the midst of infinite difficulties, to put into operation in Greece." Arguing that since the guerrilla bands in Greece had been armed by the allies, their suppression now was an allied responsibility, he voiced his "deepest disappointment when I hear of the charge here and in the United States that both I and the British Government are seeking to impose a definite form of government in Greece." Making no mention of

[90] *FR* (1944), 155-58, 165.

the regency proposal, King George reiterated his intention to issue "whatever assurance or guaranty may be asked for the ascertainment of the genuine will of the Greek people," and his readiness to "make any personal sacrifice, provided it is for the benefit of my people and is freely asked by them." Moreover, he claimed that all the major political parties supported him on this stand, and even the staunch anti-monarchist Sofoulis had urged him to exercise his "constitutional prerogatives." Accordingly, the monarch declared, "I intend, on the termination of the present crisis, to form an all-party government, for a plebiscite and free elections."[91]

This time the Greek King received little solace from the American leader. "We are not directly involved in this matter," the President replied on December 28, "and are anxious not to intrude ourselves into the internal affairs of Greece or of any other of our liberated allies." However, while welcoming assurances that the people of Greece would be given full opportunity to decide the constitutional question, Roosevelt noted that, according to his own information, "there is still widespread confusion on this issue within the country . . . which must be disposed of if unity and order are to be restored." He urged King George to undertake "courageous and patriotic action" by giving "favorable consideration to the recommendations . . . for the naming of the Archbishop as Regent. . . ."[92] Thus, this time the White House and the Department of State appeared to speak with one voice on the Greek problem. In fact, the President's letter had been drafted by the Department.[93]

[91] *Ibid.*, 163-64.   [92] *Ibid.*, 177.

[93] Memorandum of the Secretary of State to the President, dated December 21, 1944. *Roosevelt Papers*, psf, 1941-44, "Greece." Also, memorandum entitled "The Situation in Greece," dated Dec. 22, 1944 in *DSR*, 868.00/12-2644. This document indicates that in American diplomatic circles the British decision to keep Papandreou in office after the events of December 3 (for which the Athens police is blamed), and the presence in Greece of totally inadequate British

Before signing it the President had been advised of Churchill's excursion to Athens, and of his pledge that "The King does not go back until a plebiscite in his favour has been taken."[94]

Churchill's surprise descent upon Athens—to which he drove from Piraeus carrying a pistol!—provided the catalyst needed for a determined effort by all concerned to find a workable compromise. Undoubtedly his personal intercession and fervent appeal to all Greeks to end the fighting also made it easier for the extreme Left to accept defeat, particularly since the Prime Minister's arrival was soon followed by stepped-up British military action. After talks with his own advisers and with Papandreou and Damascinos,[95] it was agreed that a meeting of all political factions would be convened immediately to seek an end to the shooting and establish the foundations for a new government. The Archbishop would personally preside over this assembly and guide its deliberations.

This stormy and at first unproductive conference met during December 26-28. Its opening session was attended not only by Churchill, Eden, Macmillan, Alexander, and Leeper, but by the American and French ambassadors, and Colonel Popov (in full uniform) representing the allied

---

forces were viewed as the principal factors precipitating if not actually producing the ensuing revolt.

[94] *FR* (1944), 170.

[95] The sailors of the cruiser *Ajax*, onboard which Churchill received the Greek dignitaries, were in the midst of a wild Christmas-time masquerade party when Damascinos, wearing his colorful priestly robes, arrived to see the Prime Minister. Before the embarrassed captain could rescue his visitor the sailors, unaware of his identity, staged a frenzied dance all about him (Churchill, vi, 312-13)! According to Churchill's physician and confidant, the Prime Minister recalled after this meeting that Damascinos had expressed the hope that "the ancient claims of Greece to Constantinople might be remembered." Churchill continued: "I retorted: 'Dismiss those dreams from your mind.'" When Randolph Churchill, who was also present, inquired about the effect on the Archbishop of such a reply, his father chuckled: "He dismissed them" (Moran, p. 257).

governments.[96] Subsequently, through separate talks with the various groups and despite the prevailing bitterness and confusion, Damascinos succeeded in working out the broad outlines of a formula which he presented to Churchill on December 27. Its key component was that the Archbishop would become Regent at the earliest possible moment, and that the British Prime Minister would undertake to obtain the King's unqualified and prompt consent to this measure. A new government would then be formed which would exclude the Communists as well as the discredited Papandreou. Since ELAS would not agree to an immediate and formal truce but continued to insist on what were deemed unacceptable political demands, the fighting in Athens would be pursued with greater vigor, but the British would not assume any military responsibilities outside the Attica region. Their troops, however, would remain in Greece until a national army had been organized and trained.

Churchill gave his full endorsement to this arrangement and telegraphed the President that he was returning to London to put the "strongest pressure" on the King to appoint Damascinos Regent without further delay. He hoped that Roosevelt might do the same through a personal letter to the Greek monarch. Recalling his previous argument that the King must not be made to disregard his own Prime Minister's advice on the matter, Churchill was careful to inform

[96] For details on this conference see Churchill, vi, 315-25; Eden, iii, 580-82; Macmillan, pp. 522-26; Leeper, pp. 123-28; *E.A.M. White Book*, pp. 69-73. Popov had been reluctant to attend until he received permission from his superior in Belgrade (*DSR*, 868.00/12-2844; also Eden, iii, 581). Churchill told the assembled Greek leaders that British intervention in Athens had the support of Marshal Stalin and implied that Roosevelt had also endorsed it (Macmillan, p. 523). Following his speech to the participants he speculated for the benefit of the press that if the Greeks failed to reach agreement, their country might have to be placed under a temporary international trust. The allies could not afford, he asserted, to see whole nations drift into anarchy (*DSR*, 868.00/12-2844). For Papandreou's lengthy remarks at the conference see Papandreou, pp. 257-63.

the President that King George would be told "to accept advice of his Prime Minister, M. Papandreou, who changed his mind about three times a day but has now promised to send a telegram in his own words."[97] Churchill also mentioned that MacVeagh, with whom he had had several good talks, was also "convinced that a Regency under the Archbishop is the only course open at the moment." According to his own report on this matter, MacVeagh reminded the British leader of his suggestion for an international commission as a possible vehicle for settling the apparently insoluble political crisis in Greece. Churchill replied that he had been thinking along the same lines . . .[98] When the American Ambassador inquired if he should communicate to the President any special message from Churchill, the reply suggested that, at least for the moment, the Prime Minister had had enough of the Greek imbroglio:

> Tell him that I hope he can help us in some way. We want nothing from Greece. We don't want her airfields or her harbors—only a fair share of her trade. We don't want her islands. We've got Cyprus anyhow. We came in here by agreement with our Allies to chase the Germans out and then found that we had to fight to keep the people here in Athens from being massacred. Now if we can do that properly—and we will—all we want is to get out of this damned place. . . ."[99]

A few days later, receiving a copy of the President's letter of December 28 to the Greek King, Churchill thanked him for the timely support and added that in the event that the King refused to give in, "His Majesty's Government will advise the Archbishop to assume the office of Regent and assure him that we will recognize him and the Government he forms as the Government of Greece."[100]

On the evening of December 29 Churchill and Eden saw

[97] Churchill, vi, 319-21.   [98] DSR, 868.00/12-2844.
[99] FR (1944), 173.   [100] Churchill, vi, 321.

King George in London and presented to him the formula which had resulted from their visit to Athens. At first the King objected to the term "Regent" and to the proposed declaration that he would not return until a plebiscite had decided the issue. This time, however, the Prime Minister was "very firm and steady." Finally, at 4:30 in the morning, their meeting ended with the King, exhausted and nervous, accepting the Regency of Archbishop Damascinos.[101] The following day (December 30) the monarch issued the long-awaited statement:

> We, George II, King of the Hellenes, having deeply considered the terrible situation into which our well-loved people have fallen through circumstances alike unprecedented and uncontrollable, and being ourselves resolved not to return to Greece unless summoned by a free and fair expression of the national will, and having full confidence in your loyalty and devotion, do now by this declaration appoint you, Archbishop Damascinos, to be our Regent during this period of emergency; and we accordingly authorize and require you to take all steps necessary to restore order and tranquillity throughout our kingdom. We further declare our desire that there should be ascertained, by process of democratic government, the freely expressed wishes of the Greek people as soon as these storms have passed, and thus abridge the miseries of our beloved country, by which our heart is rent.[102]

"Greece's troubles were by no means over," commented a much-relieved Eden, "but at the least the Greek people would now have a chance to choose their destiny without fear. . . ."[103] For his part, Macmillan, whom the crisis had

---

[101] *Ibid.*; also Eden, III, 582.

[102] Churchill, VI, 322. "The Greek King," Churchill telegraphed Roosevelt, "behaved like a gentleman and with the utmost dignity . . ." (*ibid.*, 323).

[103] Eden, III, 582.

placed under severe strain, was much more anxious to affix blame. "I feel," he recorded on January 11, "that—in addition . . . to the Communist plotters of KKE—the King of the Hellenes is the real villain of the piece." He explained:

> Far back at Cairo in the winter of 1943 he twisted and turned. Had he written a clear letter (and not an equivocal one) at that time, saying that he would not return until called by a vote of the people, this powerful weapon of anti-monarchical propaganda would not have been available to the extremists. It must be remembered that Greece has always been about evenly divided between monarchists and republicans. The King has been head of a party . . . not of the State. The Venizelist tradition is similarly republican—and pro-British. But the tragic side of this division is that it disunites the bourgeois parties instead of letting them come together in opposition to Marxism and revolution. . . . The issue of the second half of the twentieth century will not be monarchism v. republicanism but a liberal and democratic way of life versus the "proletarian dictatorship of the Left" and the police State. . . . Even after Alex. and I got to Athens on 11 December, had the King immediately accepted our joint recommendation, instead of wasting three precious (weeks) in futile bargaining and intriguing, I think that the Archbishop might have stopped the fighting at that early stage. At least he would have, by his mere existence as Regent, prevented so large a rally of EAM/ELAS supporters to the extreme leadership of Siantos and the Communist Party. . . .[104]

Having formally received his mandate, Damascinos appealed for unity and the immediate cessation of the fighting. On January 4, after some hesitation, former General Nikolaos Plastiras, a man of undisputed republican convictions and integrity, assumed the office of Prime Minister and pro-

[104] Macmillan, pp. 532-33.

ceeded to form a government of moderates. MacVeagh cabled from Athens:

> With the King removed from immediate picture and with the Archbishop and Plastiras at the head of affairs some practical proof will have been supplied in addition to Churchill's repeated verbal assurances that no danger of a forced return of royalty and possible reestablishment of a Fascist dictatorship menaces the Greek people and it will then remain to be seen whether Republican Greece will (1) be satisfied that a continuance of hostilities can be of advantage only to the Communists and (2) can express such satisfaction, this last depending on how far the Communist leadership of the revolt has been able to make a genuine Red Army out of ELAS.

The American diplomat appeared satisfied with Damascinos' expectations that "Republican Greeks hitherto fighting on the insurgent side for Greek liberty and independence will gradually gravitate to the Government leaving only the relatively few Communists supposed to exist in Greece to get here with such irresponsible banditti as have been inevitably produced by the times to carry on the struggle for the breakdown of the country's social and economic life."[105]

There now appeared definite signs that the ELAS command had had enough fighting and was anxious to come to terms with the British. Indeed, if after the events of December 3 the EAM leaders had entertained serious hopes of achieving success through military superiority, they soon thought otherwise. By December 10, and before the worst of the fighting, they were already publicly urging ELAS to "hang on for a little longer, as negotiations are in progress and an Anglo-American-Russian Commission is to investigate the problem."[106] On the following day, *Rizospastis* pro-

[105] Department of State, *Foreign Relations of the United States. Diplomatic Papers.* 1945, VIII: *The Near East and Africa* (Washington, D.C., 1969), 98-99.
[106] Leeper, p. 117.

claimed editorially that "All humanity is on our side!" but reported from London that an allied military mission to Greece might be established *after* the suppression of the uprising in Athens. According to the same organ, a meeting at the Foreign Office had been attended by the American and Soviet Ambassadors, the latter pointedly declaring that he had come at the urging of his American colleague. The Soviet diplomat further claimed that his government had no firsthand information concerning events in Athens and conveyed Molotov's "personal wish" that, "regardless of the reasons which had precipitated the intervention of British troops, the internal situation in Greece might be restored to normal as quickly as possible."[107] This was hardly heady news for the men of ELAS fighting in the streets of Athens. On December 12 EAM again inquired about General Scobie's terms for an immediate truce.

From the outset the British authorities had demanded that ELAS withdraw from all of Attica, and that its supporters in the Athens-Piraeus area surrender their weapons. EAM's first response was to temporize. In its reply of December 16 it agreed to evacuate Athens and Piraeus, on condition that the Mountain Brigade and the Sacred Battalion also be withdrawn, the gendarmerie disarmed and disbanded, and the British troops confined to tasks envisaged by the Caserta Agreement so as not to interfere in the country's internal affairs. It also demanded that a new government of national unity be formed as soon as possible.[108] As London would not accept such terms but insisted on a military settlement favorable to the government, General Scobie prepared to force ELAS out of the capital.[109] A new

[107] *Rizospastis*, Dec. 11, 1944. On December 30 the Greek Ambassador in Moscow was advised that the Soviet government was appointing an ambassador to Athens (Kousoulas, p. 214).

[108] *Rizospastis*, Dec. 16, 1944.

[109] Leeper explains the rejection of these terms as follows: "Their acceptance would have meant that ELAS kept their forces intact outside Athens, that the Greek Brigade were sent away out of reach, that British troops remained neutral, and that a new Government was formed, with EAM participating in it, at the mercy of the only

wave of fighting ensued. A few days later a new ELAS peace feeler indicated that it was willing to withdraw from Athens and Piraeus, and to disarm its supporters there, but demanded that the new government be formed before the truce had become effective.[110] Again these demands were rejected and the Left was told that there would be no negotiations over political matters until ELAS had submitted to a truce. And so the shooting continued. Following the conference of December 26-28, ELAS addressed a note to the British Prime Minister himself, asserting that it had complied with Scobie's terms and asking that all operations against it cease.[111] With Churchill already back in London the reply came from Scobie who, referring to the political issues still being raised by the EAM leadership, pointed out that these matters were for the Greek government to decide. Moreover, exasperated by what Scobie and Leeper saw as devious tactics, the two recommended that the truce terms under discussion be withdrawn altogether and an ultimatum delivered to ELAS, threatening it with complete destruction. This drastic move was vetoed by Macmillan, with Eden's approval.[112]

Thus the fighting went on, with an occasional lull as new

---

armed force in the neighborhood, *viz.* ELAS" (Leeper, p. 118). A proclamation of the EAM Central Committee, referring to its meeting of December 14, presented the following terms: (1) strict observance of the Caserta Agreement regarding the noninterference of allied authorities in the country's domestic affairs, so that the solution of the current crisis could be an exclusively Greek matter; (2) formation of a regency; (3) formation of a democratic government of genuine national unity, guaranteeing popular liberties and normal political development through an early plebiscite on the issue of the monarchy and elections for a constituent assembly; (4) demobilization of all volunteer forces and establishment of a national army on the basis of regular conscription, staffed by officers to be screened by the competent military authorities; (5) faithful and honest enforcement of previous agreements with regard to the punishment of collaborators, purging of the security forces and civil service (*Rizospastis*, Dec. 16, 1944).

[110] Leeper, p. 118; *Rizospastis*, Dec. 23, 1944.
[111] Churchill, VI, 323; Leeper, p. 127.
[112] Macmillan, p. 528.

terms were put forth by the Left. However, a new British offensive on January 3 revealed to the Communists the hopelessness of their position. The ELAS command decided that further fighting was no longer possible. During January 5-6 it retreated from the Athens-Piraeus region but not before it had carried out mass executions in areas under its control and taken perhaps as many as 30,000 civilian hostages from Attica alone.[113] These atrocities, which did much to fortify the country's lasting hatred for the entire Communist movement, threatened to prolong the crisis, particularly since ELAS would not agree to surrender its hostages. Indeed, almost 4,000 of these victims of ELAS brutality were destined to die in the hands of their captors. The lingering passions stirred up by such outrages, and the desire for revenge they often inspired, were to serve as powerful contributing forces for the "Third Round" less than two years later.

On January 10 two high-level representatives of EAM accompanied by ELAS officers arrived at General Scobie's headquarters empowered to negotiate and sign a truce. This was done on the following day and the agreement became effective at 1:00 A.M. January 15. Despite the strong protests of both Damascinos and the new Prime Minister, and misinterpreting a cable from London, Scobie decided not to insist that the civilian hostages be released as a precondition for the truce, fearing that the Communists would fight on rather than comply.[114] The embittered Damascinos finally gave in on this point. "Great Britain has done so much for Greece," he told Ambassador Leeper, "that I accept the terms you bring to me. . . ."[115]

[113] Kousoulas, p. 215; McNeill, p. 189. For details regarding the atrocious treatment of hostages by ELAS see Great Britain, Foreign Office, *Documents Regarding the Situation in Greece. January 1945* (Greece No. 1: 1945) Cmd. 6592 (London: H. M. Stationery Office, 1945).

[114] Woodward, p. 363; Macmillan, p. 531; Leeper, pp. 133-34.

[115] Leeper, p. 134.

The formal act which signaled the end of the Second Round was the agreement between the new Greek government and EAM, signed at Varkiza, a small resort on the Athens-Sounion road, on February 12, 1945. It called for a plebiscite on the constitutional question, "at the earliest possible time, and in any case within the current year," to be followed by elections for a constituent assembly. Allied observers for both events were to be requested. Basic individual liberties were guaranteed, including freedom of expression, of the press, and for the trade unions. The pact further provided for the immediate demobilization and disarming of ELAS and of all Communist-controlled bands, and the formation of a national army on the basis of regular conscription. It made no mention of the Mountain Brigade, although the Sacred Battalion was to be retained and eventually merged with the new army. Actually, both units were preserved and served as the nucleus for the future national armed forces. Amnesty was granted for "political crimes" committed during the crisis, but not for "common-law crimes against life and property which were not absolutely necessary to the achievement of the political crime concerned," a clause which soon became a weapon in the hands of the authorities against the rank-and-file of left-wing resistance groups. Men of ELAS who had not surrendered their weapons by March 15, 1945, would also not be covered by the amnesty. All civilians taken prisoner by ELAS were to be freed immediately. Finally, the government undertook to purge as soon as possible the security forces and the civil service on the basis of "professional competence, or character and personality, or collaboration with the enemy or the utilization of the official as an instrument of the dictatorship."[116]

From Athens Ambassador MacVeagh, calling himself one "who loves this country and its people and at the same time has an old and deep-rooted affection for our British cous-

[116] For the text of the Varkiza Agreement see Appendix G.

251

ins," once again reflected for the benefit of the President on the causes of the recent drama and on its consequences for the future. This time he appeared to be more preoccupied with Communism than heretofore. Pointing out that newspaper accounts had tended to oversimplify and had thus rendered "poor service to the truth," he wrote on January 15:

> This attempted revolution in Greece represents no clear-cut struggle between liberalism and despotism with England lined up on the side of the latter. It is rather a bastard off-shoot of the traditional line of Greek revolutions, composed of social as well as political elements and fathered by international communism on a country economically ruined and politically distraught. The British have only played the part of midwife in this affair. It was not their fault that the child was conceived, but they have certainly lent themselves with astonishing ineptitude to its delivery, and have only themselves to thank if, in trying to retrieve their error by doing away with the child, and thus, as it were, adding murder to abortion, they have effectively stolen the limelight in a case where the chief criminals are obscure elements in the world's view.

The scholarly diplomat and philhellene saw the revolt from the perspective of the historian. "The swing to the Left in Greek politics following the Metaxas dictatorship, the exploitation of this by the communists, and the ripe conditions for social revolution created by the German occupation and fostered by German intrigue, are really the mixed elements fundamentally to blame. . . ." As for the more immediate background, and while the British Prime Minister had been right in asserting that without the British there would have been a massacre in Athens,

> . . . the fact remains that if the British had taken the political action a year ago which they have taken now, the

communist leadership of the National Resistance Movement [EAM] would never have been able to spread those suspicions which have made so many genuine Greek patriots their collaborators in an armed attempt against the State. Even as late as last Spring, when the mutiny in Cairo showed such unmistakable signs of close affiliation between the republicans and the extreme left, an overt act on the part of the British to remove all possible suspicions that they intended to support the King's return before the plebiscite (and the possible restoration of the fascist dictatorship for which he is so widely held responsible) might have averted bloodshed by giving a government of national unity, such as Mr. Papandreou's Government aspired to be, at least a chance of success. But as no such act ever eventuated, the suspicions which had already been so sedulously sown by the Communists could still be spread and cultivated, and when the charge was put about that the Papandreou Government was merely a blind to conceal the preparation of a rightist coup, this also seemed reasonable to many patriots in the light of what the British did. . . .

MacVeagh thought it encouraging that the last phase of the conflict had definitely alienated from the Communist cause many ELAS men who had not been prepared to participate in the "Red revolution which they saw being actually unleashed here." Furthermore, "Russia has given no sign of supporting this movement openly, nor can any evidence be found of her doing so secretly." He continued:

Nonetheless, taking a long view,—and if I aspired to be a prophet, which I don't,—I might hazard that after British intervention is over, the future will show a gradual reduction of the state of civil war here to one of mountain banditry . . . and that the duration of this second phase will depend not only on the wisdom and energy of the Central Government in placating honest patriots in the

253

opposition and combatting recalcitrants, but also, and to a great extent, on the efficiency of the relief and reconstruction efforts undertaken. This latter condition will indeed be of critical importance for the country-wide restoration of law and order, since without the importation and distribution of very substantial amounts of supplies, particularly of food and roofing material, during the next few months, financial stabilization cannot be effected, epidemics will almost certainly occur, and public morale will be even less able than heretofore to resist the crude temptations of anarchy and the misleading propaganda of those who batten on it.

All in all, MacVeagh believed that "the prospects for the future cannot be considered as other than dubious still."[117]

For his part, Roosevelt was apparently quite satisfied with the settlement reached in Greece and thought that the country might be made to serve as a showcase of postwar allied cooperation. On March 21 he telegraphed Churchill that he proposed to send to Greece a special international mission to develop that country's productive power rapidly and by "concerted, non-political action." He specifically mentioned Anastas Mikoyan, then Commissar for Foreign Trade, as a likely member of such a body. "It would not take them long," he asserted, "and might have a highly constructive effect on world opinion at this time." The President thought this tripartite mission might be in Greece in a month's time, but promised not to raise the matter with the Soviet government until Churchill had had the opportunity to react to the proposal. Alarmed by this suggestion, the British government quickly counterproposed a joint Anglo-American mission for Greece. This induced the President to abandon the entire idea. On April 8, four days before his death, and in his last personal message to Churchill, Roosevelt telegraphed that he accepted British objections

[117] *Roosevelt Papers*, PSF, folder "MacVeagh."

regarding Soviet participation in an "economic mission" to Greece and agreed not to proceed with the plan at the present time. However, he thought that an Anglo-American effort would be a "mistake," because it would create the impression that its participants were disregarding the decision at the Yalta Conference on tripartite cooperation in Europe's liberated areas and that "we consider Yalta no longer valid. Such is not the case. . . . We must be careful," the President concluded, "to do nothing that would weaken the effectiveness of our efforts to get the Soviet Union to honor these decisions. . . ."[118]

Not surprisingly, many of the provisions of the Varkiza Accord proved very difficult to interpret or enforce. Mutual suspicion and hatred continued to inflame many minds. But at least the fighting had ended, and Damascinos' prestige and dynamic personality gave promise that the nation, bled white by external and internal foes, might still recover.

[118] *Ibid.*, MRP, President's Messages to Churchill.

BETWEEN ROUNDS

CONSIDERING the violence of the Second Round and the emotional paroxysm which it unleashed, the Varkiza accord was no small achievement. It brought relief to a panic-stricken people and pointed the way to a stable peace. Although none of the fundamental problems which had propelled the nation into civil war had been resolved, and the tangle of partisanship, mistrust, and hatred had if anything, worsened, the military defeat of the leftist forces in the capital had made possible the removal of at least one major source of recent friction: ELAS was about to be disarmed and disbanded.

Despite its virtual control of most of the country outside the Athens-Piraeus area, ELAS and its patrons accepted surrender without evident reserve and proceeded to turn in its weapons to the appropriate government authorities. In fact ELAS produced larger quantities of every type of arms than the required minimum set at Varkiza. However, in certain cases individuals or regional bands managed to conceal some of their better weapons, thereby violating not only the government's orders but those of their superiors as well. Thus a small number of ELAS diehards, refusing to concede defeat, sceptical about the effectiveness of the amnesty and afraid to submit to the new order, took to the more inaccessible hills of northern Greece, determined to trust their fate to their weapons instead. The most notorious among them, Aris Velouchiotis, denounced by the KKE for his rejection of the Varkiza Agreement, was finally ambushed and killed by government troops. The psychological message conveyed by the public display of his bearded head in the market-

place of Trikkala could not have been lost on other guerrillas with troubled consciences. Whatever the reasons in
each case, a sprinkling of armed resistance continued, particularly in the country's northern provinces.

The problem was not simply the doing of the most in-
transigent among the leftist guerrillas. By placing beyond
the scope of the amnesty so-called common-law crimes,
which were regarded as "not absolutely necessary" for the
commission of political crimes, the Varkiza formula provided a limited and uncertain protection for those it had
been intended to benefit the most. The government's decision to punish those who had committed atrocities during
the occupation and in the recent fighting in Athens was
fully justified. Nevertheless, with the passions which the
December events had aroused, virtually all ELAS men were
exposed to the charge of having committed "common-law
crimes." In some instances and in certain areas guilt by association became the established rule: membership in ELAS
or its auxiliaries was sufficient grounds for persecution,
beatings, arrest, and prolonged imprisonment. And so tensions continued to run high, particularly as the government
made only feeble attempts to curb the activities of revenge-
seeking anti-Communists.

Even without representation in the new government and
seemingly unaware of the damage to its public image
caused by the recent upheaval, EAM declared its desire to
cooperate in the tasks of pacification and recovery. The
Central Committee of the Communist Party appealed to all
democratic forces to "join the front of democracy . . . for a
democratic rebirth, for a People's Democracy."[1] At the
same time there were unmistakable signs that the coalition
of the Left was losing its more moderate and widely respected leaders: Svolos and Tsirimokos, repelled by the

---

[1] Kousoulas, p. 200. See statement by Siantos for EAM/ELAS following the Varkiza accord in *I Symfonia tis Varkizas* (Athens, Feb.
1945), pp. 9-14.

butchery of the Second Round, officially withdrew from EAM, charging that the entire movement had been delivered to the Communist cause. In June 1945 the Secretary General of the KKE, Nikos Zahariadis, returned from a German concentration camp and hastened to give public endorsement to the Varkiza settlement. Later he would accuse Siantos of having brought about the defeat of January 1945 through bungling and indecision. However, for the moment, he appeared to accept the verdict of the Second Round and the predominance of Britain's influence in Greek affairs. In an interview arranged at his request, Zahariadis complained to Ambassador MacVeagh that under the prevailing rightist "domination and terror" free elections were going to be difficult to hold but conceded that there had been some improvement in the general situation. He said that the KKE, which he called "the most conservative party" in Greece, would conduct an intensive campaign among the peasantry which it had neglected in the past. On the basis of his impressions from this talk MacVeagh reported that a "decided shift" in KKE's orientation appeared to have taken place under Zahariadis' restored leadership which shunned all responsibility for the Second Round. "The lesson would appear to be," he concluded, that "given peace in Europe, and provided that Greek reconstruction proceeds with reasonable celerity with the help of UNRRA and the Allied economic missions, and that no unduly disturbing delays are encountered in securing a return to normal political expressions at the polls, this country has little to fear in the near future from any renewed direct action initiative on the part of the extreme Left." Instead, the American diplomat offered the view that the KKE would overtly confine itself to politics and, while working to quiet the fears of its opponents, would continue to "bore from within" in the labor organizations, the civil service, the armed forces, and perhaps even among the peasantry.[2] Indeed, the

[2] *DSR*, 868.00/6-2245.

only issue over which Zahariadis publicly disassociated himself from the government's official positions concerned Greece's territorial claims against other Balkan countries: instead, KKE's chief spokesman advocated a policy of peace and friendship with the Communist regimes to the north.

Prime Minister Plastiras soon discovered himself to be without a personal following, the prisoner of forces not of his making. Generally regarded as a staunch republican, he came under fire from the more conservative and royalist factions which accused him of attempting to play politics with the army and the security forces. His efforts to remove monarchist influences over the officer corps were also frustrated by his British advisers who were anxious to build up a politically reliable military organization. At the same time, strongly conservative in personal outlook, and blaming the Second Round entirely on the Left which he despised, he regarded EAM as a dangerously anti-national and subversive force to be suppressed and destroyed. Thus, although the charge that prior to assuming office Plastiras had secretly sworn allegiance to the monarchy is difficult to accept,[3] during his premiership his ineffective attempts to steer a course between Left and Right and his lack of political acumen made it possible for the royalists to exploit the climate created by the Second Round and to entrench themselves in the nation's decision-making process, and especially in the army command. Embarrassed and embittered, Plastiras resigned on April 7.

The new Prime Minister, Admiral Petros Voulgaris, had also acquired some notoriety in the mid-1930's for his republican convictions, and his participation in the 1935 coup had brought about his forced retirement. He returned to active duty in the Middle East where, following the mutinies in April 1944 which he helped suppress, his intense fear of the extreme Left turned him into a monarchist of

[3] Constantine Tsoucalas, *The Greek Tragedy* (Baltimore, 1969), p. 91.

sorts. He formed a Cabinet of old cronies and nonentities, with the notable exception of his very able Deputy Prime Minister and Minister of Supply, Kyriakos Varvaressos, who for several months struggled in vain to bring a galloping inflation under control and to place the nation's economy on a sound basis. Under the ineffective Voulgaris the Right continued to gain ground and began to press for national elections at the earliest possible time, confident that it would capture a powerful majority in the yet-to-be-revived parliament.

The storm of protest unleashed by the issue of the timing of the elections forced the Voulgaris government to step down in early October. As the vociferous Right would not accept a coalition with the Liberal Party, and as the socialist Left and the republican Center would not cooperate to form a new government, Damascinos was compelled to assume the office of Prime Minister on October 17, amid persistent rumors that the Right, through its armed "X" organization, was preparing to take over by force. Two weeks later Panayiotis Kanellopoulos succeeded in forming a Cabinet of impressive academicians and moderate political figures. However, mounting instability and economic chaos frightened the British government into action once again: Kanellopoulos was removed in mid-November and, over the strong protests of the Regent who felt that the Right was too strong to be left out of the government, an all-republican Cabinet under the aged Sofoulis was sworn in. The conservative Populist Party, now fully revived and confident of victory in the near future, had once again refused to work together with the Liberals, while the British wanted to avoid the appearance of an avowed right-wing government prior to the approaching elections. However, like Plastiras before him, Sofoulis discovered that in the face of London's controlling influence and the spreading rightist agitation, his own convictions counted for precious little. Beneath the facade of republican government the political pendulum continued to swing to the right.

The events of December and January had dramatized Britain's paramount responsibility in Greek affairs. Although at times uncomfortable in this master role, and often halfhearted in its measures, London sought to create conditions that would insure stability and a broadly democratic but reliably anti-Communist regime which would not be committed to work against the King's return. These objectives remained unchanged and were in fact pursued with renewed vigor by the incoming Labor government. Indeed, following the Potsdam Conference in August 1945 and the first clear signs of Soviet hostility toward Greece and Britain's presence in that country, the London government appeared more determined than ever to hold onto what it had preserved in the battle of Athens and to build upon it. In Greece all decisions of any significance were subject to a British veto. As one American observer has written, Britain's political as well as economic influence in Athens had turned Greece into a client-state whose sovereignty had all but disappeared.[4] And while political stability and economic recovery remained high on its list of priorities, the British Mission concentrated on the formation and training of reliable military and internal security forces. The political orientation of these forces was to be the principal legacy of Britain's postwar role in Greece.

This is not to say that the British set out deliberately to create a politically active army and police. If anything, the very opposite was their intention. The Military and Police Missions, which were established during the Papandreou Administration and which were given virtually free rein over their respective organizations, sought to train skilled professionals who would be careful not to meddle in politics. However, knowingly or not, following the sharp polarization caused by the Second Round, the British relied heavily upon readily available and already thoroughly politicized human material: the Third Brigade and Sacred Battalion, together with other known royalist officers, be-

---

[4] McNeill, p. 223.

came the backbone of the new army. The city police and gendarmerie were based on the security forces of the occupation years, with many of their members still belonging to the royalist "X." One result of this unhealthy situation was that some of the weapons surrendered by ELAS after Varkiza found their way into the hands of illegal anti-Communist groups which used them to terrorize their victims. In many areas anti-Communist guerrilla bands continued to move about, settling scores with the men of the now-disarmed ELAS. It was thus clear that a principal aim of the Varkiza settlement, the removal of all weapons from unauthorized persons, had failed miserably. At the same time, the high command and officer corps of the army and the internal security forces were made the willing tools of the Right, and neither Plastiras nor Sofoulis could alter that fact.[5] It goes without saying that, given the opportunity, other political factions would have done likewise: in Greece control of the armed forces has traditionally been a political objective of decisive importance.

The time had now come for the entire Left to pay for its crimes, real or imaginary. Aroused by the bloodshed of the Second Round public sentiment had little sympathy for Communists, EAM followers, ELAS veterans and their families, and viewed their persecution as a form of justice. An occasional protest from respected spokesmen of the Center parties had little or no effect. One such statement, issued on June 5, 1945 by former Prime Ministers Tsouderos and Plastiras, and by Mylonas, Kafandaris, and Sofoulis, declared:

> The terror initiated by the extreme right in the whole country after the December incidents is being amplified every day. Its development and its execution render the life of all non-royalist citizens impossible and exclude the hope that we can proceed to a free plebiscite or to elec-

[5] *Ibid.*, pp. 203-8, 226-27.

tions. The terrorist organizations of the extreme right, which had been armed by the Germans and had collaborated with them, have not been disarmed or prosecuted, but have allied themselves to the security forces in order to strangle completely all democratic thought.[6]

According to one published source, between February and July 1945, 20,000 individuals were arrested, some 500 killed by right-wing terrorist groups, while 2,961 were officially condemned to death. The same source quotes the Minister of Justice as saying in December 1945 that at that time 17,984 persons were imprisoned and that of these, 2,388 had been "legally condemned" while 15,596 were being "detained preventively"; another 48,956 were being "prosecuted for their activities as EAM/ELAS members." In all, those already under arrest or about to be charged numbered more than 80,000.[7]

These figures, which far exceed the strength of the entire ELAS force in the Athens-Piraeus area during the recent fighting, do not include the many thousands of unreported cases of persecution, beatings, and even murder in the countryside where the National Guard, assisted by local rightist elements, often took matters into its own hands. Although officially the government disapproved of such practices, privately the view appeared to prevail in many influential circles that the Left had to be eradicated by whatever means if the nation was to be rid of the Communist menace. One byproduct of this vigilantism was that former ELAS cadres who would have otherwise stayed home, began to take to the hills once again in ever-increasing numbers. By the summer of 1945 small bands had reappeared in the Mount Olympus region and in Macedonia.[8] In less than a year they would provide the nucleus for the Communist forces in the Third Round.

Under the Varkiza accord, elections for a national assem-

[6] Tsoucalas, p. 93.   [7] *Ibid.*, p. 94.   [8] McNeill, p. 241.

bly were to follow a plebiscite on the crucial issue of the monarchy's return. However, anxious to provide a longer period for passions to subside and for the unruly Left to be brought more firmly under control, the British government prevailed upon Damascinos to reverse the order of the two events and to hold elections first. Supporting this change the American government expressed the view on June 16, 1945 that the holding of elections first "appears to offer a better solution to Greek problems in that it would at an early date give Greece a representative political government which would then be in a position to make plans for a plebiscite on the question of the monarchy." The American note continued: "It may also be considered desirable that an approximate date be set for the plebiscite, preferably some six months after the convening of a duly elected constituent assembly. Thus the democratically elected government would be given a brief period in which to establish itself."[9] In September the Regent traveled to London to meet the leaders of the newly formed Labor government and ascertain their views on Greek problems. With the full support of the Truman Administration, which appeared to welcome an increasingly more important role in Athens, the British insisted upon early elections to clear the air and, hopefully, provide the country with a stable government. A statement issued by the three Western allies declared in part:

> The three Governments hold the firm opinion that elections for a revisionary assembly should be held as soon as possible. . . . Thus a government would be formed which would be based on the wishes of the people and Parliament. The formation of such a Government would facilitate the restoration of conditions of stable tranquillity in Greece. Only when these conditions are, in due

[9] *FR* (1945), 133.

course, firmly established will it become possible to hold a free and genuine plebiscite to decide on the future regime in Greece.[10]

Accordingly, with the Regent's consent, elections were announced for March 31, 1946.

Not surprisingly, the Left and Center parties protested this decision. They argued that the country was too deeply immersed in political turmoil to allow for a fair testing of the popular will and demanded that the elections be postponed. A number of prominent members of the Sofoulis government resigned over this issue and the Prime Minister himself called for a postponement until conditions of stability and order could be restored. Although few among the protestors wished to see the plebiscite come before the elections, the timing of the latter was clearly uppermost in their minds. To the delight of the royalists, the British government vetoed any change in the timing of the elections. It also refused to consider demands that the armed forces and the police be purged of royalist officers before election day. Thereupon the Communist Party and the militant Left announced their intention to abstain, charging that, with British connivance, the elections were to be a cruel hoax designed to pave the way for the return of the unpopular King.

Whether the decision of the extreme Left to abstain was a serious tactical error, as some maintain,[11] or was in fact a well-conceived maneuver to mask its lack of popular support and disarray at the top, cannot be answered with any conclusive evidence. That conditions prevailing throughout the country and the chaotic state of the election registers were bound to adversely affect the leftist vote cannot be doubted. The difficulty arises when one attempts to estimate the size of the vote which would have supported leftist candidates in any event, had they decided to take part

[10] McNeill, p. 217.   [11] Tsoucalas, p. 96.

in the contest. Immediately following the country's liberation and without the traumatic impact of the Second Round, the republican forces from Sofoulis' Liberals to the Communists would have had an easy and decisive victory over the Populists on the right, although agreement on a division of the spoils among the plethora of parties would have been tenuous at best. But the events of December, and KKE's dominant role in them, had cost the socialist Left a great many of its sympathizers and had invigorated its enemies whose more right-wing elements found their misdeeds of the past decade suddenly overshadowed by the blame heaped upon the Left for the recent fighting in the capital. The socialist-republican camp could hope to regroup its followers only if political tranquility and order were established across the country and the memories of the Second Round allowed to fade. Thus the early timing of the elections worked against the republican Left, which appeared to continue to carry the Communists as a millstone around its neck. On the other hand, irregularities in the registers, the turbulent political conditions and the actual ballot returns were such that one can bend their interpretation to support preconceived notions regarding the "real" strength of the country's alignments.

The elections of March 31, 1946, held under the proportional system which encouraged the proliferation of parties, were observed by an allied mission consisting of some 1,200 British, American, and French officials divided into several hundred teams and traveling across the country to check on campaign practices and insure the fairness of the outcome. Although invited, the Soviet Union refused to participate, displaying instead a mounting hostility toward the Greek government and its western patrons. Considering the charges and countercharges, there was in fact little violence and overt intimidation. The only major exception was a Communist attack upon the small town of Litochoro on the very day of the elections. The report of the allied mission

concluded that, under the circumstances, the election results were generally fair and indicative of the public sentiment. It must be admitted, however, that the role of the
foreign observers was largely ceremonial and perhaps even
deceptive, as most of them knew nothing about the country
and the ways of its people. Nor could they do anything
about the election registers which, ignored for a decade, remained woefully inaccurate. In any event, of the 2.2 million
registered, slightly more than 1.1 million voted, making it
possible for the Left to claim that nearly half of the population had supported it by abstaining.[12] Such a conclusion is
very probably not warranted. A well-informed American
observer estimated that in March 1946 about 20 per cent of
the voters were followers of the extreme Left.[13] To this one
may add another 10 per cent, representing the fringe of the
republican movement which may also be thought to have
abstained. Whatever one's estimates and calculations, the
results were plain enough: the Populist Party, comprising
the bulwark of the royalist and conservative cause, won an
absolute majority and its leader, Constantine Tsaldaris,
formed a Cabinet of mostly royalists. To no one's great surprise and with memories of the Second Round still inflamed
by endless rhetoric, the plebiscite on the issue of the King's
return, held in September of the same year, brought a 68.9
per cent majority in favor of the monarchy. King George returned to Athens at once. For many Greeks he served as the
symbol of the country's victory over international Communism. He died seven months later of a heart attack, leaving
the throne to his younger brother, Paul.

Unhappily no popular poll could also "settle" the country's economic problems. Despite the efforts of the British
government and of UNRRA, the Greek economy continued
to suffer from severe shortages of most goods and by
a rampant inflation aggravated by a mammoth black market
and corruption. Much like its predecessors, the government

[12] *Ibid.*, p. 97.   [13] McNeill, pp. 235-36.

of Tsaldaris looked to London for loans and other relief, with equally meager results. In September 1945 the head of the UNRRA mission in Greece had already advised London that "the Greek Government recognize their inability to cope with the economic problems facing the country without a very wide measure of foreign advice and assistance," which the Greeks hoped that UNRRA could provide. Turning the matter over to Washington, Britain's Foreign Secretary, Ernest Bevin, expressed the view that there was no choice but to allow the international agency to assume this responsibility. He argued that

> Admiral Voulgaris has always recognized his own inability to deal with economic matters and it is clear that he despairs of finding any Greek with sufficient ability to replace Monsieur Varvaressos. He has therefore appealed to UNRRA for one or more experts whose status might in theory be purely advisory but who would undoubtedly influence and to some extent direct the whole Greek economy by reason of the fact that Greece is dependent on UNRRA for all her essential imports. I am convinced that something will have to be done without delay if Greek economy is not to collapse. . . .[14]

When Secretary of State James F. Byrnes refused to endorse such a drastic expansion of UNRRA's mission in Greece, Britain's half-measures had to be continued. However, within two years this heavy burden would be shifted to the United States, as the plight of Greece appeared to reflect the tensions of the Cold War.

While turmoil and deprivation marked the domestic scene, Greece's external relations were no more satisfactory. And even though Athens was once again partly to blame, there was much that was entirely beyond its control. A detailed examination of the country's international position following liberation is clearly outside the scope of the

14 *FR* (1945), 238-39.

present undertaking. What needs to be stressed here is the fact that in the aftermath of the Second Round frustrations and fears at the international level constituted a major factor in keeping the nation in a state of unrest. Almost all controversies were of a regional nature, as they pertained to the country's territorial aspirations and affected relations with neighbors to the north, and to a much lesser extent with Turkey and Italy. The fact that some of these issues were at least in part self-induced made them no less aggravating. And, initially, ideological differences appeared to take second place to historically much more familiar and tangible Balkan feuds.

As was to be expected, from the outset Bulgaria, the enemy in the Second Balkan War, represented the focal point of national hatred and fear. The barbarous record of the Bulgarian wartime occupation of Greek Eastern Macedonia and Thrace had disclosed a deliberate policy of permanent conquest and assimilation. To make matters worse, Sofia's troops appeared to be in no hurry to evacuate Greek territory even as the Germans were stepping up their own retreat. It finally became necessary for the Soviet Union to order the Bulgarians out. Soon, however, Bulgaria, yesterday's ally of the Axis, appeared to have the full backing of Moscow and to be acting as the spearhead of dreaded pan-Slavist schemes for an exit on the Aegean Sea under the guise of an autonomous "Slav Macedonia." Moreover, after September 1944, the Bulgarian press launched a campaign of "protest" against the alleged persecution of "Bulgarians" in Greek Macedonia and Thrace and against what was termed the "mad terrorism of Greek chauvinist circles." According to these polemics, the only solution of the problem appeared to be the "liberation" of these oppressed peoples from the Greek yoke . . .

During the war years the Greek government-in-exile had done its best to keep its grievances against Bulgaria alive before allied councils and had repeatedly stated its intention to demand at the peace conference not merely substantial reparations but also a modest revision of the Greek-Bulgarian frontier so as to improve the defense of Greek territory. To the overwhelming majority of Greeks such claims were eminently fair, particularly in view of the murderous conduct of the Bulgarian troops, and no politician could resist the temptation to air his own special ideas as to what would constitute proper retribution. Public orations and newspaper editorials would often end with the old Greek battle-cry: "On to Sofia!" But if the Greeks got upset over Bulgarian propaganda, so did the Bulgarians over Greek claims. In May 1945 allied diplomatic officials expressed annoyance at reports in a Greek royalist newspaper that the occupation of Bulgaria by Greek forces had begun. On May 31 the Department of State commented to the American Ambassador in Athens that "uncontrolled Greek expansionist temper" was contributing to misunderstandings between the British and Greek governments on the one hand and the Soviet Union and its Balkan protégés on the other. Greek territorial claims were reinforcing the suspicion among Balkan states that Greece, supported by Britain, harbored "aggressive intentions" and might prove counterproductive in the long run by offering a pretext for measures hostile to Greece. Accordingly, in the Department's view Athens "might be well advised to attempt restraint of belligerent expansionist claims."[15]

Having duly communicated these warnings to a high-ranking Greek official, MacVeagh cabled back that his efforts in this regard could not be expected to succeed because of the inherent weakness of the Greek government and the "highly excited" political atmosphere in Athens. On the contrary, the "original efforts by Rightists to appropriate such claims with view to posing as only true patriots in coming elections have now stampeded Leftists into following suit and each camp appears trying to outdo other. . . ."

[15] *Ibid.*, 317.

Even the Communist Party was now willing to mouth such territorial demands.[16] Symptoms of this verbal tug-of-war were soon in evidence. In mid-July the British Military Mission in Greece was alerted to the possibility of small-scale incursions into Greek territory by Bulgarian, Albanian, and Yugoslav forces, but was instructed to leave the responsibility of guarding the frontiers to the Greeks themselves. Only in the event of a direct attack upon them were British troops to return the fire. While border incidents remained for the most part the work of irregulars in pursuit of plunder and were only magnified in excited press accounts, a war of nerves between Athens and Sofia assumed dangerous overtones, foretelling of grave complications in the near future. And, as the American diplomatic representative in Bulgaria reported in July 1945, the vociferous anti-Greek campaign in that country's press not only conveniently ignored recent Bulgarian atrocities in Greece but deliberately sought to conceal the fact that "today pan-Slavism represents far more a menace to Greece than does Greece to Bulgaria."[17]

Although not burdened by so much age-old hostility, relations with Yugoslavia soon proved to be no better. The apparent strength of Tito's Communist regime and the fear that ELAS might become a kind of fifth column in the prosecution of aggressive designs in Greek Macedonia caused grave concern not only in Athens but in allied capitals as well. In December 1944 the American government had found it necessary to call to the attention of its diplomatic representatives in the Balkans, London, and Moscow, "in-

[16] *Ibid.*

[17] *Ibid.*, 327-28. For scholarly studies of these issues by Greek authors see Dimitri Constantopoulos, *The Paris Peace Conference of 1946 and Greek-Bulgarian Relations* (Thessaloniki, 1956); Ph. Dragoumis, *Ta Ellinika Dikaia sti Diaskepsi tis Irinis* (Thessaloniki, 1949); St. P. Kyriakidis, *The Northern Ethnological Boundaries of Hellenism* (Thessaloniki, 1955); George B. Zotiades, *The Macedonian Controversy* (Thessaloniki, 1961).

creasing propaganda rumors and semiofficial statements in favor of an autonomous Macedonia, emanating from Bulgaria, but also from Yugoslav Partisan and other sources, with the implication that Greek territory would be included in the projected state." Dismissing the notion of a Macedonian "nation" as a devious fabrication, the communication expressed concern that such propaganda might represent a "possible cloak of aggressive intentions" directed against Greece. The United States would therefore hold responsible any government which tolerated or encouraged aggressive actions against Greece by so-called Macedonian forces.[18]

Such American diplomatic pressure, and the strong protests of the Greek government, seemed to have no effect, as the "Macedonian Question" appeared to be a major preoccupation of Yugoslav foreign policy. Moreover, Greece's argument on security grounds for a northward rectification of its frontier at Yugoslavia's expense was almost immediately swept away in an avalanche of counterclaims and charges which threatened to lead to violence. During the spring of 1945, Tito repeatedly declared that if the "Macedonians" living in Greek territories wished to be united with their "brethren," Yugoslavia would support their efforts. This theme was echoed in numerous official statements emanating from Belgrade, together with the assertion that the "Macedonians" of Greece were the object of systematic persecution and terrorism. In the resulting storm of public indignation in Greece, even the Communist Party had found it prudent to reiterate its position that Macedonia and Thrace constituted inseparable parts of the Greek nation. Furthermore, the Greek government complained that by reviving the Macedonian controversy the Yugoslavs were not merely interfering in Greek domestic affairs but were seeking to pave the way for the annexation of the Thessaloniki region: that was how Athens interpreted

[18] *FR* (1945), 302-3.

Belgrade's persistent demands in the spring of 1945 that the pre-war Yugoslav Free Zone in Thessaloniki, as well as rail service to the Yugoslav border, be made available again as quickly as possible.

In July, having lodged a formal complaint with the Greek government, Yugoslavia took the extraordinary step of informing Washington that the provisions of the United Nations Charter concerning human rights were being violated in Greece, "to the detriment of Macedonians, our conationals, inhabitants of the Aegean Macedonia. . . ." Belgrade also produced a list of "incidents" of alleged violations of its borders by Greek troops.[19] Reports from the American Embassy in Athens generally refuted these charges and pointed out that the Greek armed forces were too small to effectively control the movement of individuals or groups across the Yugoslav border. At the same time the American government responded to Belgrade's charges with a proposal that an allied mission be established to investigate alleged violations of the United Nations Charter in Greek Macedonia.[20] Eventually this suggestion was to lead to the creation of the United Nations Special Committee on the Balkans which was to begin its work during the opening stages of the approaching Third Round. In the meantime, the spiral of charges and countercharges continued to rise, accentuated by occasional minor skirmishes along Greece's northern borders. In May and again in June 1945 allied military authorities expressed some concern over the concentration of considerable Yugoslav forces in Macedonia, which might be employed in serious action against northern Greece.[21] Though no such attack materialized, the chorus of anti-Greek polemics had found its shrillest voice in Belgrade.

By far the most important of Greece's territorial claims, on ethnic and historical grounds, concerned northern Epirus. This controversy, together with charges that Al-

[19] *Ibid.*, 323-25.   [20] *Ibid.*, 331.   [21] *Ibid.*, 318.

bania's Greek population was the target of official persecution—and countercharges that "Albanians" in northern Greece were similarly mistreated—kept the two neighboring countries in a state of near-permanent friction, with border incidents highlighting the war of public recrimination.[22] A further Greek claim for the "return" of the island of Saseno merely added fuel to the raging fire. A side effect of this troubled situation was a strong plea from Athens to the western allies not to accord diplomatic recognition to the Hoxha regime.[23]

Compared to the rapidly deteriorating situation all along its northern borders, territorial problems between Athens on the one hand and Ankara, Rome, and London on the other were never allowed to take an ugly turn. Despite Turkish apprehensions, the Dodecanese were transferred from Italy to Greece following the peace conference; an unofficial claim for eastern (Turkish) Thrace was never pressed. Reparation claims against Italy had to be scaled down to a tiny fraction of the original figures prepared by the Greek government. Heavy reliance upon British material and diplomatic support dictated that the issue of union with Cyprus could be discussed in the mildest of terms. All in all, with the notable exception of the Dodecanese, Greece's postwar territorial aspirations and reparation claims were to be badly frustrated. Furthermore, although justified from the Greek point of view, they proved largely self-defeating because they opened the floodgates of a vicious anti-Greek campaign in the Balkans and embittered the Greek people who discovered that, at least in these emotionally charged issues, Britain and the United States were anything but strong supporters of Greek national interests.

[22] For scholarly studies by Greek authors see Ph. A. Philon, *The Question of Northern Epirus: Its Historical and Diplomatic Background* (Washington, D.C., 1945); P. N. Pipinelis, *Europe and the Albanian Question* (Chicago, 1963).

[23] *FR* (1945), 350-52, 355-57.

as Hull and Stettinius paid scant attention to his views, determined to avoid all involvement in matters which might taint American policies with the miasma of old-world power squabbles. They correctly recognized the dangers inherent in the Greek situation, and in Britain's handling of it, but wanted none of the responsibility of coming to grips with it. While approving a modest American role in relief activity, they were content to sit back and count the errors committed by the British. In all fairness, it must be added that, in the Balkans, and while welcoming American economic assistance, the British were all too anxious to go it alone. As for President Roosevelt, the strong pleas of the British Prime Minister, the need to avoid straining allied unity needlessly, the decision to direct the war effort away from southeast Europe and the absence of traditionally important American interests there, meant that Greece had to be consigned to the British zone of operational responsibility. Though such responsibility was thought to be primarily military, there was no escaping the political consequences of the arrangement, however unpalatable. The result of all these factors was a policy of noninvolvement, which in the last analysis could hardly be distinguished from a complete lack of policy.

The emotional legacy of the Second Round was that the Communists, whose many atrocities were perpetrated mostly upon innocent and defenseless hostages, came to be hated with a passion rare in the nation's history. They were now blamed for all the country's recent suffering and were branded as traitors conspiring with foreign enemies to dismember and destroy the state. Moreover, this consuming hatred was directed not only at the Communists but at all those who had been their willing or unwilling associates. Soon one-time membership in a left-wing organization made a person and his family the target of official harassment and unofficial terror. A thermidorian reaction, however understandable in view of the terrorism which the

Communists themselves had very often practiced on their opponents, kept the country in the perpetual turmoil of a mass vendetta. It also subverted recovery programs and contributed powerfully to the opening of the Third Round in the spring of 1946.

In more abstract terms the significance of the Second Round is that it represented an entanglement in which each participant's position appeared to depend upon the moves of its opponent. Locked in this desperate struggle, neither side really understood the other. Instead, each side saw the shadow of diabolic conspiracies. On the one hand the Left regarded the nation's pre-war bleak political scene as intolerable and was frantically working to prevent its restoration. On the other, conservative forces in Greece and abroad longed for the more traditional values of the past which allowed no room for the new social order demanded by the growing Left. Neither side was prepared to acknowledge any legitimacy in its opponent's aspirations, or to make allowances for them. In this frame of mind, both sides failed to perceive that, however justified from one's viewpoint a power move might be, it was bound to evoke a counter-move which would nullify the first and create the need for yet another power move. The spiraling conflict thus acquired a momentum of its own, leading inexorably to civil war. Only cool reason, the rarest of diplomatic skills, and the most profound devotion to the welfare of the entire nation could have reversed this disastrous course. It was the tragedy of Greece that in the winter of 1944 such virtues were in hopelessly short supply.

APPENDICES

THE PLAKA AGREEMENT*

Signed by representatives of EAM/ELAS, EDES,
EKKA and of the Allied Military Mission, at
the Plaka Bridge, in Epirus, on February 29, 1944.

In the interests of the total and undivided conduct of the national struggle against the Occupation and its instruments, and of the success of the Allied struggle, the liberation of Greece and the consolidation of democratic freedom, and finally of the creation of conditions conducive to the unification of the guerilla army of Greece, the undersigned representatives, authorized to undertake negotiations for the unity of Greece, have resolved:

1. They accept the proposal of EAM/ELAS for the final cessation of hostilities between ELAS and EDES.

2. The units of EAM/ELAS and EDES will maintain the positions which they occupy to-day.

3. The organisations of EAM/ELAS and EDES undertake the obligation of fighting the Occupation and its collaborators with all their forces, either independently in their respective areas or in common by prearranged agreement.

4. To ensure better opposition against the Occupation, the high commands of both organisations (EAM and EDES) in Epirus will co-operate in drafting a common offensive and defensive plan, specifying the conduct of any necessary manoeuvres by either organisation under enemy pressure within the territory of the other, provided that military necessity requires it.

5. If units of either organization withdraw from their

* As published in Woodhouse, pp. 303-4. Reproduced by permission.

positions under pressure from the Germans or their collaborators, they will return to them as soon as the enemy withdraw.

6. A Joint Military Committee, composed of representatives of ELAS, EDES and EKKA, will supervise the observation of these terms and resolve any disputes which may occur. This committee may function with only two members until the arrival of a representative of EKKA.

7. The AMM [Allied Military Mission] is asked to secure from CHQ Middle East the maximum possible supplies for the forces of all organisations in Greece, on the basis of their operations against the Germans and in proportion to the real requirements of the war.

8. The wish of all Greece is hereby expressed that those who have suffered either from German attacks or from the conflict of the organisations may receive the undivided assistance of all the organisations. The Allied Headquarters is especially asked to come to their immediate assistance.

9. From the signature of this agreement all those held by either side as prisoners or hostages for political reasons will be released and assisted to go wherever they wish, with the exception of those charged with acts of treason or serious criminal offences, whose names will be notified to the organisation concerned, for trial by the established courts-martial, of which a representative of the organisation concerned will be a member. It is hoped that these cases will be completed as soon as possible. The release of hostages will take place at the latest within a fortnight.

10. This agreement takes effect forthwith.

S. Saraphis	G. Kartalis	K. Pyromaglou
Nikolas		P. Nikolopoulos
(= Petros Roussos)		
for EAM/ELAS	for EKKA	for EDES

Chris (for Greek High Command and AMM)
G. K. Wines (for AMM, United States component)

SECRET CLAUSE

The organisations EAM/ELAS, EDES and EKKA will co-operate closely in the plans for "Noah's Ark,"* and will facilitate
the plans of GHQ, Middle East Forces, including the infiltra-
tration of special British and American units designed to
take part in the operations.

(Signatures)

* The code name for the operation leading up to the liberation of
Greece.

PRINCIPAL POINTS OF THE
LEBANON AGREEMENT*
MAY 1944

1. The reorganisation and re-establishment of discipline in the Greek armed forces in the Middle East under the Greek national flag must be carried out exclusively on a national and military basis, not on a political basis. The army will carry out the orders of the Government, and cannot possess political opinions.

2. All guerilla bands in free Greece must be unified and disciplined under the orders of a single Government. The guerilla principle of military organisation cannot be a permanent one; but no change should be made at the moment which will lead to a reduction of resistance. Consequently the present situation must be regarded as a transitional one, and the initiative in settling it can only be taken by the Government in consultation with GHQ, MEF.

3. The reign of terror in the Greek countryside must cease and the personal security and political liberty of the people must be firmly established when and where the invader has been driven out. Outbreaks of terrorism must also cease in the towns. Ministers of the Government will be in office in Greece to administer the armed forces and the liberated Greek population. As soon as the presence of the Government in Greece is possible, it must not lose a minute in proceeding there.

4. Adequate supplies of food and medicines must be sent to enslaved and mountain Greece.

* As published in Woodhouse, p. 305. Reproduced by permission.

5. Greece, when liberated, must be secured the state of order and liberty necessary to enable the people to decide, freely and without pressure, both on their constitution and their régime and Government:

- (a) The special task of the Government of National Unity will be to secure order and liberty.
- (b) The people must be enabled to make its decision as soon as possible.
- (c) On the question of the sovereign power, the political leaders who have joined the Government of National Unity are understood to retain such views as they have already expressed.

6. Severe punishment will be imposed on traitors and those who have exploited the misfortunes of the people. Since this problem concerns the post-liberation period, it is necessary to make clear that the Government of National Unity will continue beyond the date of liberation for such period as the conscience of the nation and its own political judgment may decide.

7. Arrangements will be made in advance, in concert with the Allies, for the satisfaction of Greece's material needs in the way of reconstruction, including such necessities as the provision of outlets for Greek products and freedom of emigration.

8. Full satisfaction of Greece's national claims is called for by the past services and sacrifices of the Greek people. This must include the security of our new frontiers.

LETTER TO PRIME MINISTER
G. PAPANDREOU FROM
A. SVOLOS (PEEA),
D. STRATIS (EAM), AND
P. ROUSSOS (KKE)*

Cairo, 9th July 1944

Mr. President,

We are obliged, at this sad and critical hour for the nation, to address to you the following statement—with the sincerity we have always used—as to our views on the situation and in this way to reply also to your public declarations.

We are very deeply distressed by the fact that our attempt at unity unfortunately has not succeeded, at least for the time being. Whose fault is it? You have recognized our personal effort and applauded it. But we consider it our duty to state a basic truth, that in response to our good will and readiness to reach an understanding, the Government has not only avoided taking similar steps but has handled the question in such a way that it could result only in failure.

The tactics pursued during and after the Lebanon Conference were far from contributing to the creation of an atmosphere of confidence. An outsider would get the impression that the only thing which was and is still pursued, is first to depreciate the forces which are at present offering

* I am grateful to Prof. Harry Cliadakis for the text of this letter.

resistance in Greece, and then to let them enter the Government in order to neutralize or dissolve them.

We consented to participate in a political conference in the organization of which we felt ourselves to be strangers, almost annoying intruders. Neither were equal rights accorded us nor were we permitted to make any outside contact. From the beginning we have appeared as if we were on trial. We had need of much self-control and devotion to a higher purpose in order to agree to participate.

Our organizations have heard that in the Conference not a single favorable word was spoken by the opposing camp or by you with regard to the resistance movement and its achievements, despite the fact that that movement is an honor to Greece. From the very beginning they have repeatedly heard charges against EAM and ELAS and quite official propaganda made against them by the Government both here, in Greece, and abroad; yet at the same time EAM is invited to participate in a National Union. Recently official governmental statements have spoken of abolition of ELAS at a time when the British Minister for Foreign Affairs was promising the House of Commons that he would continue to strengthen this fighting army. In the light of the above it is by no means surprising that the forces of resistance should agree to enter the Government on the condition of receiving guarantees of the fulfillment of the Lebanon Agreement, a question which—according to your own proposal, Mr. President—was left to be discussed in Cairo since, because of the unjustified and dangerous haste with which the discussions in the Lebanon were carried out, insufficient time was given to examine that question carefully. Our organizations are unable, of course, to admit that the spirit of the Lebanon Agreement meant the extermination of one side or the subordination of the other. On the contrary, there should be a spirit of sincere cooperation on the basis of the three principles we have emphasized since the very beginning:

(a) The general interest of the National and Allied war effort;

(b) The democratic principles of Allied ideology;

(c) Political equality of rights.

Only in the event that these principles were in fact respected by the Government could we have avoided the distrust which already existed before the Lebanon Conference and which resulted from a single fact: whereas, since the beginning one side was shedding its blood by fighting against the conqueror, the other side—according to your own words which appear in the Lebanon Agreement—"was absent" or only criticized the mistakes which are unavoidable in every struggle of that kind, and the unavoidable excesses.

Not the slightest discussion took place concerning the struggle itself or the strenthening of it in order to increase our contribution to the Allied victory. We were not even asked—even pro forma—under what conditions the people are fighting in the mountains. No member of the Government has considered our needs or the needs of the civilian population of the mountain areas, although from the time we first arrived we suggested that you take these needs into consideration.

We did not allow ourselves to be affected by such disappointing circumstances. We put them out of our minds and, as you well know, we avoided creating any impressions in the Mountains. Unfortunately, the Government itself has been careful to advise the resistance forces of the intentions which prevail here.

Your speeches against EAM, Mr. President, and also the speeches of others responsible for the situation here, have continued—with official inspiration, weeks after the agreement—to be spread amongst the fighting forces, and still continue. Accordingly one wonders why this was done and is still being done, if there is a real and sincere intention of cooperation. Once such a distrust has been created, could one blame the resistance forces for seeking certain guarantees, since it is neither right nor moral that the Lebanon Agreement be used against them—against those who are continuing the fight for liberation and who, if they enter the Government, will contribute to the all-important National Union an essential content?

Discussion of these guarantees was prejudiced by two more facts: The attack of Zervas against ELAS, and your broadcast of 28 June. Zervas' forces obey your orders, and your speech unfortunately had no other effect than to separate the resistance organizations and to bring inacceptable moral pressure against their representatives. It was understandable that the Mountains would reply and that they would be indignant over the attack especially at a time when—according to our information—the Security Battalions, acting for the Germans, are exterminating the fighting people in Athens and elsewhere over an unprecedentedly large area; but the Greek Government—despite our many repeated requests—refuses to take publicly the necessary stand against these executioners of the Greek People. Nevertheless, only the day before yesterday, Mr. President, you wrote to us, in regard to this question, that the Lebanon Conference "has already taken a stand." Why, then, is this specific resolution, accepted in the Lebanon after being proposed by us, not definitively stated and published?

We were also silent in regard to many other points of the Government policy which we saw and still see not only do not prepare for National Unity but positively hinder its realization in conformity with the Lebanon decision. Let any impartial person in the Middle East judge, for example, if the treatment of the military question is destined to strengthen national unity or if, on the contrary, it leads to the creation of inacceptable biases which are very dangerous because of the tendencies which they embody. Do the removal of democratic, antimonarchist elements, and the

299

assignment of responsible positions to men with fascist ideas correspond to the spirit of union and to the allied war aims against existing anti-democratic orders? Let any patriot who really desires the moral unity of the people and peace of the Fatherland judge if the treatment of the questions which developed from the events in the Army and Navy is appropriate. A new estimate of the events on the basis of more data—an estimate which could not be made in the Lebanon —will today logically lead to other measures. Is it necessary to execute sons of the People who, rising in the name of thousands of others, expressed—even in the way they did— a national desire, the desire for unity for participation in the war and the liberation of the Fatherland? Is it admissible that units of the fighting forces of the Middle East be accused of having demonstrated in order to help the enemy? Lastly, is it not true also that the general interest of the nation requires an amnesty? What kind of atmosphere of appeasement could be created without a generous policy in this matter, so that national unity may take root? Was it necessary for the political leaders of a great Allied people to point out to us that our national unity and the interest of the Allied war effort necessitate a different treatment of these questions?

Let any liberal and democratic person judge whether there are no alarming indications, whether perhaps methods are being applied which recall tendencies which have been condemned, and whether something else is being followed than the ideology and the principles of the Allied struggle which we regard as a basic condition for a smooth development of the internal and international life of nations. Finally the anti-communist propaganda is in contradiction to the general policy followed by the Allies and is of benefit only to the enemy.

We have discussed, Mr. President, the proportion of our representation in the Government. Although neither our principals nor ourselves have introduced this matter into the negotiations, we must nevertheless remind you of the following: Whereas in your statements of yesterday, you said that you had offered to us 5 seats out of 20, the fact is that during the discussion you had on 30 May with Messrs. Porfyrogenis and Roussos, you offered to us 5 seats of a total of 14 or 15 ministries, which we cabled to the mountains. Despite this fact you have completed your Government with that number, without our participation. But apart from that, is it right that Fighting Greece be excluded from ministries like those of Education, Justice, Social Welfare, and Interior, from which you excluded it in advance and without discussion, as if we were "second-class citizens" with reduced rights? Is Fighting Greece not in the service of the nation? Is it not at the disposal of the Allied struggle? Is it not connected in an equally earnest and sincere way with our great Allies? On the other hand, does not the complete monopolizing of certain ministries by the opposing side give our organizations just cause for distrust, and does it not reveal a negation of democratic ideals and of the fundamental equality of rights?

Besides that, you continuously mention ministries that are proposed for EAM, and you choose to ignore the fact that these ministries must be distributed among three groups (PEEA, EAM, and KKE) and that EAM itself is composed of many parties other than the Communist party, and that in PEEA are personalities and representatives which do not even belong to EAM. Does none of them inspire enough confidence to be assigned as Minister of Education, Justice or Interior? And we must observe that the Ministry of Interior was not requested for EAM but only for PEEA. We likewise were unable to understand why you excluded any participation in the Government by an old and historic party, the Democratic Union, when the section of it Mr. Svolos had the honor to represent at the Conference was much stronger than many other parties.

We have requested our principals in the Mountains—still

301

through your intervention because, as you know, we never have had direct channels of communication—to acquaint us with their final views on the fundamental guarantees required to insure the fulfillment of the Lebanon Agreement. Their answer (allow us to express our astonishment at seeing you use publicly a text that was addressed to you personally) is neither a retraction nor a repudiation, but only a logical interpretation and clarification of the agreement which, after such a poisoning of the atmosphere, was necessary and suitable in order to secure cooperation enjoying some prospect of success. What they want concerns chiefly the policy which should be followed by the Government *after* participation in it by our representatives so that the Lebanon Agreement might be implemented in accordance with its spirit and its moral and national aims.

The conditions contained in the cable, both in their entirety and individually—according to our verbal explanations—contribute to a general improvement of the present situation, to better prosecution of the struggle for liberation, to mental appeasement, to the future tranquility of the People, to the elimination of distrust and prejudices, and to the increase from every point of view of the prestige of the Government of National Unity; in other words, these conditions contribute to the achievement of a real unity of all and not of a superficial unity favoring one side by the extermination or subordination of the other. Unity presupposes the existence of groups which are not desired by the others. In fact, moreover, in the new Government, the influence of all responsible persons would facilitate an understanding for the fulfillment of those conditions which appeared to you absolutely necessary to state openly. Finally we declared to you that we would undertake further action to settle differences concerning specific questions. Your government has unfortunately rejected the proposals in toto although they consisted in essential acceptance of the Lebanon Agreement and conformed with its spirit, and although they would at once create, by the participation of new ministers in the Government, the beginning of cooperation.

It is sad to see how these negotiations have been conducted thus far. Our conscience is clear because *we* are not to blame but the Government which has not understood that unity must be genuine and which has done everything possible to create an atmosphere which would be destined to result in failure. The people want a solution to the question; at this time the vital question for the people is not to find out who is responsible. But every just man will admit that we cannot avoid the answer to that question, because you oblige us to give it.

In no case, for any reason, must this interruption of negotiations lead us to a break. By our actions we will demonstrate our intention not to abandon the idea and the endeavor to secure unity. Although thus far you have not done everything possible to reach an understanding, nothing can prevent an understanding from being reached in the future. A break would help only the enemy and harm the nation. We would never assume such a responsibility. For that reason and at this very critical moment we declare to you that we are ready to leave some of our representatives here with a view to permitting them to be of assistance in the task of paving the way for a new understanding. If you refuse, we have nothing else to do but return to Free Greece, where, on the basis of the Lebanon Agreement, we will strive for real unity by carrying on the struggle against the Germans and Bulgarians and by supporting all Allied military activity for the liberation of our Fatherland.

Our watchword will remain: Union for the destruction of the enemies of the Fatherland, for the protection of popular sovereignty, and for the reconstruction of Free Greece.

We beg you, Mr. President, to accept the assurance of our great esteem.

> For PEEA: A. Svolos
> For EAM: D. Stratis
> For KKE: P. Roussos

REPORT ON GREECE AND YUGOSLAVIA PREPARED BY AMBASSADOR LINCOLN MACVEAGH CAIRO, AUGUST 1944*

1. The problems in both Greece and Yugoslavia today are less military than economic and political. It is currently predicted that as the Allied pincers in Poland and France close on Germany, the Germans will withdraw their forces from the Balkans, and Allied military action is planned at present on this basis. In both countries it is contemplated to use the local guerillas to sabotage German withdrawal, and to confine actual Allied military operations chiefly to the facilitation and protection of the initial stages of relief and rehabilitation.

2. Plans for relief and rehabilitation are far advanced. They cover two periods, a military one, in which UNRRA will assist the military in the distribution of the supplies brought in by the latter, and a so-called UNRRA period to follow, in which that organization will exercise full responsibility. A military organization called the Allied Military Liaison, commanded by a British major general, has been set up in Cairo, and is now adequately staffed, though no troops have yet been assigned to it. On the staff there are some fifty or sixty American civil affairs officers. American participation in the functioning of this mission is strictly

* Copy obtained from the Franklin D. Roosevelt Library, Hyde Park, New York. Also, MacVeagh Diary, entry dated Aug. 3, 1944.

limited to collaboration in relief and rehabilitation problems. Should military action be found necessary, either to preserve order or to subdue remnants of the German forces remaining in the country, American forces will take no part in it. The chief unsettled questions in connection with the work of this mission, aside from the assignment of troops, are how to assure sufficient supplies to meet the anticipated needs, and how these supplies are eventually to be paid for. In Greece the currency question is especially acute, the pound sterling having risen from between four and five hundred drachmas to well over a hundred million.

3. In the political field both countries have suffered from the fact that their governments, which went into exile on the approach of the Germans, were newly and hastily formed affairs, while both their kings, and in particular the Greek King, enjoyed only a limited popularity with the people.

(a) As regards Greece, the Government-in-Exile is now formed of a coalition of all parties except the extreme Left, but has a strong republican complexion as a result of popular reaction against the Fascist dictatorship of 1936-1941. This situation has forced the King to agree to a plebiscite on the question of the monarchy, to be held after liberation, and also to agree not to return to Greece unless and until called for as a result of the plebiscite, or previously at the desire of his government. At present his government is against his returning before the plebiscite, but the King continues to hope that it may change its view before the hour of liberation comes. He thinks it possible that continued refusal on the part of the Communists, now controlling the largest of the guerilla organizations in Greece, to join the Government of National Unity may bring about a popular demand for his presence which his government would have to heed. However, his notable lack of personal qualities as a leader is against

305

him, as well as his long association with the recent tyranny of the extreme Right.

(b) As regards the Kingdom of the Serbs, Croats, and Slovenes, the political question is complicated by profound divisions within the country which do not exist in homogeneous Greece. These divisions have long been played upon from the outside, particularly by Italian and German diplomacy, and were acute at the time of the German invasion, which the Serbs resisted wholeheartedly, while the Croats and Slovenes in general did not. On the other hand, the most successful anti-Axis guerilla movement in the country is Croatian and Communist in origin and character, rather than Serb and Royalist, and with military aid from the Allies, granted primarily for the purpose of war against Germany, this movement now seems on its way to attempting to force its domination over Serbia and thus bring an end to the primacy which the latter has enjoyed in the conglomerate state hitherto.

4. Internationally, the Balkans remain a potential region of conflicting pressures. The war is eliminating the Anglo-German conflict of interests, but is replacing it with Anglo-Russian. Communist ideology holds no great appeal for the Balkan peoples, largely composed of peasant landholders, but the success of communist-led resistance movements in disorganized and demoralized territories supplies a dangerous opportunity for the imposition of Communist Party dictatorship. Refugees from Dalmatia, now to be seen in increasing numbers in Italy and North Africa, present unmistakable signs of indoctrination and regimentation with this end in view. Russia's interest in the Communist resistance movements of Tito in Yugoslavia and the EAM in Greece has also been clearly shown, particularly by the Soviet press and radio, though Russia continues officially to recognize the Greek and Yugoslav Governments-in-Exile, and there is no evidence that her own government is direct-

ing or financing these movements, which stem rather from the international Communism of 1917, than that of present-day Moscow. The British are intensely anxious as regards the Russian attitude, and this explains much of their activity in connection with the internal affairs of both nations. In Greece they have switched from supporting the EAM to opposing it, and in Yugoslavia they have abandoned Michailovitch and are trying to hitch the Tito movement to the car of British policy, possibly with the idea that a great accretion of recruits under British influence will over-balance and destroy its present Communist character. Evidences of growing mutual suspicion between London and Moscow have not been lacking. Shortly after Mr. Churchill began his personal correspondence with Tito, the Russians sent the latter a large liaison mission, headed by a lieutenant general, far out-ranking the local British brigadier. And when the British took strong action to quell the Greek mutinies in Egypt, which were led by adherents of the EAM, the Russian Ambassador in Cairo was outspoken in his disapproval. Further evidence of this sort was forthcoming when the Russians recently expressed displeasure and surprise over British secret operations in Rumania. This last affair has led to an attempt by London to establish a division of zones of interest in the Balkans, though only temporarily, for the war period. The attempt seems doomed to failure, largely on account of the Department's doubts as to the advisability of such action in connection with decisions taken at Teheran. But it shows that London, at least, recognizes the dangers inherent in the present situation if suspicions are allowed to grow.

5. The Rumanian peace feelers made in Cairo by an emissary of Maniu, the peasant party leader, have so far come to nothing, owing partly to a continued hope on the latter's part that the Allies could be split and negotiations carried on with the Anglo-Americans separately from the Russians, but also, it would seem, because of genuine im-

potence on Maniu's part to move against the Germans, whose control of the country up to this time has been exceedingly watchful and thorough. Bulgarian peace feelers, which have been rumored for months, seem now to be imminent, and here a hope of getting special consideration out of the supposed leniency of the Americans is clearly apparent.

6. As the war seems to be drawing to its close, postwar territorial claims and aspirations are coming more and more into the picture in the Balkans. In Yugoslavia, the Tito group is naturally the one most heard from so far. It appears to nurse dreams of domination not only over the whole of Yugoslavia, but also over the vague region known as Macedonia, including parts of Greece and Bulgaria. More serious, perhaps, are the views of the Greeks, who merit consideration for their unquestioning resistance to the Axis from the beginning. All the Greeks who have talked to me on this subject realize fully that any territorial acquisitions beyond the pre-war boundaries of the country must await decisions to be made at the peace conference. But they are nevertheless letting it be known that they regard Greece as entitled to the Dodecanese and Southern Albania, on ethnical grounds, as well as to a boundary with Bulgaria running north of the coastal range, for strategic purposes. It can hardly be questioned that the Dodecanese Islands are predominantly Greek in their population, as well as in their history, while the strongly Greek character of that part of Northern Epirus which is now called Southern Albania, including the towns of Koritza and Argyrocastro, is also undeniable.

7. American policy towards Greece and Yugoslavia is briefly, as I understand it, not to intervene in internal affairs while giving military support, during the war period, to such resistance groups as actively oppose the common enemy. British policy seems to be to insure the establishment of postwar governments favorable to British interests.

Russian policy appears, generally speaking, to be similar to the British from the Russian viewpoint. The British are very active in their direction and manipulation of the Governments-in-Exile. My Russian colleague in Cairo complained to me that the real Prime Minister of Greece is the British Ambassador. On the other hand, the Russians, while critical and suspicious of the British, appear for the most part to be holding aloof in the belief that repeated British mistakes, coupled with none on their part, will infallibly orient the sentiment of these distressed countries toward Moscow. So far, this belief may find some justification in the low ebb to which British prestige has fallen owing to the opportunist shifts of British policy toward the resistance movements, the repeated British military fiascos in Greece, Crete, and the Dodecanese, and the many mistakes in psychology which the British have committed in their handling of the Greek military and other problems.

Conclusion: Under the circumstances, I would recommend no change in American policy, but would point out that it might be made more clear to the peoples concerned. At the present moment, owing to faultily married propaganda-directives and the often loose employment of the term "Anglo-American" for activities purely British in character, American policy tends to be confused with British throughout the whole Balkan region, and we are rapidly incurring the same dislike, suspicion, and distrust which the Balkan peoples are increasingly feeling for our cousins. In addition, I believe that, in view of the great dangers for the future peace of the whole world, including ourselves, which the Balkan region continues to present as a crossroads of empire, we should maintain and even intensify our present salutary efforts to associate the Russians together with the British in all Balkan planning and activity of whatever character, from the ground up and in complete openness and confidence. Lord Moyne, the British Resident Minister in the Near East, told me the other day, that he would not recommend associating the Russians with an Anglo-American Balkan Affairs Committee, and other bodies of this sort which he was proposing, because "The Russians themselves never tell us anything." It seems to me that such an attitude can do nothing to remove suspicions already existing, and if persevered in, will infallibly produce more, with evil results.

THE CASERTA AGREEMENT*
SEPTEMBER 26, 1944

1. At a conference presided over by the Supreme Allied Commander, Mediterranean Theatre, at AFHQ, at which the Greek President of the Council with other members of the Greek Government and the Greek guerilla leaders, Generals Saraphis and Zervas, were present, the following decisions were recorded as having been accepted unanimously:

(a) All guerilla forces operating in Greece place themselves under the orders of the Greek Government of National Unity.
(b) The Greek Government places these forces under the orders of General Scobie who has been nominated by the Supreme Allied Commander as GOC Forces in Greece.
(c) In accordance with the proclamation issued by the Greek Government, the Greek guerilla leaders declare that they will forbid any attempt by any units under their command to take the law into their own hands. Such action will be treated as a crime and will be punished accordingly.
(d) As regards Athens no action is to be taken save under the direct orders of General Scobie, GOC Forces in Greece.
(e) The Security Battalions are considered as instruments of the enemy. Unless they surrender according to orders issued by the GOC they will be treated as enemy formations.

* As published in Woodhouse, pp. 306-7. Reproduced by permission.

(f) All Greek guerilla forces, in order to put an end to past rivalries, declare that they will form a national union in order to co-ordinate their activities in the best interests of the common struggle.

2. In implementation of these decisions, General Scobie has issued the following orders, with which the Greek representatives agree:

(a) General Zervas will continue to operate within the territorial limits of the Plaka Agreement and to co-operate with General Saraphis in harassing the German withdrawal within territory between the northern Plaka boundary and Albania.

(b) General Saraphis will continue to operate in the remainder of Greece with the following exceptions:

(i) ATTICA PROVINCE. All troops in this province will be commanded by General Spiliotopoulos, acting in close co-operation with representatives of the Greek Government and assisted by a liaison officer nominated by General Saraphis. To be under Command Force 140.*

(ii) PELOPONNESE. Troops in this area to be commanded by an officer recommended by General Saraphis in agreement with the Greek Government, assisted by a British Liaison Mission. To be under Command Force 140.

(iii) At a later stage Thrace (including Salonika) to be under command of an officer nominated by the Greek Government.

(c) The task of both commanders will be to harass the German withdrawal and to eliminate German garrisons.

* The official designation of General Scobie's forces. British troops already in Greece were Force 133.

(d) As territory is evacuated both commanders are personally responsible to Commander Force 140, for:

    (i) Maintenance of law and order in the territories where their forces are operating.

    (ii) Prevention of civil war and killing of Greeks by Greeks.

    (iii) Prevention of infliction of any penalty whatsoever and of unjustifiable arrest.

    (iv) Assistance in the establishment of the legal civil authority and the distribution of relief.

A map showing the operational boundaries has been issued to both commanders.

Signed: H. Maitland Wilson
General,
Supreme Allied
Commander,
Mediterranean
Theatre

G. Papandhreou
Prime Minister of Greece

S. Saraphis

H. G. Macmillan
British Resident
Minister
AFHQ

N. Zervas

POLITICAL AND ECONOMIC OUTLOOK OF THE EAM ON THE EVE OF THE GREEK CRISIS (DECEMBER 1944) PREPARED BY THE OFFICE OF STRATEGIC SERVICES, RESEARCH AND ANALYSIS BRANCH

R. & A. No. 2821*

JANUARY 5, 1945

SUMMARY

Analysis of two issues of the official EAM review, *New Greece*, discloses the intellectual position of EAM and its fundamentally Greek outlook and orientation on the eve of the December crisis. Although the review is radical in tone, it is chiefly remarkable for its intense and peculiarly Greek nationalism.

In dealing with domestic policy, several authoritative writers stressed the necessity for orderly and disciplined support of the Papandreou Government, in order to frustrate royalist and reactionary plans to provoke foreign intervention. An article on economic policy advocated maintenance of private enterprise, subject to broad over-all controls.

* Copy obtained from the National Archives and Records Service, Washington, D.C.

Remarkably moderate articles on foreign policy stressed the importance of close relations with all of the great Allied powers, demanded retribution on the part of the Axis governments, advocated a peaceful settlement with Albania, and expressed hope that Cyprus would be ceded to Greece by Great Britain.

I. INTRODUCTION

This analysis is based on a study of the authoritative fortnightly review of the EAM Central Committee, *New Greece* (NEA ELLADA), two issues of which had appeared (5 November and 20 November 1944) before the outbreak of hostilities in Athens. The editor of the review is the well-known leftist literary figure, N. Karvounis, who was one of the Athens delegates to the PEEA National Council and subsequently served in the Bureau of Information of the National Government.

The two issues of the periodical contain over twenty-five articles contributed by such prominent individuals as General Sarafis (head of ELAS), Elias Tsirimokos (EAM Minister of National Economy), Maria Svolos (noted feminist and wife of Professor Alexander Svolos), Professor Petros Kokkalis (PEEA Minister of Social Welfare), Kostas Gavrielidis (leader of Agrarian Party and PEEA Minister of Agriculture), and Metropolitan Antonios of Elis (leader of the EAM in Peloponnesus). The articles cover a wide variety of subjects, ranging from the domestic problems and foreign policy of Greece to the Beveridge Plan and the reelection of President Roosevelt.

II. DOMESTIC PROGRAM

The fundamental note struck by the review on the question of domestic policy is the absolute necessity for maintaining strict order and discipline, and for supporting Premier Papandreou's National Unity Government. The explanation, which is frequently repeated, is that the royalists and reactionaries, realizing that they lack the support of the great mass of the Greek people, are seeking to provoke disorders with the aim of forcing foreign (i.e., British) intervention and eventually bringing about the return of the King.

The accomplishments of the Papandreou Government after its return to Greece are freely acknowledged and enumerated—stabilization of the currency, fulfillment of immediate relief requirements and temporary sheltering of the inhabitants of the burned villages. It is added, however, that the war aims of the United Nations involve the extermination of fascism in all its forms, the restoration of democratic liberties, and the assurances that the people will be free to settle their internal problems in accordance with their desires. In fulfillment of these aims it is insisted that a plebiscite must be held at the earliest possible moment in order to settle the question of the King's return. The result of the plebiscite, it is confidently asserted, will greatly weaken the position and influence of the "anti-national, anti-allied, fascist reaction," and will render much simpler the solution of the remaining problems.

Among other domestic problems, special mention is accorded to the formation of a democratic national army, the purging of the civil service of fascist elements, the trial of quisling collaborators, and the reconstruction of the devastated country. Individual articles on these various problems are markedly moderate in tone. Elias Tsirimokos, who was a member of the three-man committee on measures to be taken against quislings, specifies in his article that rumor and hearsay cannot be accepted as evidence in judging suspected collaborators, that no one will be convicted without an opportunity to present his case, and that all convictions must be based on positive and concrete proof.

An article on social and economic reconstruction specifically rejects the two "extremist" policies of (1) a return to the pre-war "laissez-faire" operation of "blind economic forces" or (2) the introduction of state control of all branches of the national economy. Instead a "middle of the road" policy is recommended, along the following lines: government aid to self-governing agricultural cooperatives; industry to be left to private enterprise, but to operate under an overall plan which will determine the quantity and nature of its output; abolition of monopolies and of other restrictions on commerce; and guaranteed living standards for workers.

III. FOREIGN POLICY

Moderation is evident also in the articles on foreign policy. Concerning relations with the great powers, it is stated that Greece's position in the Mediterranean and her post-liberation relief needs require close cooperation with Great Britain and the United States. Similarly, it is said, Greece's position in the Balkans calls for correspondingly friendly relations with the Soviet Union. "Those who urge that Greece should orient her foreign policy towards only one of the great allied Powers," the magazine says, "are fifth columnists, actual enemies of the war effort of the Allies and of the United Nations."

As regards claims against the former occupation states, the following demands are made: (1) that Bulgarian, Italian, and German officials responsible for atrocities committed in Greece be surrendered to the Greek Government and be put on trial for their crimes, and that the Bulgarian, Italian, and German Governments pay in full for the damages wrought in Greece; (2) that Bulgaria, which is excoriated as the most dastardly of the occupation powers, be required to evacuate all Greek territories and be forced to accept frontier rectifications in order to prevent further aggression; (3) that Italy should surrender the Dodecanese.

On the controversial Southern Albanian question, the

first issue of the review stressed the friendly relations between the Greek and Albanian peoples, who have fought and are fighting against common enemies, and concluded that a peaceful settlement could be negotiated in a direct agreement with Albania. This position was attacked by the conservative, nationalistic newspapers of Athens, but the editor of *New Greece* held his ground, and in the second issue he wrote a full length article reiterating and elaborating his thesis. Stating that Albania is one of the United Nations and is so recognized by Great Britain, the United States, and the Soviet Union, he revealed that the first Albanian anti-fascist national liberation congress held in Permet (May 1944) included representatives of the Northern Epirote (i.e., Greek) minority and that a certain Manolis Oikonomos was included in the Provisional Government as a spokesman for the Northern Epirotes. Finally, the editor denounced the extreme Greek claims to Albanian territory as being akin to the Hitlerian conception of "living space."*

Concerning Cyprus, to which Greece unofficially lays claim on the ground that it has an overwhelmingly large Greek population, it is noted that Britain signed the Atlantic Charter and that "our great Ally always keeps her word and honors her signature."

IV. INCIDENTAL OPINIONS

The second issue of the review introduced two new departments entitled "Intellectual Life" and "Fortnightly Chronicle." The latter section briefly summarized international developments and expressed warm praise for the policies of General de Gaulle. The reelection of President Roosevelt was also acclaimed as a great contribution to the cause of world peace and security.

Under "Intellectual Life," contributors urged the formation of a National Theater which, unlike the previous "Royal

* Cf. Greek Territorial Claims and Aspirations, R. & A. No. 2662, forthcoming.

Theater," should cater to the needs of the masses of the people and should give expression to Greek culture rather than ape "foreign styles."

V. CONCLUSION

The review is permeated with expressions of an intense nationalism, an exuberant pride and love for Greece. Metropolitan Antonios refers again and again to "our beloved and sweet country." Although radical in tone, and interested in the USSR to the extent of including an article on the October 1917 Soviet Revolution, the review is nevertheless unmistakably and even belligerently Greek. It is completely unlike the 1918-1919 Greek revolutionary periodicals, which had a doctrinaire, international proletarian character. On several occasions the EAM is referred to as a modern version of the 1821 secret revolutionary organization, *Philike Hetairia*. In short, the contributors obviously feel themselves to be patriots, champions of their country rather than of a class, and acting in harmony with the historic traditions of the nation.

THE VARKIZA AGREEMENT*

FEBRUARY 12, 1945

ARTICLE I. LIBERTIES

The Government will secure in accordance with the Constitution and the democratic principles everywhere recognised, the free expression of the political and social opinions of the citizens, repealing any existing illiberal law. It will also secure the unhindered functioning of individual liberties such as those of assembly, association and expression of views in the Press. More especially, the Government will fully restore trade union liberties.

ARTICLE II. RAISING OF MARTIAL LAW

Martial law will be raised immediately after the signature of the present agreement. Simultaneously with this action there will be brought into force a Constitutional Act similar in all respects to Constitutional Act No. 24, whereby the suspension of those articles of the Constitution to which reference is made in Act 24 shall be permitted.

Articles 5, 10, 12, 20, and 95 of the Constitution shall be suspended forthwith throughout the country. This suspension shall continue until the completion of disarmament, and the establishment of administrative, judicial and military authorities throughout the country. As regards Article 5 in particular, this suspension shall not take effect in the cities of Athens and Piraeus and their suburbs. Especially,

* As published in Woodhouse, pp. 308-10. Reproduced by permission.

however, as regards persons arrested up to the present day it is agreed that Article 5 of the Constitution is not in force, and that they will be liberated within the shortest possible period of time, the necessary orders to this effect being given to the competent authorities.

Followers of EAM who may be held in captivity by other organisations shall be set free as soon as possible.

ARTICLE III. AMNESTY

There shall be an amnesty for political crimes committed between the 3rd December, 1944, and the publication of the law establishing the amnesty. From this amnesty shall be excluded common-law crimes against life and property which were not absolutely necessary to the achievement of the political crime concerned. The necessary law will be published immediately after the signature of the present agreement. From this amnesty will be excluded any person who, being under obligation to surrender their arms as being members of the organisations of ELAS, the National Civil Guard or ELAN, shall not have handed them over by the 15th March, 1945. This last provision concerning exclusion from the amnesty shall be annulled after verification of the fact that the disarmament of ELAS has been effected, since there will then be no further cause and justification for it. Guarantees and details of the amnesty to be provided are contained in the draft law attached to the present agreement.

ARTICLE IV. HOSTAGES

All civilians who have been arrested by ELAS, or by the National Civil Guard (EP), irrespective of the date on which they were arrested, shall be set at liberty immediately. Any who may be held on the charge of collaboration with the enemy or of commission of any crime shall be handed over to the justice of the State for trial by competent courts according to law.

ARTICLE V. NATIONAL ARMY

The National Army, apart from the professional officers and NCOs, shall consist of the soldiers of the classes which shall from time to time be called up. Reserve officers, NCOs and other ranks, who have been specially trained in modern weapons, shall remain in service so long as there is a formation requiring them. The Sacred Squadron shall remain as at present, since it is under the immediate orders of the Allied High Command, and shall thereafter be merged in the united National Army in accordance with the above principle. The effort will be made to extend regular conscription to the whole of Greece in accordance with the technical facilities existing and the necessities which may arise. After the demobilisation of ELAS, those men who belong to classes which are to be called up shall report for enrolment in the units already existing. All men who have been enrolled in the units now existing without belonging to the classes being called up, shall be discharged. All members of the permanent cadres of the National Army shall be considered by the Councils for which provision is made in Constitutional Act No. VII. The political and social views of citizens serving in the army shall be respected.

ARTICLE VI. DEMOBILISATION

Immediately on the publication of the present agreement the armed forces of resistance shall be demobilised and in particular ELAS, both regular and reserve, ELAN and the National Civil Guard. The demobilisation and surrender of arms shall take place according to the detailed provisions of the protocol drawn up by the Committee of Experts.

The State will settle all questions arising out of requisitioning carried out by ELAS. The goods requisitioned by ELAS, including beasts, motor vehicles, etc., which will be handed over to the State according to the detailed provisions of the protocol which has been drawn up, will be regarded thereafter as having been requisitioned by the Greek State.

Article vii. Purge of Civil Service

The Government will proceed, by means of committees or councils, to be established by a special law, to the purging of the personnel of the public services, officials of public companies, local Government officials, and those of other services dependent on the State or paid by it. The criteria of which the purge will take account will be either professional competence, or character and personality, or collaboration with the enemy or the utilisation of the official as an instrument of the dictatorship. Officials of the above services who, during the occupation, joined the forces of resistance will return to their positions and will be considered in the same manner as other officials. The above-mentioned councils will also consider the cases of officials who have taken part or collaborated in the manifestations which have taken place between the 3rd December 1944, and the date of signature of the present agreement. Those of them who are found to have been concerned may be placed at the disposal of the State as provided by law. The final disposal of such officials will be decided by the Government which shall result from the elections to the Constituent Assembly. Officials who have already placed "en disponibilité" by decisions of the ministers, will be submitted to the decision of the council above mentioned. No official will be dismissed solely on account of his political opinion.

Article viii. Purge of Security Services

The purge of the Security Services, the Gendarmerie and the City Police will be carried out as soon as possible by the special purge committee on the same basis as the purge of the civil service. All officers and other ranks of the above corps who fall under the provisions of the Amnesty Law, who during the period of the occupation joined the ranks of ELAS, ELAN, or the National Civil Guard, will return to their positions and will be considered by the purge councils in the same manner as the rest of their colleagues. All the officers and other ranks of the above corps who left their positions between the 3rd December, 1944, and the date of signature of the present document shall be placed "en disponibilité," their final disposal being left for the decision of the councils to be constituted by the Government arising from the elections.

ARTICLE IX. PLEBISCITE AND ELECTIONS

At the earliest possible date, and in any case within the current year, there shall be conducted in complete freedom, and with every care for its genuineness, a plebiscite which shall finally decide on the Constitutional question, all points being submitted to the decision of the people. Thereafter shall follow as quickly as possible elections to a Constituent Assembly for the drafting of the new Constitution of the country. The representatives of both sides agree that for the verification of the genuineness of the expression of the popular will the great Allied Powers shall be requested to send observers.

Of this present agreement two identical copies have been made, whereof the one has been received by the Government Delegation and the other by the Delegation of EAM.

In Athens, at the Ministry of Foreign Affairs, 12th February, 1945.

Signed: I. Sophianopoulos   G. Siantos
       P. Rallis   D. Partsalidhis
       I. Makropoulos   E. Tsirimokos
       for the Hellenic Gov-   for the Central Committee
       ernment   of EAM

BIBLIOGRAPHY

I. Manuscripts and Unpublished Records

Forrestal, James V., Diaries and Papers. Princeton University Library, Princeton, New Jersey.

Hopkins, Harry L., Papers. F. D. Roosevelt Library, Hyde Park, New York.

Communist Party of Greece (KKE). Central Committee records of telegraphic messages, October-November 1944 (incomplete).

Kingdom of Greece, Archives of the Ministry of Foreign Affairs, Athens.

MacVeagh, Lincoln, Diaries and Correspondence. Private collection.

Roosevelt, Franklin D., Papers and Correspondence. F. D. Roosevelt Library, Hyde Park, New York.

Stimson, Henry L., Diaries. Yale University Library, New Haven, Connecticut.

United States Department of State. Diplomatic Records, 1942-45. National Archives, Washington, D. C.

United States Office of Strategic Services. Records. National Archives, Washington, D. C.

II. Published Documents

Great Britain. *Documents Regarding the Situation in Greece–January 1945* (Greece No. 1: 1945). Cmd. 6592. London, 1945.

Great Britain. *Report of the British Parliamentary Delegation to Greece–August 1946.* London, 1947.

Great Britain. *Parliamentary Debates* (Commons). Vol. 402 (1943-44); 406 (1944-45).

I Symfonia tis Varkizas. Athens: Directorate of Press and Information, February 1945.

National Liberation Front (EAM). *White Book: May 1944–March 1945.* New York: Greek-American Council, August 1945.

Royal Institute of International Affairs. *Documents on International Affairs, 1947-1948.* London: Oxford University Press, 1952.

United States Department of State. *Foreign Relations of the United States, Diplomatic Papers–1942.* Vol. II. Washington: Government Printing Office, 1963.

United States Department of State. *Foreign Relations of the United States. Diplomatic Papers–1943.* Vol. IV. Washington: Government Printing Office, 1964.

United States Department of State. *Foreign Relations of the United States. Diplomatic Papers–1944.* Vol. V. Washington: Government Printing Office, 1965.

United States Department of State. *Foreign Relations of the United States. Diplomatic Papers–1945.* Vol. VIII. Washington: Government Printing Office, 1969.

United States Department of State. *Foreign Relations of the United States. The Conferences at Malta and Yalta–1945.* Washington: Government Printing Office, 1955.

U.S.S.R. Ministry of Foreign Affairs. *Correspondence Between the Chairman of the Council of Ministers of the USSR and the Presidents of the USA and the Prime Ministers of Great Britain During the Great Patriotic War of 1941-1945.* New York: Capricorn Books, 1965.

U.S.S.R. *The Tehran, Yalta and Potsdam Conferences–Documents.* Moscow: Progress Publishers, 1969.

III. BOOKS

Barker, Elizabeth. *Macedonia–Its Place in Balkan Power Politics.* London: Royal Institute of International Affairs, 1950.

Borkenau, Franz. *European Communism*. New York: Harper, 1953.

Bryant, Arthur. *Triumph in the West*. New York: Doubleday, 1959.

———. *The Turn of the Tide*. New York: Doubleday, 1957.

Byford-Jones, W. *The Greek Trilogy: Resistance–Liberation–Revolution*. London: Hutchinson, 1946.

Byrnes, James F. *Speaking Frankly*. New York: Harper, 1947.

Capell, Richard. *Simiomata. A Greek Note Book, 1944-1945*. London: MacDonald, n.d.

Chandler, Geoffrey. *The Divided Land–An Anglo-Greek Tragedy*. New York: Macmillan, 1959.

Churchill, Winston S. *The Second World War*. Vol. v: *Closing the Ring*. Boston: Houghton Mifflin, 1951: Vol. vi: *Triumph and Tragedy*. Boston: Houghton Mifflin, 1953.

Condit, D. M. *Case Study in Guerrilla War: Greece During World War II*. Washington: Department of the Army, 1961.

———, et al. *Challenge and Response in Internal Conflict*. Vol. ii: *The Experience in Europe and the Middle East*. Washington: Social Science Research Institute, 1967.

Constantopoulos, Dimitri S. *The Paris Peace Conference of 1946 and the Greek-Bulgarian Relations*. Thessaloniki: Institute for Balkan Studies, 1956.

Deane, John R. *The Strange Alliance*. New York: Viking Press, 1946.

Dedijer, Vladimir. *Tito Speaks*. London: Weidenfeld and Nicolson, 1953.

Djilas, Milovan. *Conversations With Stalin*. New York: Harcourt, Brace and World, 1962.

Eden, Anthony. *The Memoirs of Anthony Eden*. Vol. iii, *The Reckoning*. Boston: Houghton Mifflin, 1965.

327

Feis, Herbert. *Churchill, Roosevelt, Stalin*. Princeton, N.J.: Princeton University Press, 1957.

————. *From Trust to Terror*. New York: Norton, 1970.

Fergusson, Bernard, ed. *The Business of War*. New York: Morrow, 1958.

Hull, Cordell. *The Memoirs of Cordell Hull*. 2 vols. London: Hodder and Stoughton, 1948.

Iatrides, John O. *Balkan Triangle*. The Hague: Mouton, 1968.

Kofos, Evangelos. *Nationalism and Communism in Macedonia*. Thessaloniki: Institute for Balkan Studies, 1964.

Kolko, Gabriel. *The Politics of War*. New York: Vintage, 1968.

Kousoulas, D. George. *The Price of Freedom: Greece in World Affairs, 1939-1953*. Syracuse, N.Y.: Syracuse University Press, 1953.

————. *Revolution and Defeat. The Story of the Greek Communist Party*. New York: Oxford University Press, 1965.

Kyriakides, Stilpon P. *The Northern Ethnological Boundaries of Hellenism*. Thessaloniki: Institute for Balkan Studies, 1955.

Kyrou, A. A. *I Nea Epithesis Kata Tis Ellados*. Athens: Aetos, 1949.

————. *I Synomosia Enantion tis Makedonias*. Athens: Aetos, 1950.

Leahy, William D. *I Was There*. New York: McGraw-Hill, 1950.

Lee, Arthur S. Gould. *The Royal House of Greece*. London: Ward Lock, 1948.

Leeper, Reginald. *When Greek Meets Greek*. London: Chatto and Windus, 1950.

Librach, Jan. *The Rise of the Soviet Empire*. New York: Praeger, 1964.

Lukacs, John A. *The Great Powers and Eastern Europe*. New York: American Book Co., 1953.

Macmillan, Harold. *The Blast of War*: *1939-1945*. New York: Harper and Row, 1967.

McNeill, William H. *The Greek Dilemma*: *War and Aftermath*. New York: Lippincott, 1947.

————. *America, Britain and Russia*: *Their Cooperation and Conflict, 1941-1946*. London: Oxford University Press, 1953.

Moran, (Lord). *Churchill. Taken from the Diaries of Lord Moran*: *The Struggle for Survival, 1940-1945*. Boston: Houghton Mifflin, 1966.

Morrell, Sydney. *Spheres of Influence*. New York: Duell, Sloan and Pearce, 1946.

Myers, E.C.W. *Greek Entanglement*. London: Rupert Hart-Davis, 1955.

Naltsas, Christoforos. *To Makedonikon Zitima kai Sovietiki Politiki*. Thessaloniki: Institute for Balkan Studies, 1954.

Nicolson, Harold. *Diaries and Letters*. Vol. ii: *The War Years, 1939-1945*. New York: Atheneum, 1967.

O'Ballance, Edgar. *The Greek Civil War, 1944-1949*. New York: Praeger. 1966.

Papaconstantinou, Th. *I Mahi tis Ellados*. Athens: Galaxias-Keramikos, 1966.

Papadakis, B. P. *Diplomatiki Istoria tou Ellinikou Polemou, 1940-1945*. Athens, 1957.

Papandreou, George. *I Apeleftherosis tis Ellados*. Athens, 1948.

Pentzopoulos, Dimitri. *The Balkan Exchange of Minorities and Its Impact Upon Greece*. Paris: Mouton, 1962.

Philon, Ph. A. *The Question of Northern Epirus*. Washington: Greek Government Office of Information, 1945.

Pipinelis, P. N. *Europe and the Albanian Question*. Chicago: Argonaut, 1963.

Ponomaryov, B., *et al. History of Soviet Foreign Policy, 1917-1945*. Moscow: Progress Publishers, 1969.

Pyromaglou, Komnenos. *I Ethniki Antistasis*. Athens, 1947.

329

Pyromaglou, Komnenos. *O Doureios Ippos.* Athens, 1958.
————. *O G. Kartalis ke I Epohi Tou.* Athens, 1965.
————. *Ti Ipa sto Livano.* Athens(?): E.O.E.A. Press, 1944.
Reid, Francis. *I Was in Noah's Ark.* London: W. and R. Chambers, 1957.
Roosevelt, Elliott. *As He Saw It.* New York: Duell, Sloan and Pearce, 1946.
Sarafis, Stefanos. *Greek Resistance Army. The Story of ELAS.* London: Birch Books, 1951.
Seton-Watson, Hugh. *The East European Revolution.* New York: Praeger, 1956.
Sherwood, Robert E. *Roosevelt and Hopkins.* New York: Grosset and Dunlap, 1948.
Stavrianos, L. S. *The Balkans Since 1453.* New York: Holt, Rinehart and Winston, 1961.
————. *Greece: American Dilemma and Opportunity.* Chicago: Regnery, 1952.
Stettinius, Edward R. *Roosevelt and the Russians.* New York: Doubleday, 1949.
Sulzberger, C. L. *A Long Row of Candles.* New York: Macmillan, 1969.
Toynbee, Arnold and Veronica M. Toynbee, eds. *The Realignment of Europe* (*Survey of International Affairs, 1939-1946*). London: Oxford University Press, 1955.
Trukhanovsky, V. *British Foreign Policy During World War II, 1939-1945.* Moscow: Progress Publishers, 1970.
Tsatsos, Jeanne. *The Sword's Fierce Edge.* Nashville: Vanderbilt University Press, 1969.
Tsoucalas, Constantine. *The Greek Tragedy.* Baltimore: Penguin, 1969.
Tsouderos, Emmanuel I. *Ellinikes Anomalies sti Mesi Anatoli.* Athens: Aetos, 1945.
————. *Diplomatika Paraskinia, 1941-1944.* Athens: Aetos, 1950.
Voigt, F. A. *Pax Britannica.* London: Constable, 1949.
Voukmanovitch-Tempo, Svetozar. *Le Parti Communiste de*

Grèce dans la Lutte de Liberation Nationale. Paris: Agence Yougoslave d'Information, 1949.

Wolff, Robert L. *The Balkans in Our Time.* Cambridge, Mass.: Harvard University Press, 1956.

Woodhouse, C. M. *Apple of Discord. A Survey of Greek Politics in Their International Setting.* London: Hutchinson, 1948.

Woodward, Sir Llewellyn. *British Foreign Policy in the Second World War.* London: Her Majesty's Stationery Office, 1962.

Xydis, Stephen G. *Greece and the Great Powers, 1944-1947.* Thessaloniki: Institute for Balkan Studies, 1963.

Zafeiropoulos, Dimitri. *To K.K.E. ke I Makedonia.* Athens, 1948.

Zotiades, George B. *The Macedonian Controversy.* Thessaloniki: Institute for Balkan Studies, 1954.

IV. ARTICLES

Kitsikis, Dimitri. "La Grèce entre l'Angleterre et l'Allemagne de 1936 à 1941," *Revue Historique* (Paris), 238 (July-September 1967), 85-115.

————. "La Famine en Grèce (1941-1942). Les Conséquences Politiques," *Revue d'Histoire de la Deuxième Guerre Mondiale* (Paris), 74 (April 1969), 17-41.

Lukacs, John. "The Night Stalin and Churchill Divided Europe," *New York Times Magazine* (October 5, 1969), 36-49.

McNeill, William H. "The Outbreak of Fighting in Athens, December 1944," *American Slavic and East European Review,* VIII (1949), 253-61.

————. "Greece: A Permanent Crisis?" *Foreign Policy Reports,* XXVII (April 15, 1951).

Sacker, David. "The Background of the Greek Crisis," *Contemporary Review,* No. 963 (March 1946), 155-59.

Stavrianos, L. S. "Greece: The War and Aftermath," *Foreign Policy Reports,* XXI (September 1, 1945), 174-87.

Stavrianos, L. S. "The Immediate Origins of the Battle of Athens," *American Slavic and East European Review*, VIII (1949), 239-51.

———. "Present Day Greece," *Journal of Modern History*, XX (June 1948), 149-58.

Vovolinis, Constantine. "Pos Efthasamen Is Tin Tragodian tou 1944," *Eleftheros Kosmos* (Athens) (February-May 1948).

Xydis, Stephen G. "The Secret Anglo-Soviet Agreement on the Balkans of October 9, 1944," *Journal of Central European Affairs*, xv (October 1955), 248-71.

———. "Greece and the Yalta Declaration," *The American Slavic and East European Review*, xx (February 1961), 6-24.

Zahariades, Nikos. "Greetings from the Communist Party of Greece," *For a Lasting Peace, for a People's Democracy!* (October 24, 1952).

V. OTHER SOURCES

Rizospastis (official organ of the Greek Communist Party).
United States Department of State *Bulletin*.

INDEX

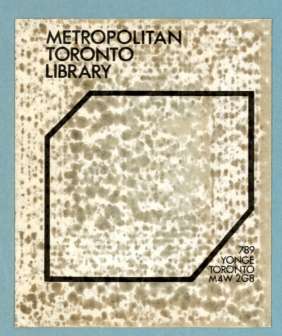